WALKING
WITH THE
WISE
Entrepreneur™

**55 Inspirational Mentors and
Millionaires Teach the Secrets of
Prosperity in Business and Life!**

Compiled by

Linda Forsythe

Foreword by

Susan Gilbert

MENTORS Publishing House, Inc.
San Diego, California

Need Inspiration Information or Mentoring?

Visit our Website!
www.mentorsmagazine.com

- **FREE** newsletters filled with guidance, from our nationally recognized mentors

- **FREE** online subscription to MENTORS™ magazine

- **FREE LIVE TELESEMINARS** by mentors and millionaires who interact and coach you toward success

- **COMING SOON...**
  www.Mentors4RealEstate.com
  www.Mentors4ThinkAndGrowRich.com

Mentors™
magazine.com

Dedication

*W*alking with the Wise Entrepreneur
is dedicated to all of the trailblazers of
enterprise. It is the entrepreneur moving
forward with courage that inspires us all.

WALKING WITH THE WISE ENTREPRENEUR™

ISBN 0-9729875-4-1

Printed in the United States of America

6 5 4 3 2 1 – 1 0 9 8 7

Published by MENTORS Publishing House, Inc.

This book is available at quantity discounts for bulk purchases and for branding by businesses and organizations. For further information, or to learn more about Mentors magazine™, mentorsmagazine.com™, Walking with the Wise™, or Mentors 4 Real Estate™ and other products and services of Mentors Publishing House, Inc, contact:

MENTORS Publishing House, Inc.
11609 Aspen View Drive
San Diego, CA 92128
Telephone: (858) 486-4297
email: linda@mentorsmagazine.com
Web: www.mentorsmagazine.com

Graphic Design, Art Direction by Ariane Thorne
Mentors Lighthouse Logo Design by Ariane Thorne
Illustrations by Kim Muslusky
Editing by Tammy Gann and Scott Hamashige

The publisher would like to acknowledge the many publishers and individuals who granted us permission to reprint their cited material or have written specifically for this book.

Foreword

How to Love Your Life as an Entrepreneur

by Susan Gilbert

"Would you tell me please, which way I ought to go from here? That depends a good deal on where you want to get to..."

— Lewis Carroll, from "Alice in Wonderland"

I love my life as an entrepreneur and there's nothing I want more for you than that you feel the same about YOUR life. Maybe you've been "entrepreneuring" for a very long time like me (it's been over twenty years now), or perhaps you're just considering your first entrepreneurial endeavor.

Either way — Beware! People consider entrepreneurs simultaneously as both misfits and geniuses. Some entrepreneurs enjoy huge successes, while others play in the entrepreneurial minor leagues; there's one question I think we could ask both groups and get the same answer:

Q: Would you like to work less and make more money?

A: YES!!!

Then my advice is to: "Do what you love to do, and work at perfecting your area of expertise on a daily basis."

I know. You've heard that before. But bear with me for a minute.

Here are two ways to do this:

1. Discover what you do best and find multiple ways to benefit from it.

For example, let's say someone loves to cook. A good suggestion would be to start a newsletter (e-zine) on cooking, write an e-book, make a video, create recipes and sell them, teach cooking classes online or in their home town, etc. ... Do you see what I mean? An entrepreneur has one focus (cooking) yet creates multiple products from that one focus.

5

2. No matter what your focus is, make it unique in some way. Inject your personality into everything you do. Don't call your e-zine "Sarah Jean's e-zine" — call it "Sarah Jean's Kickin' Cooking Secrets" — get the idea?

Born or made?

Many people have debated the question, "Are successful entrepreneurs born or made?"

Coming from first hand experience, I believe that it's a combination of natural tendencies combined with life circumstances. When I became a young widow with very little education and no specialized training, it was "sink or swim." My father worked long hours in the steel mills of Pittsburgh, so I had no family modeling of what "self-employment" looked like; however, I did possess a "can do" attitude. I didn't qualify for a good job, so I decided to create my own! My natural self-confidence and my impatience helped push me into entrepreneurial endeavors (I didn't want to "put the time in" for a degree). I gravitated to things I loved to do. I started with a commission-only sales job (I love people). Then I owned and operated a bakery/café coffee house (my mother passed along the love of baking and great java). Later, I started a publishing company — first traditional, then online (I'm a voracious reader).

Here's a great example of this with a more well-known entrepreneur.

The fourth son of a schoolteacher mother and a restless jack-of-all-trades father, Walt Disney worked on his high school newspaper. He took photos, drew drawings and studied cartooning on the side in order to fulfill his dream of becoming a cartoonist.

After serving in France and Germany during World War I, Walt worked in a commercial art studio in Kansas, Miss., where he met a friend. Together, they established a studio of their own. They bought a second-hand movie camera and made one-and two-minute animated advertising shown in local movie theatres.

Walt did what he loved and the rest was history. He moved to California, created Mickey Mouse, Donald Duck, feature length animations and Disneyland. Of course, there were critics, "naysayers" and dubious bankers along the way, but Walt "DID it," and he always said, "Just remember, it all started with a mouse."

I will tell you a secret in a minute about an important five-letter word that described what Walt did....

Can there be a problem with doing what you love?

Sometimes, while pursuing my passions, I end up with too many projects at the same time and end up stressed out and abandon projects. Sound familiar?

I usually have a lot of tasks that I want to accomplish and so I create a 90-day plan in order to focus on the specific sets of tasks I need to accomplish each week; focusing on "ONLY ONE" main area each week.

And normally, this system works to keeps me focused, but, ironically the act of creating the 90-day plan and looking at all I need to accomplish in the coming three months can overwhelm me.

Have you ever experienced that? I think we all have at one point or another.

There IS a solution. A few minutes ago, I promised to tell you a simple secret to Walt's success. Can you guess what that secret is?

Here's a hint. It's not really a secret at all. In fact, everyone knows about this. Unfortunately, though, not everyone knows what to do when they're feeling overwhelmed by stress.

Ready? ... The secret is ACTION!

Yes, ACTION. You may be thinking, "Hey, wait a sec, you just said you were feeling overwhelmed; how can action possibly solve that?"

Napoleon Hill, in his book "Think and Grow Rich" said, "Action is the real measure of intelligence." Thomas Huxley said, "The great end of life is not knowledge but action."

I knew what I had to do this week and yet I struggled to do it. I even had a 90-day marketing plan with each week spelled out for me I still felt stuck. I got unstuck when I realized I felt paralyzed, so I decided to do something about it. I decided to take action.

Have you heard of "Kaizen"?

Kaizen is a Japanese word which means "continuous and incremental improvement."

What I like about Kaizen is that it means taking small-action steps over time to solve problems. The beauty of this approach lies within its simplicity. You begin something that seems daunting, which overwhelms you by focusing on one small step that you can take to help improve the problem or get you closer to your goal, but in fact, it is the small easy step that helps you bypass the feelings of fear and stress that lie between you and the completion of your task. After a little while, you can then introduce another small step, which continuously helps to improve the situation or problem until you've conquered it.

So, this way you CAN take action even if it is very small, and then slowly over time each action you take has an effect, which builds on all the others creating an unstoppable force until your problem has been solved. The fact that the action is so small makes it easy for you to do SOMETHING and not focus on how much you have to do.

Maybe a short example will help. Last year, I wanted to create an "infopreneuring e-course and a training class" to support and market it.

7

However, I kept putting this off because I had a bunch of other stuff I needed to get done as well; this was a major focus for me. Finally, what I decided to do was to just write my chapter headings. Then, I picked one chapter to outline (I started with my favorite — you don't have to write them in order), breaking it down so that I only had to worry about one chapter at a time. This REALLY helped me make some progress in this area without worrying about how many there was. Before long, I had several chapters written and I was beginning to "see" how the whole picture would develop on it's own natural unfolding. My excitement took me right out of "overwhelmness" and head first into this project with a jet fuel called passion.

Anytime you have a fear to conquer or an overwhelming situation to deal with, try to identify a small step to take: one that won't take much time. Then, increase those steps incrementally, and before you know it you will have solved your problem or completed your task.

OK, back to "Are entrepreneurs born?"

OR, are they taught to turn their passion and ideas into great companies?

U.S. universities have poured $1 billion into the subject in the past 10 years in order to find answers to that question. Along the way, they've uprooted business schooling — adding hundreds of instructors and thousands of classes on entrepreneurship. Educators want to create more entrepreneurs like Earl Graves Sr., the founder of "Black Enterprise" magazine, whose success landed him on Daimler Chrysler's board of directors. Graves, 69, sold Christmas cards when he was seven years old — imitating his father, who held three jobs at once. "I was always thinking of where I was going to make more money — and how," he says. "People who don't have ambition — they get a regular job."

Here's another great example. With a mother like his, no wonder Richard Branson became an entrepreneurial dynamo. His Virgin Group straddles dozens of ventures — from music to cars to cell phones and bridal gown sales. Yet, it's Branson's Virgin Atlantic Airways that his independent-spirited mom may have influenced most. After all, Eve Branson, 80, once talked her way into a glider pilot training program by masquerading as a man.

"There are definitely traits which I inherited," says Richard Branson with a grin.

Branson started his British empire at 17 years old with a high school magazine. More than 30 years later, Virgin Group employs 35,000 people and has $7.9 billion in annual revenue. Branson, 53, famous for such over-the-top antics as donning a wedding dress to promote his bridal business, inherited his mother's tenacity.

Entrepreneurs like Branson are born — though skills can be taught too. Entrepreneurs inherit many traits that contribute to their success: creativity, drive,

and a willingness to take risks. Their education can then "fine tune" their craft of choice.

Arthur Blank, co-founder of Home Depot, recalls the risk his father took starting a pharmaceuticals supply business. The elder Blank, a father of six, started the business venture while in his late 30s. He died five years later when Arthur was about 15 years old. Arthur's mother, Molly, refused to give up on the family firm and successfully took over — they later sold the business.

Blank says, "That never-say-die spirit can't be taught."

But with education, he says, "If somebody has that potential, that kernel within ... it can be nurtured."

Pearls of Wisdom Within These Pages....

Lucky for you, you have an amazing book that you are holding between your hands right now! You can read and learn from the pearls of wisdom offered by some remarkably successful entrepreneurs.

Have you ever wondered why some entrepreneurs make a fortune while so many others with equally good products or services always seem to struggle financially?

What are the acquired skills needed for business and personal success?

Caution! The very qualities that can make you a good entrepreneur can end up hampering your business further down the line. One of the biggest strengths of successful entrepreneurs is their ability to take an idea, fly with it, and then stick with it through thick and thin.

But this very stubbornness can prevent entrepreneurs from listening to other ideas and suggestions — the constant "noise" from their market — which might benefit their business, and by extension, their own life.

Entrepreneurs hold their own beliefs very strongly, but they often won't adjust those beliefs when they get information from the market. Entrepreneurs focus so much on their businesses that they might not pay attention to trends and developments that might ultimately affect that business. In effect, they become a bit myopic.

Be Willing to Adjust Your Focus

Maybe you are stuck at a certain level with your business and you can't seem to change the channel or increase the volume. You've tried the vertical hold. You've messed with your brightness settings, but there's only one thing to do when you can't get a clear picture of what will make the difference.

9

Focus on these six things:

1) You are exactly what you believe and think about all day long. What you focus on grows and expands. Constantly guard your words and thoughts.

2) The primary purpose of business is to create and keep customers. Marketing and innovation should produce those results. All other business functions just cost you money. Focus on your marketing.

3) Find out what works in your business and then do more of it. First, focus on doing these things above any habitual needs. Utilize these few basic and profitable things over and over to build your business rapidly and successfully.

4) Visualize and see the results of your goals constantly. Focus on this vision intensely with positive feelings and emotions. Seeing the results of your goals here and now, will stimulate your mind to see new "light bulb" ideas to get what you need done.

5) Have fun. When you enjoy your work, your personal satisfaction and your level of satisfaction with your business will skyrocket. Remember, you're doing what you love. Have fun with it!

6) Experience is not what happens to you, but it's what you do with what happens to you that counts. Thomas Edison failed in his first 1,000 attempts to create the light bulb. Lucky for us he kept on trying, or we would live by candlelight. Your business is no different — it takes time to build. Focus on future growth with incremental steps taken today, then continue to educate yourself and learn how you can do what you do even better!

Take action now with one small step. Devour the stories and teachings within this book.

Combine doing what you love with action, focus and education. Not only will you be wildly successful, you just may be an author in the next "Walking with the Wise" book!

If you like what you've read ... check this out!

FOOTNOTES ⟨⟩

*As America's Focus Expert, **Susan Gilbert** helps individuals and organizations focus on what matters to create the results they desire. Author of the award-winning book, **"The Land of I Can,"** Susan is also co-author of **"The Complete Idiot's Guide to Starting and Running a Coffee Bar"** and a contributor to **"Chicken Soup for the Working Woman's Soul"** as well as many **"Walking with the Wise"** books and magazines. A successful entrepreneur for over 25 years, Susan knows what it takes to "fly solo." Learn what attributes you already have or need to develop to be a thriving entrepreneur by taking our free, short quiz: **www.WiseEntrepreneurQuiz.com*** ᗞᗞᗞᗞᗞᗞᗞ

TABLE OF CONTENTS

SECTION I – THE ENTREPRENEURIAL WAY: Taking the Right Roads to Your Destination.

"Follow these secrets of prosperity to guide you on your entrepreneurial quest."

SECTION II – HOW TO OVERCOME OBSTACLES ON YOUR JOURNEY TO PROSPERITY.

"Fortunate entrepreneurs share their personal success stories, inspiration and guidance."

SECTION III – THE WAY YOU THINK DETERMINES YOUR LIFE

*"Thinking about prosperity, your belief system, and using
spiritual wisdom lends to prosperous results."*

13

SECTION IV– TIPS FOR MAKING YOUR BUSINESS A SUCCESS

"Business secrets from the masters."

SECTION V– RARE EXCLUSIVE INTERVIEW WITH CHUCK AND GENA NORRIS!!!

In this Special Section, Linda Forsythe conducts an interview with Chuck Norris and his beautiful wife Gena for "Mentors™ Magazine." This transcript of the LIVE interview has been printed for your enjoyment. Learn about the obstacles that Chuck and Gena had to overcome on their road to celebrity success and how they live the lives of entrepreneurs .... with true prosperity and abundance.

"Mentors™" INSIDER INFORMATION: Chuck also reveals how the "KickStart" program is going to revolutionize high schools everywhere!!!

BEFORE You Begin Reading The Book ... Read This Introduction!!!!

by Linda Forsythe

It worked!!! Very few people stop to read the "Introduction" in a book, and I was determined to create a way for you to do so (snicker, snicker). I guess you can tell I'm an entrepreneur. Now that you're here ... I don't want to waste your time, so I'll make this good. You really do need to read this Introduction to see if you have what it takes to be an Entrepreneur because we're a special breed. We are the "mavericks" who love to prove people wrong, and figure out a way to do something that has never been done before. We also need more people in our club because very few have what it takes to be extremely good at it.

The ability of the entrepreneur to overcome insurmountable odds is an entertaining thing to witness. There is also a certain amount of drama behind the story of the *journey* the entrepreneur loves to regale. People who want to be as successful as the person telling the story will generally sit and listen with rapt attention. It's amazing how the successful entrepreneur loves to tell their heroic tales to anyone willing to listen; hence, the creation of this book. Our ultimate goal is we want to make business life easier than what we had when we grew our own businesses. This book of entrepreneurial wisdom is a true "win-win" situation for both the article contributor (mentor) and the reader. The article contributor is able to give you benefit of their experience of what works and what doesn't (and ultimately exploit our war stories). You, the reader, can learn what roads will be easier to take for your journey because this is part of your road map.

History abounds with fascinating tales of successful entrepreneurs dating back thousands of years and around the globe. These stories have one common denominator as do all stories of success — the indestructible spirit. It is the spirit that can "overcome" all. The spirit can make the physically weak strong, the emotionally weak indomitable and the financially weak rich. Does this sound like more drama? Well allow me to illustrate my point. ...

Viktor E. Frankl wrote interesting observations in his book, "Man's Search for Meaning" when he gave insight into our inner most psychological make up. Frankl told of his horrific experiences as a captive in Nazi Germany's concentration camps of World War II. Most of us are now aware of the inhumane conditions of that particular period, which involved torture, starvation, apathy and the attempt for genocide of an entire race. The dismal environment of horror surrounding concentration camp captives were hopeless and without escape. How does one go on? For what purpose? One of the key observations Frankl made was, it wasn't the most physically fit, intelligent or healthy that made it through, but the individual who had the "indomitable spirit." They were the ones who focused on the end result of freedom and wouldn't let that focus die.

While the journey of an entrepreneur isn't as dismal as it was for World War II concentration camp survivors. ... Most self-made successful entrepreneurs will tell you that the journey certainly *felt* that way. WHEW!!!

The American Heritage College Dictionary, Third Edition, supplies the following definition of an **Entrepreneur**:

*"An individual willing to establish enterprise, especially one of some scope, complications and risk. Industrious with systematic activity, especially when directed toward profit. Willingness to undertake **new** ventures with creativity and initiative."*

Creativity that is ever so prevalent in the entrepreneur stems from the ability to problem solve. The ability to "think on their feet" with absolute persistence. If there isn't a system to go by, the entrepreneur will create one and succeed through a great deal of trial and error. The true entrepreneur feels there isn't any question that doesn't have an answer somewhere, and it is they who will find it. They are the trailblazers in life who will mow down obstacles in their path like over-grown weeds. Entrepreneurs are the eternal optimists who deny failure through continued forward action. They've learned that failure only "happens" when they quit. They've learned the lessons of failure, and in turn, trudge through the thick mire of adversity until they ultimately achieve their goal.

With that statement made ... Let's put the "indomitable spirit" under a microscope and begin by looking at how it is born.

"Changing the Way you Think:" Do you want to know if you are thinking correctly? Take a look at your surroundings. What do you see? Everything you see and experience began with a "seed of a thought" at some point in time. This is a strong statement, but if you take the time to really evaluate the true beginning of what ultimately has manifested in your life…you will realize the power of your thoughts. You created the life you are living right now. You decided to accept or deny what was given to you. You nurtured that "seed of a thought," which grew into action and created a reaction. A life of peace and prosperity begins by accepting blessings and refusing curses. The Bible is an excellent reference on how to live a true life of abundance and it certainly does not teach that the accumulation of money is the answer. Becoming a successful entrepreneur goes MUCH deeper than finding and implementing the knowledge to become rich. It's about loving your fellow man. "Do unto others as you would have them do unto you." I absolutely guarantee if you follow this simple principle of the golden rule…YOU WILL PROSPER!!! The fruit surrounding you can now grow if you continue to nurture your existing thoughts, OR if you can plant different thoughts in your mind for a

17

different garden. This is true whether or not you are an entrepreneur. Good seeds of thought produce good fruit and bad seeds of thought produce weeds. If you want a different life…change your thoughts, but in any case, evaluating thoughts and the fruits they produced is the place to begin.

"No Complacency:" When an individual has made the decision to "accept" life as it is and remain comfortable with this decision — complacency is the tenuous house they live in. Entrepreneurs ARE NOT complacent. The individual who shuns complacency and has become restless with their inadequate surroundings has a "seed of a thought" planted to evoke change. Thus, producing the death of complacency. The death of complacency doesn't come easily. Change is not something we as humans are comfortable with, therefore, it must take a "life-altering" situation or crisis to push us out of our house of complacency. A number of people have found this unfortunate fact out when they were laid off from well-paying corporate jobs they thought they would have for life. Unfortunately, for most people when life-altering situations happen, the choice is to grieve the hardship and still maintain the status quo or wish for "what used to be." The thought of change seems to make a crisis situation worsen because of the added stress level of moving away from what you knew. This appears to be true even if the situation was uncomfortable — or in some cases — unbearable. Stepping out into the unknown without guaranteed "positive results" appears to be too great of a risk for most. It is the entrepreneurial spirit and the faith of believing, "There MUST be a better way!!!" that opens up a new beginning for a better life. Therefore, the birth of an "indomitable spirit" has begun. Transformation through change is eminent. Man has never won a better life or made discoveries because of complacency. So, the next time you have a crisis — know that it is nature's way of giving you a nudge toward change of rich opportunity.

"No Room for Failure:" A majority of very successful self-made entrepreneurs have not had a "soft place to fall" nor a safety net to rely on; therefore, giving up was not an option. Giving up leads to destruction. Does this surprise you? Let's take a closer look by examining the psychology of *why*. If a journey is rocky or uncomfortable, bruises are inevitable and obstacles appear insurmountable as deep chasms surround you on both sides ... the curves of life are very sharp. ... What is the typical human reaction? If there is a soft place to fall, then we usually tend to take it because continuing the journey to the final destination of a goal doesn't appear to be worth it. As an example, let's look at society today ... we have unemployment insurance, life insurance, car insurance, home insurance, fire, flood, tornado, earthquake, mudslide, tsunami, funeral, divorce, terrorist, attorney and even pet insurance. The list goes on, and on, and on. Then we have the ultimate insurance of the Social Security system that is purported to give us a comfortable retirement or golden parachutes for the person laid off from a job. A life of complacency abounds with a false sense of security, and therefore, multiple reasons to end the journey. This is just a forewarning for the true entrepreneur to avoid looking too much into tempting road blocks and mirages along the way. Proper preparation is good, but the thoughts of complacency that can rise because of it are NOT. In the book, "Think & Grow Rich," there is a true story of a 14th-century warrior-general who was faced with overwhelming odds of fighting an army three times the size of his with inadequate and limited weaponry. To solve his dilemma, he gave the unthinkable order to his fellow warriors to "Burn the boats!" This seemingly insane order gave his small and ill-equipped army no place to retreat; with the sea at their backs and the illusion of insurmountable odds of survival facing them. He then told his men, "You see these boats going up in smoke? ... this means that we cannot leave these shores alive unless we win! We now have no choice — we win — or we perish!" Guess who won and why? Yupp, you guessed it ... the small and ill-equipped army! Did they have a "soft place to fall?" Did this warrior-general possess an "indomitable spirit?" The bigger question is, "Did the larger and better prepared army, who was ultimately slaughtered, become complacent the day before battle because of an illusion of having the better odds of winning?"

The decision to be an entrepreneur will place you in the company of great men and women as the list is long and distinguished. The majority of inventions, artwork, medical advancements and business innovations that humanity benefits from today came from the maverick and trailblazer. It came from the individual who made every moment count with a vision, an indomitable spirit and absolute determination to realize a worthy goal. Because of this they achieved!!! This person made a difference when they took the first step in faith and ultimately succeeded because they decided to NEVER quit. You, as the reader have all the help you need and please know that every single person who contributed an article in this book wants to see you complete your journey!!! Now it's a matter of *your* choice.

If you like what you've read ... check this out!

FOOTNOTES

Linda Forsythe is the founder of MENTORS International, MENTORS™ magazine, www.mentorsmagazine.com, and the Walking with the Wise™ book series. She has dedicated her life to guide others toward a life of abundance. This has led her to create multiple forms of media that include wisdom from mentors around the globe. Linda is highly sought after to appear in print, television, radio and seminars. She encourages you to contact her and let her know how this book helped you. You can contact her at Linda@mentorsmagazine.com.

SECTION I

THE ENTREPRENEURIAL WAY:

Taking the Right Roads to Your Destination

© 2005 Kim Muslusky

The Decision and Determination to Succeed

From "NO B.S. Business Success"

by Dan Kennedy

"Men are anxious to improve their circumstances, but are unwilling to improve themselves. They therefore remain bound."
— James Allen, "As a Man Thinketh"

Contrary to a great many textbook assertions, having the best product, better mousetrap, a whiz-bang new idea, the top location, the best market, the smartest accountant, the neatest bookkeeping system, a ton of capital — or all of them together — does not ensure success. On the other hand, having the worst product, a mediocre mousetrap, a silly idea, a bad location, a weak market, an accountant who can't count, a shoe box and paper bag bookkeeping system, or no money — or all of these things together — does not ensure failure.

I have seen people succeed under the most improbable conditions. I've also seen people who have everything going for them still manage to screw it up. In all of these cases, it's the person making the difference. That's why there really are no business successes or failures; there are people successes and people failures.

Entrepreneurial Success Is Mostly a Matter of Decision

A partnership, friendship, intimate relationship, or marriage that succeeds or fails, a book that gets written or remains a jumble of notes in a drawer, the garage that gets cleaned out Saturday or put off until next week — these are all the result of decision and determination to make the decision right. Making the *right decisions* is often a lot less important than determining to make your *decisions right*. Only by making a decision and acting on it can you get into action and move forward. By waiting to make only the perfect decisions, you remain inert and cannot move forward at all. To quote my friend, legendary ad man Gary Halbert: "Motion beats meditation."

Most people go through life making decisions by default, choosing only from narrow options dictated by others or by evolving circumstances. One millionaire friend of mine grew up in a very small town where, as he put it, there were two career options: working at the factory or raising pigs and chickens. With only a few exceptions, everybody he went to school and graduated with chose one of those two options.

21

I am often amused when I'm traveling and get asked what I do; when I describe my job as best I can, I often get the envious sigh, the gee-I-wish-I-could-do-that, and then the laundry list of complaints and dissatisfactions from my fellow traveler about present career or business or life. I'm amused because he apparently does not know he can change those circumstances by decision. Similarly, when I told fellow travelers that I lived in "sunny Phoenix" (where I lived for more than ten years), I'd often hear the envious sigh, the gee-I-wished-I-lived-there-instead-of-in-X, then the litany of unpleasant things about their home city. This amuses me because apparently they haven't noticed the highway signs in their town pointing the way out.

Successful entrepreneurs learn to be much more assertive, proactive, and creative in making decisions to change things as they prefer, to make things happen. If you are to succeed as an entrepreneur, you have to break free of your old reacting and responding mode and switch to the assertive, proactive mode. *You have to reject the entire idea of limited choices.*

As an entrepreneur, you need to reject every single piece of programming you've ever received about limited options or prerequisites for exercising certain options.

> It's amazing how people spend their lives in prisons entirely of their own making, the key dangling right there in the lock, no jailer in sight.
>
> I find it very hard to work up much sympathy for most of these "sad sacks." I remember listening to a 40-or-so-year-old guy working behind the counter at a neighborhood convenience store where I sometimes stop for coffee complaining loudly — even poetically — about his miserable job, low income, and lousy lot in life. I asked where he lived and which way he drove to work. After he answered, I asked if he'd noticed every day, twice a day, he drove past the public library, a gigantic repository of free help for changing your career, your finances, your life. As you might guess, I might as well have been speaking Martian. If pressed, I assure you, he'd tell you he was too busy or too tired to read, or didn't like to read, or had bad eyesight when he was in school, or some other pitiful excuse. Pfui.

Just for example, you probably believe that certain options exist only for people with particular education, licenses, or certifications. Sure, you can't just up and declare yourself a heart surgeon or airplane pilot. But you can certainly be a CEO, and you can certainly make as much money as you choose.

Here's a little jolt: one of the highest-paid marketing consultants and coaches works with Realtors, a man who is paid millions of dollars a year from real estate agents for his advice, has never been in real estate, and does not have a real estate license. His name is Craig Forte, and he is a longtime client of mine. For four years, I had the largest business training company serving dentists and chiropractors, working with more that 10,000 doctors, but I am neither a DC nor DDS. I give you this one example as food for thought.

www.mentorsmagazine.com

Warning: Your Entry Point to Entrepreneurship May Be a Handicap to Overcome

For many people, the decision to pursue the entrepreneurial lifestyle is the by product of an evolving dislike for their jobs, frustration with their bosses, or a sudden loss of employment. They may be downsized, Enron'd, forced into early retirement, or just fed up enough one day to tell the boss to "take this job and shove it." The employees-turned-entrepreneurs out of default or disgust lug a lot of mental and emotional baggage with them. The habits, attitudes, and behaviors that work for the employee in the corporate bureaucratic environment do not work well at all in the entrepreneurial environment and must be left behind. The reason why so many new businesses fail is that the owners are unable to leave their old attitudes behind.

Personally, I've only held one job in my entire life, for one year, immediately out of high school. I secured a territory sales position with a national book publishing company, a job that was supposed to be for a college graduate with sales experience. I got it through a combination of bluster, white lies, and agreeing to work on "free trial" for three months — no pay, no company car. Although I excelled at the work itself, by year's end, I and my sales manager both agreed I was fundamentally unemployable. Thus, I became entrepreneurial.

However, I'd always intended to be my own boss, and I was very fortunate to have some preparation for it in youth as my parents had been self-employed my entire life. Like other kids, I read comic books and filched my father's "Playboys," but I was also reading "Think and Grow Rich," listening to Earl Nightingale tapes, working in the business, riding with my grandmother on job deliveries to clients, and writing up my list of life goals. This is not a mandatory prerequisite to later success. I know plenty of wildly successful entrepreneurs who came from much less helpful backgrounds. But I did have the edge of clear intent from the start of my adult life and little time to acquire the bad habits of thought and behavior that most longtime employees of other people have to shed when switching to entrepreneurship.

I think that to succeed, you must not only make a firm and committed decision to do just that but you must also decide to quickly, even eagerly, give up long-held attitudes and behaviors that fit fine in your previous environment but do not work well in entrepreneurial life. Although I don't swim, I imagine it'd be tough to swim across a good-sized lake while clinging to a boat anchor. Letting go of anchors from your formal life as you dive into entrepreneurial waters is essential.

Hey, That's Not Fair!

A lot of people respond to various handicaps, problems, and disappointments with the complaint, "It's just not fair." And it sure isn't. For

23

starters, we don't get to pick our parents. There's a flaw in the system right there! Next, most of us aren't moviestar gorgeous. But all this pales in comparison to the biggest injustice and mystery of all, the frequency with which bad things happen to good people.

A young man, Donald R., an honor student, considerate, courteous, and athletically talented, had an accident on the high school trampoline, landed on his back across the frame, and wound up paralyzed in both legs and both arms for life. He had to make a choice. He could have retreated into isolation, devoted his life to self-pity and bitterness, and lived as a helpless invalid. Instead, Donald R. learned to focus the entire force of his personality through his voice so he could use the telephone, the only tool that lets him travel anywhere in the world while in a wheelchair, to become an enormously successful businessman.

Dialing with a pencil clenched in his teeth, he became one of the most proficient telemarketers in his chosen industry. He supported himself with dignity. He made the money to have a beautiful home custom built with every imaginable convenience and gadget to help him function as if he weren't handicapped. He became an inspiration to others in his field and to other handicapped people. He was influential in his community, generous to good causes, completely productive, and proud. He enjoyed an active social life and a happy marriage.

There is no argument that Donald got dealt a lousy hand. Bad things *do* happen to good people, and sometimes we have little or no control over such things. However, we *can* control our reactions to the cards we are dealt. After Donald had his accident, he dumped a few cards, drew a few new cards, and changed his hand by choice.

I knew Donald R. personally many years ago, when I was in direct sales. More recently, I've appeared on a number of seminar events where Christopher Reeve was another of the speakers. Imagine suddenly being dealt his hand. Going from a physically imposing, athletic, dynamic actor known to many as "Superman," to someone completely immobilized, wheelchair captive, totally dependent. He still chose to pursue a multifaceted career as a professional speaker, author, actor and producer, even though the very act of getting out of bed was a Herculean project. He even forced the medical establishment to very reluctantly reconsider its position that certain spinal cord injuries are irreversible.

That's why there are always people who pull themselves out of the worst ghettos in America to become successful, prominent businesspeople, top athletes, and good family men and women. Oprah Winfrey is just one example of someone who proves this point. She emerged from the horror of child abuse to become the top female talk show host in America, a talented actress, and a savvy entrepreneur.

We choose our reactions. We decide what happens next. Complaining, whining, and proclaiming the unfairness of the situation does nothing to improve it.

I'm sort of an unjustified success. I'm woefully unqualified for just about everything I do.

As I recall, I got a C in high school speech class and probably deserved worse. I had a rather severe stuttering problem three different speech therapists failed to cure. If you had seen me stuttering and stammering as a kid, you wouldn't have wagered a nickel on my future as a professional speaker. Incredibly, I rose to success and prominence, including nine consecutive years on the biggest, most-envied-by-other-speakers seminar tour in America. The tour included dozens of cities each year with audiences as large as 35,000; I appeared with former U.S. presidents, world leaders, Hollywood celebrities, famous athletes, and other top speakers. By any reasonable appraisal, I didn't belong there. I chose to be there.

The fact that I earn a large income as a writer would be a heart attack-sized surprise to my English and journalism teachers. In total, I've had nine books published. My first business book, "The Ultimate Sales Letter," has become something of a "bible" for advertising copywriters and has been continuously available in bookstores since 1991. That kind of longevity is rare. My books have been translated in five different languages, published in 20 different countries.

Over the years, I've talked to a lot of people *thinking about* writing a book. Many hold back because they feel they aren't qualified. That's a double whammy; a self-deficiency and an inaccurate appraisal of the way the marketplace works. Others have written books but not done what is necessary to market them. Generally, everybody's waiting for somebody else to discover them, certify them, anoint them, invest in them — instead of deciding to make happen what they want to happen.

I'm also responsible for the sale of tens of millions of dollars of merchandise each year through the advertising that I create, but I have no formal training in that field.

I could go on with other resume items, all the result of decision, not of qualification.

Personally, I prefer being an unjustified success rather than a justified failure.

One corner of my office is graced by a huge, stuffed Yogi Bear. He's there to remind me of his favorite saying: "I'm smarter than the average bear." That's me: smarter than the average bear. I'm not necessarily better educated, or better qualified, or better capitalized, or better connected. But "street-smarter." Go-ahead, I say, run your best at me. I'll keep figuring out new ways to win faster than anybody else can manufacture new obstacles! *That* is the attitude of the entrepreneur who makes it big.

Some cynic once said, "There is no justice. Only power." As an entrepreneur, you have tremendous opportunity to acquire the power of control over all aspects of your life. I'm not talking about the kind of power you lord over

25

everybody — bullying power, brute power. I mean the power to arrange your life as you desire it to be. To associate with people you really enjoy and benefit from being with, to earn an income truly commensurate with your contributions, to live where you most want to live, to travel or to stay home. Your finances are not controlled by some corporate bureaucracy or the whim of a boss. You write your own paycheck.

I have, for example, arranged my business affairs so that I can take many minivacations, linked to business travel, as well as extended vacations without worry. I can work at home and let my office run itself. I never have to sit in rush-hour traffic. I get to pick and choose clients and projects.

You get the power by deciding to have power.

If you like what you've read ... check this out!

FOOTNOTES ❦

Dan Kennedy is a highly-paid direct-response copywriter, consultant, coach and advisor to thousands of his 'Inner Circle Members' worldwide, and a confidante to over 100 first-generation, from-scratch millionaire and multi-millionaire entrepreneurs. He is the author of nine books, including the "No B.S." series of books published by Entrepreneur Press. Information about Dan is available at www.dankennedy.com.

Do YOU Have The Entrepreneurial Spirit?

by Cynthia Peavler Bull

Entrepreneurs are a special breed, and although obsessed with reaching their *own* goals, are genuinely concerned to use their experiences to help others. They dedicate themselves to years of hard work, sometimes experiencing failure, but they push forward and don't take "no" for an answer — even when they feel like quitting. They possess determination, drive and guts. Some might say an entrepreneur is simply possessed!

What distinguishes an entrepreneur from another person? An entrepreneur **ACTS** on his thoughts, instincts and talents and actually **DOES** something — despite the odds. His passion is breath itself with tremendous power and it propels him to take risks. Even when that "creative spark" dims and he is immersed in doubts, the entrepreneurial spirit just keeps igniting, pushing him beyond self-imposed or external limits.

"That's scary!" you say, and indeed it is. But for the entrepreneur, that spark is the life force in its purest form. Somehow the entrepreneur continues to burn the midnight (and early a.m.) oil, sweats and stews details and frustrations ... and turns it all into **$uccess**.

Make excuses? Entrepreneurs have heard them all and known some of them personally on their journey to success. Do entrepreneurs hold a biased view? Most assuredly! Because they seek to improve life for themselves and others by making it richer, fuller and happier, and almost always get paid for doing what they love to do!

What makes entrepreneurs special?

It's important to understand their mind, their "psyche" and what motivates them. As a group they're dedicated, determined, driven to realize a dream deep within the spirit that ignites the creative spark that pushes them forward. When faced with disappointments, they find inspiration to continue toward their goals — and that spirit just keeps igniting. They are **ACTIVE DOERS** despite the odds. But they also push themselves even further, finding new challenges to take

27

on, reaching new heights. Along the way, they earn the respect of peers and even adversaries as they continue building a reputation of excellence.

What transformation takes place that turns an ordinary person into an entrepreneur? What sets them apart as an acknowledged leader, a person with knowledge or expertise? **When their efforts produce results that clearly distinguish them from others**. Part of it is sweat and toil, trial and error, success and failure, long hours, feast and famine; real-life situations that they transcend. In one way or another, they "pay their dues" and log hard hours to gain the knowledge and experience that puts them ahead of the pack. Part of their mystique is a continuing search for elusive ideas and the desire to make them REAL. It's a combination of experience, opportunity, timing and knowing when to pick up an option, sometimes, repeating the drill and then stepping in at the right moment.

Yes, being an entrepreneur can be scary. It takes guts to pursue dreams, and entrepreneurs have realized dreams many times over. Their success comes from having a proven formula, character, business and personal ethics, and from dealing fairly with people who have come to trust them.

Have you ever wondered why entrepreneurs help YOU make money?

In the Internet world, entrepreneurs are certainly busy making money for themselves. But what you might not realize — or want to believe — is that most entrepreneurs truly want to help **YOU** succeed! WOW! Are you *really* aware of that? **BELIEVE IT!** Sure, they'll make even *more* money by helping you, but the ones I've met are called to a higher purpose than the proverbial buck.

We're **ALL** ears when it comes to making money, but truly successful people **share** their experiences, holding back little because they realize there is a greater good and that by sharing the wealth of knowledge, their fair share comes back to them. They support and live the theory, the principle, the universal truth of reciprocity.

Today, there are Internet entrepreneurs in every area imaginable to tell you "everything you need to know about, blah, blah, blah," and "Ten Steps for better, blah, blah, blah." If you want warehouses filled with $$ practically overnight, believe me, free-flowing ideas on how to do just that are probably seven out of 10 mouse clicks away. But finding truly reputable entrepreneurs requires careful searching — and *LUCK*. Is it an accident that you and they become linked? I doubt it.

When you encounter entrepreneurs and have an opportunity to work with them, you're going to get mega doses of support to encourage, nurture and inspire your efforts and to celebrate your successes. They are genuinely interested in helping you to improve your life and to make it more meaningful, both for you and others in your present as well as in your future. And, if they can show you how to get paid for doing what you love, then you have helped them reach yet another of their goals.

Are entrepreneurs the same?

How many entrepreneurs do you know and do they really fit the stereotypic mold of an entrepreneur? If you can think outside the box, then entrepreneurs may be all around you — in disguise!

Most people think of entrepreneurs as people who step out from the crowd, take a risk and somehow make lots of money, while the rest of us stand on the sidelines of life. However, what about those entrepreneurs not so recognizable — those "in disguise!" Who are they?

I ask you now to expand your thinking and consider who **else** might have the entrepreneurial spirit, someone whose goal is not just making money.

Webster's Tenth Edition defines an entrepreneur as
- One who organizes, manages and assumes the risks of a business or enterprise.

Business we understand. Enterprise is defined as
- A project or undertaking that is difficult, complicated and/or risky.
- Readiness to engage in daring action; initiative.

... which brings us to ...

The unexpected ("silent") entrepreneur

Let me introduce you to Helen, a well-educated, well-trained and experienced lady who has always worked for someone else and always fulfilled her commitments. Helen received her RN degree in '68, a B.S. in '71 and her Master's in '77, and for a time taught psychiatric nursing in New Jersey. She has three kids and has outlived two husbands. Her first husband died in '57 when her children were ages 10, five and six months. When her children were little, she wanted to join the Army, but put her dreams aside and honored her family commitments. She remarried in '71, the same year she earned her B.S. degree.

After her husband's retirement in '77, the family moved to a small seaside community, where Helen says she "came kicking and screaming." She had just earned her Master's and was looking forward to continuing her nursing career in New Jersey, but she began working as a psychiatric nurse for a community agency, continuing there after her second husband's death in '85. Helen eventually retired after 26 years of service, **BUT** she always held on to her dreams.

So, what is it about Helen's story that parallels the entrepreneurial spirit? Well, here's the **neat** part.

While Helen has passed the age to enter the Army, she has taken another route to fulfilling her dreams. In March 2003, Helen applied to the Peace Corps and was in the final processing stages one year later. Helen was scheduled to be

29

in Washington, D.C., in March 2004, and to leave for Albania, Europe, later that month to begin teaching maternal and child health care, nutrition, diet and other health-related topics.

What's the **truly amazing** part?

According to Webster's definition, Helen meets the criteria as an entrepreneur. She has organized, managed and assumed the risks of undertaking a difficult and complicated project. According to MY definition, her readiness and initiative certainly led her to engage in daring action.

Now, for the **SUPER AMAZING** part!

Helen is over 70 years old.

What does she want to do after her two years of Peace Corps service? Re-enlist — if they'll have her.

I've always admired this remarkable lady for many reasons. She's a no-nonsense person who sees things as they are and somehow manages to clear away the cobwebs despite all the spiders.

Is she an entrepreneur? You **bet** she is!

What can you learn from Helen? Essential characteristics of every entrepreneur.

Are YOU an entrepreneur?

Do YOU have the spirit it takes to succeed, to transcend the ordinary? If you've ever found yourself in one of these situations, then you might be an entrepreneur:

- You get up in the middle of the night scrounging around for a pencil/pen and the tiniest piece of paper to write down ideas because you *know* that getting back to sleep doesn't guarantee you'll remember them in the morning.
- You wake up — again! — at 3 a.m., your mind racing with thoughts of how to improve your website, write copy, how to approach new partnerships and you end up going to the computer to "get it all down."
- While driving, you stop by the roadside to write down notes while they're still fresh in your mind. Thank goodness in your excitement you remember to pull off the road!
- You leave home because there's no "space" for you to think and regroup your ideas, and then drive around for three hours until it's safe to go home when everyone's asleep and you can sit quietly and "create!"
- You tell your spouse (significant other), "I'm tired, can we do IT later?" Then, after lying without sleep for what seems like hours, get up in the dead of night to write copy, create a product or plan marketing strategy.

30

If you've ever done any of these, then **You've Got It!** This sometimes delicate quality makes you hard as nails and **drives** you to do "whatever it takes" to realize your goal, your dream, your passion. Dare to dream and become the entrepreneur you were destined to become!

"May we each soar to the heights we are destined to reach and always be receptive to the visions we have yet to imagine." © 2005 CYN-R-JE Consultants

If you like what you've read ... check this out!

FOOTNOTES ♀

*Cynthia, founder of CYN-R-JE Consultants, LLC™, has helped many international authors, marketers and speakers reach new heights and add greater value to their products through her writing and editing services. Contact her at **www.cynrje.com** for a 50% discount on your next writing or editing project.*

Take a Chance on Yourself & Small Business!

Your twelve-step program to free yourself from Corporate America.

by Robert DeLaurentis

One of the most defining moments in my life occurred in 1992 when Partner Bob, for whom I'd worked long, hard and cheap for, called me in and said, "Robert, your services are no longer needed." Those seven words, uttered without emotion or explanation, sounded like a death knell. I remember thinking, "Welcome to the real world ... oh poor pitiful me!"

I had experienced adversity before: I served my time in the North Arabian Gulf during the Persian Gulf War, I'd lost friends and family members without warning and I'd previously cheated death. However, the stunned sense of helplessness I felt when Partner Bob took away my livelihood hurt as powerfully as any pain I'd ever known. In an instant, Partner Bob took away everything I had been preparing for since childhood. What about my plan to take the world by storm, to scramble to the top of the Corporate American heap? And, what about wealth? Let's not forget that. All of it was gone, thanks to Partner Bob.

On the way out the door that day, laden with a pathetic look and my little box of belongings, I looked up as someone told me, "Bob just did you the biggest favor of your life. You just don't realize it yet."

Truer words were never spoken. For the first time in my professional life, I was headed in the right direction. By following these twelve principles, I would soon achieve financial freedom.

Find a mentor or partner to guide you through rough waters.

I did not pursue my first business venture alone. I found a skilled partner who had been in business for several years. Author and entrepreneur, Susan Gilbert, took me on sales calls, showed me that my aggressive style didn't always work in small business, taught me skills that I lacked, and even lent me a door to put between two filing cabinets to use as my first desk. Two minds *can* be better than one. Others can help share the load (and risk) until you feel ready to take your first step.

Don't be afraid to take a chance. If you don't try, you will not succeed.

My partner and I took our two best business ideas to market at the same time. We paid for equipment with a credit card so we could get started. One venture involved implanting digital voice chips into stuffed animals so customers could record personalized messages and give the toys as gifts. We sold the finished product to deploying soldiers at military bases around San Diego. The second venture involved buying the rights to do computerized hair, weight and character imaging to help men and women find a new look that worked for them. The computerized imaging concept took off; however, the talking stuffed animals flopped. We sold the recording equipment and toy inventory for a profit and focused on the computerized imaging business. We wouldn't have succeeded if we hadn't taken the chance.

Mitigate the risk.

Start by negotiating. Every dollar you save as a result can lessen your risk. Let's use buying real estate as an example. If you do a good job of negotiating, you shouldn't pay more than about 90 percent of market value. If you buy a property and find you have bitten off more than you can chew, you can always sell it. After closing costs and fees, you should still break even.

Do something every day to get closer to your goals.

When I decided I wanted to focus on real estate, I read every book I could find on the subject. I went to the library and read books that applied to financing and buying rental properties for close to nothing down. When I exhausted the library's free resources, I went to the bookstores. I attended three seminars as my friend's guest; my cost was the price of the hotel room we stayed in. As a matter of habit, I read a book chapter each day until I got to where I could read a whole book and only learn one or two new things. The things I learned, and what you could learn using the same methods, helped me make the next deal.

Tell the Universe that you want to be an entrepreneur in control of your financial future.

During the war, I was stationed on a guided missile cruiser off the coast of Kuwait, and each day I wrote in my journal about my experiences and what I envisioned for my life in the future. I looked at that journal a few years ago and my jaw dropped when I read, "What a great life it would be if I could continue to buy real estate, live off the positive cash flow, work part-time and travel the world." That's exactly the life I lead today.

Learn to use leverage to achieve your business goals.

Your job has to do more than just sell your time; it must pay you a residual or help you to achieve leverage. I learned this concept from my brother-in-law

33

and sister who own two successful insurance agencies. Every time a customer renews a policy, they get a commission check. They don't have to talk with the customer; the checks just keep coming in — it's a good plan. They are the least stressed people I know, they have plenty of time to spend with their family, and their big home on the golf course doesn't hurt either. I achieved my leverage with real estate. If I buy a million-dollar house with 10 percent down and the real estate market in San Diego appreciates 23- to 33-percent a year, like it has for the last decade, I make $230- to $330K a year before I even get out of bed. That's a healthy return on my money, and I get to live in the house, to boot!

Smile in the face of adversity until it surrenders.

Starting a small business can be difficult at times, but the rewards can greatly exceed the cost. Be your own hero. If you aren't, who will be? As an entrepreneur, you are doing something for yourself. Every ounce of your blood, sweat and tears will pay you dividends. If this chance to earn your financial freedom doesn't make you smile, nothing will.

Track the dollars.

Any business needs cash flow. You must have a firm grip on what comes in and goes out. When I consider purchasing a property, I do conservative cash flow projections based on current numbers, and on what I believe I can rent the property for after renovations. If I can't make $500 positive cash flow on each renovated property, it's not worth my time. I move on to the next opportunity.

Be flexible.

You will never know whether your business plan will work until you test it. I have a friend who built a $200,000 ice cream store, only to discover that his location didn't work. He found that multiple mall carts and a catering service that featured his ice cream were much more cost effective than the expensive storefront. Your business can guide you in the direction it wants to go based on demand. Listen and watch for the signals. When I bought my second rental property in San Diego, it had an attached granny flat that rented for $300. I painted the unit and raised the rent to $600. When I showed it, a crowd of thirty people clamored to see it, which told me I needed to start buying small units as fast as I could to take advantage of the tremendous demand.

Don't be afraid to fail.

You will never learn a lesson as quickly or as completely as you do when you fail. Ninety-five percent of small businesses fail, so be prepared to try different ideas to ensure that yours doesn't. Each effort will teach you more. There is no shame in making an attempt and giving it your all. My first attempt at small business was to sell a cash savings guide through the newspaper. It didn't work. I didn't sell a single copy! My failure didn't stop me. I just moved on to the next project a "wiser entrepreneur."

Don't be afraid to ask.

The military has a policy of "Don't ask, don't tell." My policy is, "Don't ask, don't get!" What does it hurt to ask for a discount? I was at Lowe's the other day, buying a couple thousand dollars worth of supplies, and I asked a manager if she had a 10 percent off coupon for a good customer. She handed me one — a $75 rebate coupon for the washing machine I was buying. In that moment, I made four times what Partner Bob paid me for a day of mentally exhausting work. If you don't know, ask. The answer may surprise you.

Do it one step at a time, and eventually you will arrive.

Rome wasn't built in a day. Your small business, too, needs time to grow. It took me five years and three small business ventures before I found the one that would more than match my corporate salary. Today, I earn 57 times more per year than what Partner Bob paid me in the salt mines, and I only work 20 hours a week doing what I enjoy. Eat your heart out, Partner Bob. You *did* do me the biggest favor of my life.

If you like what you've read ... check this out!

FOOTNOTES

*The founder and president of San Diego-based Innorev Enterprises, Inc. and Cyprias Enterprises, LLC., **Robert DeLaurentis** owns and manages over 100 houses, condos, apartments, and storage units. Learn how you, too, can be a real estate mogul. Receive Robert's **"Insider Real Estate Secrets"** at www.realestatetips.biz.*

Capitalizing on Your Strengths

by Brian Tracy

One of the qualities of high achievers is self-reliance. They accept complete responsibility for themselves and everything that happens to them. They look to themselves as the source of their successes and as the main cause of their problems and difficulties. They say, "If it's to be, it's up to me." When things aren't moving along as fast as they want, they ask themselves, "What is it in me that is causing this problem?" They refuse to make excuses or to blame people. Instead, they look for ways to overcome obstacles and to make progress.

Most people in America start off in their careers with little more than their ability to work. More than 80 percent of the millionaires in America started with nothing. Most people have been broke, or nearly broke, several times during their young-adult years. But the ones who eventually get ahead are those who do certain things in certain ways, and those actions set them apart from the masses. Perhaps the most important thing they do, consciously or unconsciously, is to look at themselves strategically, thinking about how they can better use themselves in the marketplace, how they can best capitalize on their strengths and abilities to increase their returns to themselves and their families.

Your most valuable financial asset is your earning ability — your ability to earn money. It's like a pump. By properly applying it to the marketplace, you can pump tens of thousands of dollars a year into your pocket. All your knowledge, education, skills and experience contribute toward your earning ability — your ability to get results for which someone will pay money.

And your earning ability is like farmland. If you don't take excellent care of it, if you don't fertilize it and cultivate it and water it on a regular basis, it soon loses its ability to produce the kind of harvest that you desire. Successful men and women are those who are extremely aware of the importance and value of their earning ability, and they work every day to keep it growing and current with the demands of the marketplace.

One of the greatest responsibilities in life is to identify, develop and maintain an important marketable skill. It is to become very good at doing something for which there is a strong market demand.

In corporate strategy, we call this the development of a "competitive advantage." For a company, a competitive advantage is defined as an area of excellence in producing a product or service that gives the company a distinct edge over its competition.

In capitalizing on your strengths as the president of your own personal-services corporation, you also must have a clear competitive advantage. You also must have an area of excellence. You must do something that makes you different from and better than your competitors. Your ability to identify and develop this competitive advantage is the most important thing you do in the world of work. It's the key to maintaining or increasing your earning ability. It's the foundation of your financial success. Without it, you're simply a pawn in a rapidly changing environment. But with a distinct competitive advantage, due to your strengths and abilities, you can write your own ticket. You can take charge of your life. You can always get a job, and the more distinct your competitive advantage, the more money you can earn and the more places in which you can earn it.

There are four keys in capitalizing on one's strengths. They are applicable for people who work in huge companies, such as General Motors, for candidates running for election and for individuals who want to accomplish the very most in the very shortest time.

The first of these four keys is specialization. No one can be all things to all people. A "jack-of-all-trades" also is a "master of none." That career path usually leads to a dead end. Specialization is the key. Men and women who are successful have general skills, but they also have one or two areas where they have developed the ability to perform in an outstanding manner.

Your decision about how, where, when and why you are going to specialize in a particular area of endeavor is perhaps the most important decision you will ever make in your career. It was well said that if you don't think about the future, you can't have one. A major reason why so many people are finding their jobs eliminated and finding themselves unemployed for long periods of time is because they didn't look down the road of life far enough and prepare themselves well enough for the time when their current jobs would expire. They suddenly found themselves out of gas on a lonely road, facing a long walk back to regular and well-paying employment. "Don't let this happen to you."

In determining your area of specialization, put your current job out of mind for the moment, and take the time to look deeply into yourself. Analyze yourself from every point of view. Rise above yourself, and look at your lifetime of activities and accomplishments in determining what your area of specialization could be or should be.

And by the way, you might be doing exactly the right job for you at this moment. You already might be capitalizing on all your strengths, and your current work might be ideally suited to your likes and dislikes to your temperament and your personality. Nevertheless, you owe it to yourself to continually expand the scope of your vision and look toward the future to see where you might want to go in the months and years ahead. Remember, the best way to predict the future is to create it.

You possess special talents and abilities that make you unique, different from anyone else who has ever lived. The odds of there being another person just like you are more than 50 billion to one. Your remarkable and unusual combination of education, experience, knowledge, problems, successes, difficulties, and challenges — and your way of looking at and reacting to life — make you extraordinary. You have within you potential competencies and attributes than can enable you to accomplish virtually anything you want in life. Even if you lived for another 100 years, it would not be enough time for you to plumb the depths of your potential. You will never be able to use more than a small pair of your inborn abilities. Your main job is to decide which of your talents you're going to exploit and develop to their highest and best possible use right now.

So what is your area of excellence? What are you especially good at right now? If things continue to stay as they are, what are you likely to be good at in the future — say, one-or two-or even five-years from now? Is this a marketable skill with a growing demand, or is your field changing in such a way that you are going to have to change as well if you want to keep up with it? Looking into the future, what could be your area of excellence if you were to go to work on yourself and your abilities? What should be your area of excellence if you want to rise to the top of your field, make an excellent living and take complete control of your financial future?

You can become almost anything you need to become, in order to accomplish almost anything you want to accomplish; if you simply decide what it is and then learn what you need to learn. This is such an obvious fact that most people miss it completely.

Early on in my professional life, after working as a copywriter for some years, I decided that I wanted to get into real estate development. Using the same process that enabled me to excel at copywriting, I went to the library and began checking out and reading all the books on real estate development. At the time, I had no money, no contacts and no knowledge of the industry, but I knew the great secret: I could learn what I needed to learn so that I could do what I wanted to do.

Within 12 months, I had tied up a piece of property with a $100 deposit and a 30-day option. I put together a proposal for a shopping center, and I tentatively arranged for major anchor tenants and several minor tenants that together took up 85 percent of the square footage I had proposed. Then, I sold 75 percent of the entire package to a major development company in exchange for the companies putting up all the cash and providing me with the resources and people I needed to manage the construction of the shopping center and the completion of the leasing. Virtually everything that I did, I had learned from books written by real estate experts — books on the shelves of the local library.

As you might have noticed, the fields of copywriting and real estate development are very different. But these endeavors, and every other business situation I have been in over the years, had one element in common: success in each area was based on the decision, first, to specialize in that area and, second, to be extremely knowledgeable in that area so that I could do a good job.

In looking at your current and past experiences for an area of specialization, one of the most important questions to ask yourself is, "What activities have been most responsible for my success in life to date?" How did you get from where you were to where you are today? What abilities seemed to come easily to you? What things do you do well that seem to be difficult for most other people? What things do you most enjoy doing? What things do you find most intrinsically motivating? What things make you happy when you are doing them?

In capitalizing on your strengths, your level of interest, excitement, and enthusiasm about the particular job or activity is a key factor. You'll always do best and make the most money in a field that you really enjoy. It will be an area that you like to think about and talk about and read about and learn about. Successful people love what they do, and they can hardly wait to get to it each day. Doing their work makes them happy, and the happier they are, the more enthusiastically they do it, and the better they do it as well.

In capitalizing on your strengths, the second key is differentiation. You must decide what you're going to do to be not only different, but also better than your competitors in the field. Remember, you have to be good in only one specific area to move ahead of the pack, and you must decide what that area should be.

The third key in capitalizing on your strengths is segmentation. You have to look at the marketplace and determine where you can best apply yourself with your unique talents and abilities to give yourself the highest possible return on energy expended. Which customers, companies, and markets can best utilize your special talents and offer you the most in terms of financial rewards and future opportunities?

The final key to capitalizing on your strengths is concentration. Once you have decided the area in which you are going to specialize, how you are going to differentiate yourself, and where in the marketplace you can best apply your strengths. Your final job is to concentrate all of your energy on becoming excellent in that field. The marketplace pays extraordinary rewards only for performance that is extraordinary.

In the final analysis, everything that you have done up to this point is simply the groundwork for becoming outstanding in your chosen field. When you become very good at doing whatever people need when they need it, you begin moving rapidly into the top ranks of working people everywhere.

If you like what you've read ... check this out!

FOOTNOTES ✪

*Brian Tracy is one of the top professional speakers in the world. He addresses more than 450,000 people each year throughout the United States, Canada, Europe, Australia and Asia. His keynote speeches, talks and seminars are customized for each audience. They have been described as "inspiring, entertaining, informative and motivational." He has worked with more than 500 corporations, given more than 2,000 talks and addressed millions of people. For full information on booking Brian Tracy to speak at your next meeting or conference, visit **http://www. briantracy.com**, call **858-481-2977**, or write to Brian Tracy International, 462 Stevens Road, Solana Beach, CA, 92075.*

10 + 1 Secrets of Inspiring Personal Leadership ... And the Profitable Results!

by Carol-Ann Hamilton

How Do You Walk in the World?

"**D**id you leave a trail of kindness behind you today?" Ever since a colleague shared this wonderful phrase, it has become a guiding light for my work and life. Think about it. If we were to engage with everyone this way, wouldn't ours be time well-lived?

Unfortunately, my quarter-century corporate career more often than not saw me on the receiving end of unkind leadership. However, I have come to sincerely thank these toxic bosses. For, without their example of how NOT to treat people, my commitment to transform the workplace would not be as bone-deep.

Yes, these soul-wounding leaders gave me my purpose, and I am honored as a result of their difficult lessons because they permit me to now offer you positive opportunities — entrepreneurial and otherwise — through your personal leadership.

In turn, you will be called to action–to do whatever it takes to become a beloved leader. People will go to the ends of the Earth for the beloved — even when painful actions and decisions are required. No matter what, the best leaders achieve their stellar results precisely because they bring loving kindness to everyone they meet. To become beloved is to embody what respectfully ought to be your singular mission: *"What can I do to make sure the people around me never forget how treasured they are?"*

Converse with me as you read. Adopt an attitude of questioning and discovery. Challenge yourself by holding an invisible "mirror of examination" to your behaviors and beliefs. Ask, *"How do I leave the people whose paths I cross feeling? Do I leave a trail of kindness where I go?"*

Who Are You as a Personal Leader?

You see, personal leadership has nothing to do with the nature of your business, your latest entrepreneurial pursuits or your job description. You can be a CEO, president, or principal without acquiring followers or you can hold a non-managerial title and yet inspire everyone around you by walking your talk.

So, what creates the magic? The answer lies in your personal integrity, attitude, vision and values. It is through your unique personal style that others accord you the right to lead. Position power doesn't cut it. Personal power does.

It's just that with our hurry-up sickness in North America, we tend to hugely under-value "being" in favor of "doing." Doing takes an active form and can be evidenced in bottom-line results. It is easier to see doing — even if often in the form of "ready, fire, aim."

Being, on the other hand, is perceived as less tangible. Being is how we achieve results — the character traits we exhibit to realize gains. An enterprise can achieve the most impressive numbers, but if they come at the hands of beleaguered employees, shoddy practices and questionable ethics, one wonders how satisfying was the win at day's end?

Let me ask you some questions: "Do you and your team produce passionately versus passively? Are employees fully present — engaging their full capacity at work? Or did they leave their best talents at the company gate — becoming 9-to 5-drones?"

The performance difference stems from personal leadership. It starts with who you *are* as a personal leader. Personal character will define your ultimate accomplishment.

The Top-Ten List

More specifically, personal leadership is about uplifting others, acknowledging their essence and igniting their enthusiasm — thus answering the soul's yearning for meaning and belonging. Inspiring personal leadership is about consistently living your principles. It is about accountability for how you walk in the world.

So, here's my invitation; please consider this Top-Ten list as the secrets for not only being an inspiring leader in business, but in your own life.

1. **Outer transformation begins with your inner world.**
Personal leaders accept full responsibility for demonstrating authenticity. By modeling sincerity, they encourage others to do the same. True leaders recognize openness as a necessary ingredient to being trusted. Authentic personal leaders drop their masks, show emotions and get real.

2. **"How we *really* are around here" starts with your leadership.**
Inspiring leaders' character and values show courage of conviction; they take tough stands on others' behalves. Instead of "shooting the messenger," they invite truth-telling from everyone — especially the front line. These gutsy leaders operate completely opposite to valueless workplaces — recognized by the beautiful lobby wall plaque listing corporate values that no one actually practices on the job.

41

3. Think of yourself as a "servant" to others.

With an interest toward what's best for all rather than "what's in it for me," personal leaders insist on service from everyone. They never tolerate behaviors contrary to the greater interest. Those who lead have earned the right through their own credibility with followers. Even if skilled, wayward individuals are not allowed to prevail.

4. Remember what is really important in life.

Work-life balance is a way of being, one lives and not a programmed-one "does." Compassionate leaders point out unhealthy behaviors rather than laud those who put in sixteen-hour days. Their investment in wellness creates a more resilient workforce; able to prosper in a competitive global environment. Nurturing leaders transform people by caring — reminding even the staunchest workaholics that no one wishes he or she had spent more time at the office on his or her deathbed.

5. Build relationships first.

Personal leaders know solid relationships are the leverage to achieve results; inspiring leaders believe this is counter-intuitive. Striving toward personal mastery, they never make others wrong. At the same time, they never back away from difficult conversations when necessary.

6. Bring out the best in others.

We have entered the age of the individualist. Wise leaders ignite freedom of expression and thus meet diversified needs with diversified responses. As an outcome, these uplifting leaders attract the bright and enthusiastic team players they seek to hire and retain — becoming employers of choice in the process.

7. Adopt people-centered practices.

Soul-inspiring environments support getting the job done by making it straightforward for people to succeed. Inspiring leaders remove bureaucracy, clear roadblocks and grant employees the authority plus responsibility to satisfy customers and shareholders alike.

8. Acknowledge your fellow human being.

Rather than see people merely as human "doings," personal leaders recognize them as human beings, valuable for that reason alone. They appreciate others' uniqueness. As simple as stopping by someone's work station, they know looking for opportunities to make colleagues feel cherished pays back many times over through enhanced performance.

9. Be prepared to question your very notions about work.

Business needs to overhaul its traditional assumptions by discarding the outmoded attitude, *"they should just be grateful to have jobs."* No more, are employees willing to function as mere cogs in the organizational wheel. Inspiring leaders accept in this era of massive upheaval that to do anything less, is to risk becoming obsolete. New work options must serve the individual *and* business goals.

10. Answer peoples' yearning for a sense of meaning and purpose.

Hearts everywhere are yearning for meaningful work. Sorry! — monopoly-sized market shares do not necessarily resonate with the soul. Visions that rouse peoples innate desire to contribute do. Employees long to have their time at work make a difference rather than be mindless.

Plus One ...

We save the most provocative statement for last. It is the one that fundamentally challenges existing business norms.

11. Profit is an outcome, not a goal!

Profit is the end result of doing a number of things right by starting with treating people right. Profit is not an over-arching goal; it is a by-product. First, there must be basic human respect and dignity on the part of leaders toward their team members, then people will bring their whole selves to work. Productivity and profitability flow in direct proportion to how you treat employees, not the other way around. While this premise is contrary to "standard operating procedures," imagine any other reality is to guarantee eventual bankruptcy.

Why Should We Care?

This brings us to why it's important to care.

Inspiring leaders and entrepreneurs know people will increasingly decide where and with whom they partner to share their valuable store of creativity. An unrecognized talent war is about to inevitably shift the labor market's power balance.

Here's the issue, demographics will soon wallop organizations everywhere; promoting a massive talent exodus of seasoned employees that will overwhelmingly impact growth and productivity. Coupled with radically shifting workforce expectations, all industries face a crisis of a magnitude never before seen — no exceptions.

Forward-looking entrepreneurs and business leaders know that the solution to this brewing revolution is to respond proactively to the swelling demand for transformational leadership. They promote inspiring personal leadership as the means to build high-performance cultures where people maximize their potential *while* achieving abundance.

Entrepreneurs: "How readily do you attract and retain the bench strength you need to thrive, not just to survive? Already, it's not easy to find loyal people resources, and it's about to become lots harder. No longer are there 10 in line behind each person maltreated or otherwise disenfranchised.

Employees: This is great news for you. No longer must you tolerate the havoc wreaked by even one soul-wounding leader. Contrary to popular belief, no company can afford to let talented people burn out or leave. The marketplace cost of a poor reputation is simply too high. People can and will vote with their feet leaving "dinosaur" organizations in the dust.

There you have it — the business case for inspiring personal leadership.

While the imperative to build soul-inspiring environments currently stems from the combined power of demographics and changing attitudes, I profoundly look forward to the day when treating your team right is taken for granted as the right thing to do. Generating outstanding profits and nurturing the human spirit are not mutually exclusive — they are synonymous.

Amongst those entrepreneurs who already appreciate this truth, loyalty, commitment and high performance naturally ensue from leaders' desire to foster the respect and dignity for which employees yearn. From them, we can draw great hope. As for those who refuse to get on board, they will shortly see that whether one buys this reality or not, unstoppable forces will usher in a new way-of-being to the workplace — and by extension — the world.

The Call to Action

When we started our journey, I challenged you to consider who you are as a personal leader — in both the visible and invisible moments of truth (like when nobody is looking).

As you examined your inner core, you recognized it is a choice whether to leave a trail of kindness or destruction in your relationships. No matter your various roles in life, business and otherwise, it is singularly up to you to generate a legacy of either soul-wounding or soul-inspiring.

You learned how you can make your mark to transform the workplace; if you choose to assume the mantle of conviction and courage that characterizes an inspiring personal leader.

The rest is up to you!

Parting Question for Reflection

We stand at a hugely promising time for humanity. The vital questions people everywhere are asking themselves about what's really important can translate into all aspects of life — entrepreneurial and more.

Imagine what could happen across the planet if we listened with a generosity that dignifies the individual. What extraordinary learning could be unleashed if we promoted one another's self-actualization? All is possible when we harness and encourage others' untapped potential — mining their in-born wisdom and gifts.

The way I see to tap into this powerful time is to become that soul-

inspiring leader who transforms the workplace by leaving a trail of kindness wherever they go.

With greatest respect, allow me to thus leave you with two parting questions that may make all the difference in how you walk in the world from today forward:

1. What if you considered every interaction with the people in your life to be your last?

2. How would that thought change the quality of your relationships?

If you like what you've read ... check this out!

FOOTNOTES ✝

Carol-Ann Hamilton; pioneer-visionary and toxic boss healer is the co-author of "The A to Z Guide to Soul-Inspiring Leadership," and is an inspirational coach to leaders worldwide in transforming workplaces by maximizing people potential while attaining bottom-line prosperity. Book your complimentary organizational assessment at www.ChangingLeadership.com, and while you visit, download your FREE Leadership Report.

It's Your Movie.
Let Your Clients Play Director

by David C. Stone

Successful entrepreneurs are inquisitive creatures by nature constantly seeking interaction with other entrepreneurs feeding off the mutual transfer of expertise and experience. My association with *Mentors Magazine*™ has been an invaluable link in this information exchange as I have gained incredible insight from each and every person that appears in this book. And in being asked to contribute my own article to this anthology, I am eager to live up to my end of the bargain and leave you, the reader, my personal contribution to the information exchange.

When I began preparing this article, I let my mind wander back over my life as an entrepreneur and scrolled through the myriad of experiences that helped me get to where I am today. I spent time revisiting each phase of my career, the highs and the lows, searching for the thread of success that always managed to survive and to weave its way through the tides of my early triumphs and defeats. At every turn in that reflective journey, I recognized the one crucial characteristic that always enabled me to overcome my challenges to enhance my successes, and ultimately, to propel me to the creation of multi-million dollar corporations. This one, intrinsic and critical characteristic — *Flexibility.*

The ability to adapt to the changing needs of my clients allowed me to continuously grow and to become an ever more reliable and dependable partner for my clients. Not only was flexibility the key to surviving the ebbs and flows of my entrepreneurial endeavors, but I would argue that flexibility is the very cornerstone of entrepreneurship. In an analogical nod to Mr. Chuck Norris, a featured contributor to this anthology, I contend that while your entrepreneurial dream is certainly *your* movie, the box office success of your movie depends on letting your clients play director.

Every entrepreneur has a basic outline to build his or her dream. Many actually have a detailed blueprint highlighting everything down to the finest of details, and while it is imperative to have a clear understanding and detailed map of where we want to go if we expect to get there, we have to understand that there will inevitably be obstacles along the route we map out for ourselves. Standing your ground in the face of a challenge can contribute to success, but at times inflexibility in the face of a challenge can insure failure. Only the entrepreneur with the inherent flexibility to adapt to unexpected challenges will be able to successfully overcome the roadblocks that invariably lie ahead.

When I started out on my entrepreneurial dream, I had just graduated from Penn State University and set up shop in a spare bedroom in my home. I filled my "office" with the necessary tools for printing sales in the 1980s, including a $98 desk, a $700 cell phone (that had to be carried in what could be considered a small suitcase) and a $1,800 fax machine that no one would describe as being a "space saver."

The product offering for my initial foray into the print management industry consisted mainly of business forms and documents. If a client needed to put print to paper, I could get it done. Whatever printed materials a client needed to conduct business — be it invoices, business cards, requisition forms, envelopes, labels, etc. — I sought to fulfill those needs with superior service and competitive prices. Flashy? Certainly not, but I was filling a basic and critical need for my clients — more importantly — my entrepreneurial plan was in motion.

I had the good fortune of facing my first real unexpected challenge relatively early in my career. One day, I got a call from a large prospective client that I had met only a few weeks prior and says, "We've gone over your proposal, and we'd like to use your services." Excellent! My business was still in its infancy stage and here I was landing a new, huge account! Then he added, "And we have about one hundred pallets we'd like you to store for us." One hundred pallets?!?! The bedroom was nice and relatively roomy, but there was no way I could store one hundred pallets in it. "Absolutely," I said. "I'll pick them up on Monday." Immediately after hanging up the phone, I went to work identifying and securing a storage area large enough to house the pallets, as well as the equipment and manpower necessary to have them picked up. It hadn't been part of my original blueprint, but by incorporating flexibility into that plan, my company now officially offered storage and distribution services.

The majority of my service expansion came about through similar situations. I would find myself faced with a client needing something outside the scope of my product and service line and had to find a way to fulfill that need. If I failed to do so, I would be confronted by the prospect of losing not just that particular project, but perhaps the entire account. Through my early experiences, I quickly realized a viable, successful and long-lasting business would require the flexibility to constantly adapt and enhance my service offerings to better serve, maintain and expand my client base.

My "entrée" into commercial printing shows how being a flexible and inquisitive entrepreneur can not only result in increased business opportunities, but also can garner significant media exposure and enhanced credibility. In the early '90s, a client came to me with the following objective: his business needed to include a puzzle and a floppy disk in a direct mail piece, and he also needed to be able to use the piece as a trade show handout. I knew business forms and documents inside and out, but I certainly wasn't an expert in commercial printing. Being flexible, I decided to find a way to fulfill my client's needs, and

47

being inquisitive, I turned to colleagues who *were* experts in the various aspects of the project and drew on their collective expertise to create a solution.

Using the information I gathered, I created a promotional mailing piece with a design that not only met the client's objectives, but ultimately surpassed his expectations by reducing postage costs and increasing response rates. And, in a fortunate turn of events, not only did the project satisfy my client, but it also garnered media attention as a printing trade-press "Gold Award" winner. In this case, flexibility not only allowed me to meet a client need, but propelled me to becoming an 11-time award winning a commercial printing supplier, specializing in marketing, advertising, direct mail, ad specialty items and promotional product services to an ever-expanding client base.

In time, I also discovered that training myself to approach each situation and challenge with a flexible mindset enabled me to manage the expectations and perceived needs of my clients. In those instances where I determined that adapting my services to fulfill a perceived need was not the best option, I could, instead, use flexibility to alter the specific details of the client's perceived need.

To illustrate this point, I once found myself competing for a client who needed an annual run of 3 million credit card applications—a rather significant account for any print management firm. This retail company had over 700 stores, each with its own identity code, and the applications sent to a particular store had to be marked with that store's ID code so that the company could track how many applications each of the locations filled out. The current service provider was printing the various codes on the entire 3-million-run of applications, and then storing them separately in 700 individually labeled warehouse bin locations. I could have simply bid on the project using the same specifications, but since I had trained myself to approach each challenge with a flexible mindset, I immediately saw a better option.

I proposed storing all of the applications in a single-bulk section rather than 700 different ones, and then print the various codes in smaller runs more frequently instead of doing the entire run once a year. This would save the client significant storage costs, and since each of the code printing runs would still be in significant quantities, the printing price difference would be minimal. Also, having opened offices in Chicago and San Diego, I could offer less expensive, more time-efficient distribution services by storing the applications in more geographically centered locations to the client's respective stores, rather than having to ship them out across the country from a single warehouse.

I won the contract—I did so not because of the flexibility in my service offering, but because of my ability to incorporate flexibility into the client's perceived need.

Flexibility in business also allows you the potential to specialize in areas and create niche markets for clients who may traditionally be underserved by your industry. Oxford Print Management has been working with credit unions for more than 20 years, and a perfect example of flexibility leading to the development of a niche market product is the creation of the "Oxford Member Xceptance Program," which I designed specifically for my small to medium-sized credit union clients.

Several of my smaller credit union clients approached me with the idea of working with them to develop a program that would allow them to pre-screen their members and promote loan specials via direct mail pre-approval offers. Many of the largest credit unions in Southern California were my clients, and I knew that the larger credit unions had the financial means and manpower necessary to conduct direct mail pre-approval programs on their own. I also knew that even a simple credit bureau pre-screening program could prove too much of a financial burden for the smaller credit unions, let alone a full blown, man-hour-intensive direct mail effort.

So, working in tandem with my smaller credit union clients, and drawing on the resources available to a full-service print management firm, we designed a turnkey, cost-effective program that allows credit unions to simply submit their target list and have Oxford do the rest: work with the credit bureaus on their behalf for pre-screening services; design and print a customized mailer; and take care of the entire mailing process including postage. By incorporating flexibility into our business strategy, we created a product that makes it economically and physically feasible for small- to medium-sized credit unions to effectively reach out to their members to promote special offers and great rates, thereby cultivating a steady stream of new loan revenue.

My entrepreneurial dream—my movie—started with a simple plan. Incorporating flexibility into that plan has enabled me to go from working out of a bedroom office to running multi-million dollar corporations with offices in Chicago and San Diego. Never lose sight of the fact that your entrepreneurial dream is *your* movie, and by letting your clients play director can make your movie a box office smash.

If you like what you've read ... check this out!

FOOTNOTES ⚱

David C. Stone is president and CEO of Oxford Print Management and Printex Designs. With offices in San Diego and Chicago, Mr. Stone has been providing print management services to clients nationwide for more than 20 years. For more information, visit www.ioxford.com or call 619-282-0005. To receive your Free Monthly e-Specials, send an email to sales@ioxford.com.

It's Easier Becoming An "Infopreneur"

by Wayne Van Dyck

Entrepreneurs thrive during periods of rapid change, and we are living in such a time right now. The good news is that the more rapid the change, the greater the opportunities available to entrepreneurs.

The explosion of new technologies make this an unprecedented period in economic history for entrepreneurial opportunities: cheap computers, new software applications and digital networks — namely the **Internet** — are powerful tools available to everyone who wants to create financial independence and improve his or her lifestyle.

The Money Game

I've been a student of business since I began my career as a venture capitalist on Wall Street. Over the years, I raised millions of dollars to finance numerous entrepreneurs and start-up companies until I decided to become an entrepreneur myself and financed my own companies in broadcasting, alternative energy, software and telecommunications. I was the CEO of the company that built the first digital network in Moscow, in 1990, and started one of the first B2B Internet service providers.

It's from this perspective that I see fantastic **new entrepreneurial opportunities** unfolding, and nowhere is this more apparent than in the world of communications and information.

Because information and communication are fundamental components of every human interaction and business transaction, each new communication medium — the telegraph, telephone, radio and television — has had a successively greater impact on the world, and created great fortunes for those who rode each wave of change. The Internet will be the most significant wave of all.

The Internet

The Internet now makes it possible to reach almost any person, anywhere in the world in only a few seconds and for only a few pennies, but what makes it even more significant is that computers can convert all the traditional analog forms of information (sound and voice, printed words, pictures and data) into a common **digital medium** for transmission over the Internet. This capability is radically changing existing businesses and creating vast new entrepreneurial opportunities.

While the Internet is affecting every business in every industry, its greatest impact will be on the **information industries'** products and services. Think of some of the biggest businesses in the world. Think entertainment (music and movies), think broadcasting (news, information and entertainment), think publishing (books and magazines) and biggest of all, think training and education (books, courses and continuing education).

To see the **Internet's** potential impact, let's look at one small, well-established medium: the book.

Analog Economics

A physical book requires harvesting trees to make paper, onto which a story or information is transferred via a printing press. Then many hands and lots of energy are required to move the book from manufacturing plant to retail store and, finally, to the consumer. This process is resource, labor and capital intensive.

To see how this works in financial terms, let's consider how an author of a book would benefit from this:

In the analog world he or she writes their book and receives 10 percent of every sale, or $2.50 on each $25 book sale. The publisher retains the remaining $22.50 for manufacturing, distribution and selling expenses. Let's further assume that the publisher pushes hard and sells 25,000 copies in one year, a decent number in the **offline** publishing world. Our author would then earn **$62,500** ($2.50 x 25,000 copies) for their creative efforts.

Digital Economics

The same book can be produced and packaged in a digital form known as an "eBook," and delivered anywhere in the world in seconds, at 1/100th the cost and with almost no environmental impact.

So, let's assume our author writes that same book, but decides to become an **entrepreneur** in the **digital world** by setting up a small Web business and selling their eBook online over the Internet to a worldwide market, and for the sake of this example, let's assume that it sells the same number of books at the same price.

Looking at the costs of doing this, over the year the author would spend about $2,500 to build the Web site, $4,000 a month for a half-time web-master, $150 per month to host the Web site (that sells and collects money 24-hours a day, seven days a week) and an additional $10,000 per month to buy pay-per-click ads on Google to get traffic to his or her site.

At the end of one year their expenses ($2,500 for construction, $48,000 for the web-master, $1,800 for hosting and $120,000 for advertising) would total about $172,300. On the income side, revenues ($25 per copy x 25,000 copies) would total $625,000. When we subtract the expenses from the revenues, our author is left with **$452,700**. Cheap **digital tools** and the Internet's reach provide the author with the leverage to do a little more work…but make a lot more money.

51

He or she could never enjoy this sort of success in the offline world.

This simple example shows the amazing leverage of becoming an entrepreneur and selling information products in the new digital world. Whereas in the physical world, our author earned 10 percent of the revenues ($62,500), in the digital world, earnings are more like 70 percent ($452,700), or **seven times more income**.

The New Capital

This new digital world shifts the advantage from those with, or having access to, financial capital, to those with **intellectual capital** — and that's exciting.

In the analog world of physical publishing, setting up the systems to manufacture, store, ship, distribute and retail books requires lots of financial capital. Plants and offices have to be built to hold the equipment, people and inventory. Trucks have to be purchased to transport the books to the stores that have to be opened to sell them. As a result, entrepreneurs have had to start almost any venture by first raising a lot of financial capital, commonly known as venture capital.

Again, the **Internet** changes all this.

In the digital world, the business infrastructure is embedded inside computers and networks, and increasingly intelligent software replaces most of the manual and clerical functions critical to any business. Setting up a digital business requires intellectual capital but relatively little financial capital. Thus, the power shifts from the people with the money to the people with the ideas and intellectual horsepower to recognize, harness and leverage the new information technologies.

The Economic Tsunami

Already, we've seen 30-year-olds start with little or nothing on the Internet and become multimillionaires (even some billionaires) while large companies run to the courts in an effort to hold back the **economic tsunami** brought on by these new technologies and quick-witted entrepreneurs.

We first saw the digital world impact the music industry; now it's affecting Hollywood's monopoly on film and video distribution, and soon we'll see it affecting the publishing and education fields. Much faster, lower cost digital systems are replacing traditional, slow physical manufacturing and distribution systems.

As the older physical systems crumble under the economics of the new technologies, countless jobs and careers are being lost in the process. We see long-term employment disappearing; pensions are on the way out; salaries are not what they used to be, and this comes at a time when the cost of living continues to rise.

As a result, we all need to begin thinking more about becoming entrepreneurs — to understand and take advantage of these new digital technologies by creating new information products and services that will leverage our skills and expertise.

Traditionally, entrepreneurs have not only had to have the ability to envision something new, they had to raise the capital and build complex organizations to supply their new product or service, thus, requiring skills to lead, coordinate and manage.

Infopreneurs

What makes the Internet and information publishing businesses so exciting is that they don't require the traditional skills of money raising, organizational development and management to launch and build. This opens the new financial doors to a much larger group of potential entrepreneurs.

Entrepreneurs capitalizing on the new areas of digital information publishing are becoming known as **infopreneurs**. They think and work differently.

Infopreneurs are the new entrepreneurs who envision ways to apply new information technologies and systems to satisfy market needs and wants. They can see and create new economic models. They don't need to raise capital; they create it, instead. They don't manage large organizations; they guide small teams. They don't work in corporate office complexes, but in bedrooms across America. They don't have on-site employees, they have contractors spread around cyberspace, and they make a lot of money. This is the new breed.

The businesses they build are also different.

Virtual Businesses

Infopreneurs are creating a whole new category of opportunity known as **virtual businesses**. Virtual businesses exist almost entirely inside computers and networks. Most of the business functions that are handled by teams of people in the offline world are now embedded in software applications. Virtual businesses are automated collections of hardware and software connected to their customers via digital networks. They **operate 24/7**, selling and delivering information products to **worldwide markets** with minimum human intervention.

Virtual businesses receive their customers over the Internet and respond with **automated product presentations** and **virtual salespeople**. Automated eCommerce engines process transactions, and products are shipped and delivered electronically. Software systems provide supervision, control and management.

Virtual businesses exist today that were started on shoestrings. Yet, they serve the same number of customers and produce the same level of profits as venture-backed companies launched with millions of dollars and significant investments in plants and equipment. There are virtual businesses run from bedrooms that make more than companies with hundreds of employees. This is truly an entrepreneurial heyday.

www.mentorsmagazine.com

Benefits of Becoming an Infopreneur

If you've often thought about becoming an entrepreneur, or you've looking at your existing economic world quaking and shaking, if you no longer see a bright future in a big organization, if you're worried about your financial outlook, if you long for something different or more lucrative, consider becoming an infopreneur.

Becoming an infopreneur offers many significant benefits.

- **You get to be your own boss.** Working for yourself brings the freedom to work on what you want, when you want.

- **You can work anywhere.** Since all your activities take place via the Net, you can be anywhere in the world...on the beach in Hawaii, in a mountain cabin in the Alpsor or at a Starbucks in Manhattan.

- **You don't need much capital.** Info businesses can be launched on a shoestring and throw off capital instead of consuming it. The only significant capital you'll need is the intellectual capital you create by learning how to exploit these new technologies.

- **You can start in your spare time and at your own pace.** You can start slowly and maintain your 9- to 5-gig while you learn the ropes and develop the confidence and income to make the big leap to independence.

- **You don't need employees.** All the specialized talent, skills and help you'll require can be hired over the Net on a contract basis, there's no overhead or burn rate to keep you up at night. You don't even need any real management skills.

- **You can make a lot of money.** I personally know infopreneurs that make millions each year and employ only a few outside contractors. One is making more than $8 million after expenses with just nine employees, that's the leverage of virtual companies.

Internet information publishing is the most accessible entrepreneurial opportunity you will see in your lifetime. It's the easiest, fastest and least risky way to create financial independence or build a fortune. Best of all, you can do it on your terms, with no venture capitalists or shareholders telling you what to do.

Maybe **you** should consider becoming an infopreneur

If you like what you've read ... check this out!

FOOTNOTES ✪

Wayne Van Dyck is the CEO of Six Degrees Media Inc., in Sausalito, Calif., and a developer of online businesses including SellersVoice.com and SimpleMoneyMachines.com. To get a free copy of his book, go to www.YourRoadToAMillion.com or email to wvd@sbcglobal.net.

Training Young People to Become Self-Motivated Entrepreneurs

by Rhea Perry

Will Rogers once said, "Even if you're on the right track, you'll get run over if you just sit there." As a mother of seven, I've learned that if I want my children to develop their full potential, it's better to train them to motivate themselves rather than drag them through life kicking and screaming. How else will they learn to make wise decisions and develop the confidence they need to influence their world?

To do that, I had to regain control of my life because juggling the never-ending activity that comes with having so many kids had begun to overwhelm me. So, after reading the book "Margin" by Dr. Richard Swenson, we left society and moved to a farm at the "Backside of Nowhere."

Mom Had to Change Her Thoughts on Education

Out of sheer frustration with an "academically challenged" 14-year-old, (who is a lot like Thomas Edison) we sent our oldest son Drew to spend a month in Idaho with one of his first mentors, stock market specialist Chris Verhaegh. When Drew brought his entrepreneurial mindset home, I began incorporating it into our daily education. I started giving my children what Thomas Edison's mother gave him: lots of time, freedom and equipment to experiment with.

Convinced that the path to financial freedom meant earning passive residual income, Drew tried breeding dogs, rabbits, goats and cows. You've probably guessed that we learned some great management lessons and usually lost more money than we made.

So, when we realized that breeding wasn't for us, we sold most of the animals and set up six gumball machines in local businesses. Once a month, I drove the kids to service the machines, and Drew kept track of the profits.

About that time, my husband and I purchased 13 houses in a "nothing down" deal. Less than two weeks after closing, we had one of those "drive an hour to fix the toilet in the middle of the night" events. Yes, the frozen plumbing in the only empty house had thawed, and the neighbors called to inform us that water was pouring out from under the door.

Unable to get off work the next day, my husband sent Drew, instead. Drew hired the appropriate contractors and had the house repaired in just three days. Within five days, it was rented.

He came home that first day and said, "Mom, I love this!"

Trust me those are the words every mother wants to hear.

Seeking Success Includes Investing Heavily in Education

So, Drew changed directions again and became a real estate investor at age eighteen.

It seemed like a good idea to learn about this real estate investing thing from somebody who knew something about it, so to cut years off our learning curve, Drew and I flew all over the country to attend conferences of all kinds — and boy, did we get an education! Drew didn't just learn the technical aspects of real estate, negotiating and business philosophy — he also learned how to travel and how to network with others to build beneficial relationships.

We invested the equivalent of the cost of a college education in our escapades, but considering the knowledge and experience we both gained, it was worth it. Besides learning several other ways to make money from home, there's no way to estimate how much money we saved on lessons we would have learned "the hard way." Some people just don't seem to be cut out for college, and Drew is one of them. After all, in college, you have to sit still.

When Drew learned how to buy houses, he bought 13 in two years. By the time he was twenty-one, he had bought or managed 21 houses and accomplished one of his many goals.

He bought one house for $880 and sold it six months later to a rehabber for $15,000, clearing a profit of $10,000.

When he purchased a nice brick house in the country, and sold it, he swapped the down payment for a brand new 4-wheeler that had only been out of the garage three times. We agreed before the former owner delivered it that we would sell it before we fell in love with it. No problem.

After the new homeowner delivered his down payment and drove away from our farm, we stood there staring at that wonderful, powerful, shiny new blue machine all covered with racing stickers that was just begging someone to drive.

Drew and I looked at each other. Then we looked at the 4-wheeler.

"Maybe we'll just keep it for a few days," we agreed.

Within a week, the boys had bush-hogged a racetrack, complete with ramps, through the uncut sage grass in our six-acre front field. For at least a month, they lived in "Dirt Track Heaven" with only a few minor incidents and only one damaged fence. When our HVAC repairman saw the 4-wheeler, he agreed to trade three central units plus installation for it.

It was a sad day.

A year or two later, Drew accidentally bought a house on eBay™ ... in New York (we don't live in New York). One of his friends had forwarded him an auction, but he hadn't had time to read it, so he entered his proxy bid and left. The next day, he discovered that he had won the house for $4500. About six months later, he sold it for a profit ... on eBay.

I won't tell you about the lesson that almost cost him $100,000. He now focuses on failing fast in order to learn the lesson as soon as possible.

Careers Develop with Time and Experience

When people found out Drew was selling houses on eBay, they started asking him to speak at real estate investment conferences, which launched his career as a professional speaker.

So, when he graduated from managing the farm into the world of investment real estate, he passed the gumball machine route down to the next brother. But by then, his second brother had started going to professional conferences with us and had learned how to make money on the Internet. At 15, he understood the value of passive residual income, so it didn't take him long to figure out that servicing machines required leaving home. He preferred to earn his living through the click of a mouse. So, he quickly passed the gumball machine route down to the third brother, who had asked for "a source of income" for his ninth birthday.

The first time these two boys serviced a machine together, I sat in the van and watched through the window as they added more gumballs and spilled half of them on the floor! I held my breath to see if they were going to sweep them up and put them into the machine anyway. They didn't.

I breathed a big sigh of relief!

I mean, with boys, you just never know.

When they came back to the van, I didn't have to say a word — I know you won't believe this, but I didn't.

Success Stories Turn into an Annual Conference

When we moved to "The Sticks," I discovered the Internet and eventually started my own Yahoo! Group™ where I told the boys' crazy stories to friends all over the world. So, when I invited the members to come over to our farm for a one-day education workshop, 100 people came from 18 states. Four even flew!

57

The next year, we did it again, and a one-of-a-kind family learning experience was born. Now we host our own annual business conference for parents and teens to learn various ways to make money from home with our mentors and other experts. Some of our special guests have been Mark Victor Hansen, Troy McClain of NBC's "The Apprentice," and Internet millionaire Armand Morin. Drew has become one of our speakers and now teaches how to sell houses on eBay. We call it Rhea's Entrepreneur Days. They call it "Rhea's Days."

3 Keys to Practical Education

Education should be an adventure to enjoy while you solve the mystery of finding what you love to do. When my children discover a new interest, we focus on getting the skills and knowledge they need. Then, I encourage them to set and pursue goals with deadlines, which motivates them intrinsically and provide direction for making decisions.

Here is how we do it:
1. Use living books and resources written by authors who love their topic.
2. Structure meaningful projects.
3. Provide quality time with wise mentors and teachers who offer direction and advice based on experience.

Casey Stengel said, "If you don't know where you're going, you might end up somewhere else."

They key to raising an entrepreneur is this: "don't let fear of failure or fear of what others think steal your child's dream. You might discover that life holds more for you than you ever thought. After all, your child just might become the next Thomas Edison who changes the world! Dare to do something different!"

If you like what you've read ... check this out!

FOOTNOTES

Rhea Perry has educated her seven children at home since 1988. She shares success stories and offers encouragement to parents and teens in her bi-monthly newsletter and at her annual family business conference, Rhea's Entrepreneur Days. To get a copy of Drew's $880 house story, visit www.EducatingforSuccess. com/wwtw.

Avoid the Entrepreneur's Curse

by Drew Miles

I have to share this story with you because it could save your financial life. I am an attorney (for seventeen years) and I own several successful businesses. In fact, I've been involved in business for most of my life, having grown up actively involved in the family business and starting my own law firm immediately after passing the New York Bar exam. My experience tells me that the fastest path to lasting wealth is through owning your own business.

I say all that to make a point: "There is a right way to be in business and there is a wrong way. Most entrepreneurs are so busy with making money (doing the next deal, closing the next sale, etc.) that they leave themselves horribly exposed. This is what I call, 'The Entrepreneur's Curse.'"

You see, being in business the wrong way could ruin you financially. It's as if every business owner should have a neon sign in his or her office, which says:

Warning! Don't make one more dollar without reading this. You are only one lawsuit away from financial disaster.

Let me explain, recently, an acquaintance of mine (he's a body shop owner — I'll call him "Jim" for privacy purposes) had a life changing experience with a customer. She had been rear ended in a collision and brought the car in for repairs. The techs repaired the damage, refinished the rear quarter panel and trunk and got the vehicle back to factory-seconds.

Before the shop would release the car to the customer, they prudently told the insurance company they wanted to check out the front alignment with a measurement on an alignment machine (the shop was accustomed to going the extra mile for its customers and were being their conscientious best). Unfortunately, the insurance company wouldn't spring for the extra $60, so they released the car to its owner.

Later that day, the lady was driving on the interstate when the left front wheel came off her car. Her car got smashed and she was taken to the hospital complaining of chest pains and anxiety.

The next thing you know, her lawyers are calling and threatening to sue Jim for a faulty repair. Jim says, "My guys never touched the front end — we repaired the rear. Besides, I wanted to check out the front end, but the insurance company wouldn't pay me to do it. I can't afford to work for free."

"Tell it the judge," says one lawyer. "We're coming after you, your business and your million dollar house; this time next year, I'll be living in it." Then the line went dead.

This is no laughing matter Jim's lawyers explained, "You've got a real problem on your hands. We better settle with them as soon as possible."

"You see, your corporation could be giving you a false sense of security and leave you even more exposed," says one lawyer. Jim says, "What about that 'S' corporation you set up for me a few years ago? You told me that would protect my assets." Well, they explained, "When you were doing business as a sole proprietor, all of your assets were at risk, even your house, your car and your bank accounts. Setting up a corporation is a good first step, but you could have done more. You see, thousands of corporations have been set aside (the lawyers call it piercing the corporate veil) and everything in them is sold at auction. That means the business itself, your accounts, your equipment — right down to the paint inventory and the desks and chairs. Everything goes at one of these auctions."

Jim was beside himself. "What the heck am I paying you guys $300 an hour for. Why are you telling me this after the fact? How come you didn't do something BEFORE this happened," he asked. The lawyer replied, "Well we did the best we could at the time. You see, we don't really specialize in asset protection. We're business attorneys and that's what we're really good at."

"We'll do the best job we can settling this thing for you. It'll be all right. We try to get them to take payments. Maybe we can spread the $1 million out over 5 years…," says the lawyer.

Each year, there are millions of lawsuits across this county. It's not a matter of "if" you'll be sued; it's just a matter of "when," and it doesn't stop here. Statistically, the average person is involved in five- to seven-lawsuits in his life. Twenty-five percent of business owners will be sued this year. However, you don't care about statistics, and I don't blame you for that — you care about your family and your business.

Let me share another true story about my friend Larry. Larry and his family were in the auto body supply business for 30 years and had developed a very successful paint and jobber store. They did 12 million in annual sales and supplied over 100 body shops throughout the State of Florida with 35 employees.

One day, one of his employees decided to take a company delivery truck to run some errands. (He called it errands; Larry called it "joy riding"). With a cup of coffee in one hand, and the other hand on the CD selector, he blew through a red light and "T-boned" a car with a mother and son inside.

Thankfully, the employee and woman were OK, but the boy suffered life-altering injuries. A helicopter rushed him to a hospital that specialized in head trauma and by the time the police cleared the scene and the highway workers cleaned up the debris, Larry and his family were being served with a lawsuit.

The family's initial reaction was "don't worry, that's what we've got insurance for," but the insurance company felt differently. They informed the family because the employee was "joy-riding" on his own time, they would not cover the entire claim, not the damages to the cars, not the damage to the personal property and not the boy's medical expenses, which were now approaching half a million dollars. So, they settled out of the case early on.

The family realized quickly that they had to go into damage control mode. They paid their attorneys $50,000 to defend the claim. Nevertheless, the jury awarded the boy $10 million. Without further insurance coverage, the lawyers could seize the family's homes, their cars and their bank accounts to pay for the medical expenses.

Following a family meeting, the decision was made to do the only thing they could at that point — to salvage this horrific situation. They would sell the family business and use the proceeds to pay for the little boy's expenses.

This horrendous tragedy could have been avoided — if Larry and his family knew what to do. That's what makes my work so fulfilling.

You see, I grew up in a family business (my grandfather started a building supply company on Long Island, N.Y. after WWII and then my father took it over after that), so I know what its like to have a lot tied up in your business. Let's face it, other than with your family, you spend more time at your shop than anywhere else.

Yet, the fact is, there are creditors and predators out there that would rather sue you than work hard and build their own business. Maybe it's the lottery or the ridiculously high-paid athletes. Maybe it's the "me generation," but whatever it is, it seems everybody wants it NOW — no one wants to work for it anymore.

There are two Major Obstacles to your continued success. If you don't address them, you'll suffer unnecessarily...

The first one was the discussion of lawsuits. They can come in and tear your world apart almost overnight.

The other major obstacle is taxes. Taxes work against you differently, more slowly. Taxes are like Chinese water torture — drip, drip, drip and drip. On and on until you finally break, and by the time your done paying them or overpaying them, there is hardly anything left for you.

Taxes are one of your biggest expenses. Don't take my word for it, check it out. After your equipment, paint and supplies — your tax bill is right there.

Most entrepreneurs are paying 30- to 50-percent in taxes. Even with all the help from your CPA and accountant, and between federal taxes, state taxes and Social Security or self-employment tax (what I now call the invisible tax killers) you are losing about fifty percent of everything you earn — **that's tragic**. It's time to stop getting ripped off from overpaying your taxes.

The problem is that the more you make, the more you pay in taxes. Now, like you, I don't mind paying my fair share of taxes, but this is out of control. How are you supposed to get ahead when you're giving up half of everything you earn? I'll bet you're feeling the same way I was feeling — ripped off and taken advantage of. I'll bet you would like to reduce your tax bite, right?

The world is a funny place. The irony is that while you are paying about fifty percent or more in taxes, the wealthiest people in this country (people like Ross Perot, Donald Trump and Bill Gates) pay only single digits ... reportedly between four- and five-percent. That's because they can afford the cost of high-priced tax attorneys and CPAs. Odds are you don't have $100,000 or more to invest in high-priced experts. That extra money should be in your pocket!

The good news is that the incredible tax savings comes from using strategies, not from paying for high-priced experts. When you learn strategies you'll enjoy the savings too.

In 1988, I saw a television interview with Bill Gates. Although it was fairly early in his Microsoft career, he was already a very successful businessman. The interviewer asked him, "Mr. Gates, what is the single most important thing that you can attribute your success to?" Wow, that question really got my attention. I stopped dead in my tracks. I just HAD to learn the secret to Gate's success from the man himself.

Instantly, my mind started to race ahead. I figured he'd talk about things like perseverance and hard work, dedication and being a visionary. After all, he is responsible for bringing a whole new industry into being, but Gates mentioned none of that. Instead, what he said blew my mind and put my career on a whole new path.

Gates said that the secret to his (and your) business success is a good working knowledge of the tax code. Frankly, I was disappointed. You see, his answer wasn't very inspiring or sexy. In fact, I thought it was pretty dull until later that day when it finally hit me. You see, the power in his answer was in this subtle truth. It's not how much you make, its how much you keep that counts. This is what Gates knew; what I didn't yet appreciate. When you unnecessarily pay upwards of 50 percent in taxes, you're not keeping very much of your money, are you? You can do better than that!

From that moment on, I became obsessed with learning the secret tax strategies he was referring to. I knew that these strategies would save me (and my clients) thousands and thousands of dollars — and they can do the same for you.

62

Unfortunately, if you are depending on your accountant or CPA to save you money, you will be sorely disappointed and tens of thousands of dollars in the hole.

I spent hundreds of hours in the library researching; I read every book I could get my hands on. I attended seminars sponsored by the best business and accounting minds in this country. I acted like a private investigator on a mission. My mission was to learn the wealth secrets contained in the tax code.

You are probably using the "family" accountant just like I was. As my research continued, I called up my "family" CPA — Lenny. Lenny had done tax returns for my parents for 17 years and they trusted and relied on him. I called him one day and asked, "Lenny, did you know that under sections 105 and 106, my business can pay for the cost of ALL of my medical bills and insurance premiums, even things that my insurance policy doesn't cover like wellness care and alternative medicine including deductibles and co-payment — with no cap or limits at all?

Lenny said he wasn't aware of that; OK, I thought. No one knows everything. I can't fault him for missing one deduction.

I went back to my research.

A week or so later I called Lenny about another big deduction. I asked him, "Are you aware that under section 74 your company can give away two tax-free awards worth $1,600 each year?"

Lenny was not aware of that deduction, either. This is when I became concerned. I was starting to realize that I was missing some valuable tax saving deductions. **Knowing the information is not enough. You must proactively design and implement a methodical program to legally maximize your deductions.**

A short time later, I called Lenny to inquire about another big tax saver. I had uncovered the fact that "C" corporations are taxed at the low rate of only 15 percent on their first $50,000 of net income. Wow, I thought, that's much less than the 40- or 50-percent I'm used to paying.

This time Lenny's response almost floored me. This time, he was well aware of the strategy I was referring to. In fact, he was adamant about it. He said proudly, "Of course I know that. I've been a CPA for over 20 years and I've known about that one for a long time."

But I became more disturbed than ever because I realize that knowledge is one thing, but "applied knowledge" is another. As Forrest Gump said, "Stupid is as stupid does." You see, you don't get the tax benefit from simply knowing about these deductions; you must apply them to get the savings.

So, I just had to ask Lenny one more question, "Lenny, if you know about

63

the 15 percent rate for "C" corporations, then why don't you have me in a "C" corporation?"

There was dead silence — disturbing silence. Lenny didn't have a good answer. You see, all his knowledge was not doing me or any of his clients any good if it wasn't being used. It was then at that moment I knew people needed a resource. Someone who could proactively help them identify the tax deductions, which they are legally entitled to.

No "Gray areas" and no "Red Flags," just the safe, secure and certain tax deductions that can benefit you the most. I have lectured all over the U.S. and Canada and taught over ten thousand people how to save thousands and thousands of dollars in taxes every year and protect themselves and their families from creditors and predators.

Whether you are making $50,000 or $500,000, I can show you how to slash your tax bill to the legal minimum.

Let me give you some examples:
• There are over 300 deductions that are available to small businesses like yours. Most business people are only using about 30 deductions, so you're probably missing out on 90 percent of the tax-saving deductions you are entitled to.
• Properly structured LLCs and corporations can protect your assets and save you thousands in taxes each year. Improper structuring of your business can be disastrous.
• Upstreaming income is a method of shifting income from one tax year to another and from a high tax entity to a low tax entity. This single strategy can save you tens of thousands of dollars.
• You must learn to make your assets bullet proof. You'll be so protected that the predators of the world would be worse off if they sue you then if they left you alone in the first place.

Permit me to share some tax saving case studies with you.

Stephanie had two small businesses that brought in about $50,000 net income. Her family accountant had worked with her diligently to keep her taxes down. With his help, she was paying $4,500 in state and federal taxes and $7,500 in Social Security. After she signed up for our program, she called me very upset one day. She said she had spoken to her accountant who told her she was wasting her time and money. In fact, he told her that the best she could hope for was to break even on the program. She said, "Drew, I don't know what to do, you see, I trust your opinion, but he's been our family accountant for 15 years. What can I do?"

I assured her that I personally stand behind our guarantee. If we couldn't uncover at least $10,000 in legitimate savings, I'd immediately refund her investment — plus 10 percent. Then, I suggested she get her CPA on a conference call.

Now, understand that I take a great deal of pride in my work. Every single

day I work with business people, from beginners to seasoned professionals who are unwittingly overpaying taxes and suffering as a result. Their businesses suffer. Their lifestyle suffers, and their relationships suffer as a result. It's important to me to do the best job possible for each and every person I work with.

After some preliminary discussion, we got down to the heart of the matter. Her CPA identified Stephanie's largest expenses and said, "but there is no way you can find any more deductions than we've already taken." I just love those kinds of challenges. So, during the next 15 minutes, I outlined three specific strategies for Steph and her CPA. After discussing the first one (and securing his approval), I asked her CPA to calculate how much Steph would save. Realizing that CPAs are conservative by nature, I wrote the figure down. I repeated the process for the next two strategies and added up the figures.

In just 15 minutes using only three strategies I had saved Steph $11,200 by his calculations! How would you like to have a similar experience?

Another of my clients, Dr. Perry, was already a successful chiropractor — making about $750,000 when we met. Yet, despite the best efforts of his accountant, his overall tax rate was about 35 percent. That's a tax bite of over $260,000. In one of our very first sessions, we discussed one of his "hobbies" — raising and showing horses. Between the boarding, feedings, trailer, vet bills and other related costs, his hobby was costing him almost $100,000 per year. I was able to show Dr. Perry how to turn his hobby into a viable business, which allowed him to write off all of those expenses. By his CPAs calculation, we were able to shift $96,000 from pre-tax dollars to after-tax dollars, saving him over $48,000 in the process. Now, his new horse business has added tens of thousands of income to his bottom line!

I love this stuff; I can go on and on. My message to you is simple — to build lasting wealth you must structure yourself and your businesses properly. Doing so, will ensure that your assets are bullet-proof and that you are paying your fair share of taxes and no more than that.

The rich really do play by a different set of rules, but once you learn them, you can put those rules to work for you.

Drew Miles
The Wealth Building Attorney
www.pfbs.com
www.taxloopholesoftherich.com
(888) 695-2765

If you like what you've read ... check this out!

FOOTNOTES ♕

Drew has combined what he learned during his formal legal education, his "informal" education and 25 years of business experience in the development of programs designed to teach people how to build and preserve lasting wealth. In addition to being an attorney, he is an author, teacher and international speaker in the areas of asset protection, and tax-saving and wealth-building strategies.

65

How the Wealth was Won

by Adam Ginsberg

There is a lawyer in New York unknowingly setting a cowboy in Western Montana off on his very own personal road to riches. ...

eBay™ is not for everyone. As was true for the 19th century settlers of the West, it takes a pioneering spirit and a tolerance for risk, perhaps even a certain attraction to it, to make the great continental crossing. It takes a burning desire to take the reins of one's own future, and with stallion, saddle and spur, embark on a quest with a simple end in mind: the freedom to work and live by one's own rules. Somewhere beyond the Mississippi valley lies the promise of fortune.

As it approaches its first decade, eBay is not only ripe for the 21st century pioneer, but its potential as an earnings bonanza swells by the day as new markets in Asia, South America and Europe outpace the growth of those in our own backyard. Equipped with an Internet connection, a mouse and a camera, anyone who thinks they have the right stuff can jump on the bandwagon today — there is plenty of room and more horses are on the way.

I didn't necessarily hop on the bandwagon with an eager skip in my step and a gold pan in my satchel as much as I was pushed into a moving carriage by none other than my mother, Sheila Ginsberg, nearly four years ago. I'd gone from overseeing business development for a highly unprofitable but wildly fashionable Internet start-up, replete with stock options worth the weight of my future yacht in gold, to running a decently performing and utterly lusterless furniture shop, which I commonly referred to as my sore neck from the whiplash of the Great Internet Bust. I had a couple of pool tables in stock and Mom, who had been selling her Beanie babies on eBay for the past year, suggested — no, insisted — that I sell one of my tables on this "fabulous eBay thing — you won't believe how many friends I've made all around the country!"

"Thanks, Ma, but no thanks."

Sure enough, 37 phone calls and three weeks later, I had listed a pool table on this fabulous eBay thing. I figured that once I proved to her that eBay was no place for me, let alone one of my billiards tables, she'd get off my case and let me peddle my wares the old-fashioned way. It was on the last night of my first auction that I felt the other side of the Internet whiplash snap my neck right back into place: I sold the pool table, and for several hundred dollars above my retail store pricetag. I called my supplier the next morning. "Manny, I'm making another order, but I need you to ship to Philadelphia."

"Philadelphia? Did your wife leave you?"

"No, Manny, I'm still in L.A., but I sold a table in Missouri."

"Yeah, ok Adam. It's gonna cost you extra."

"I found a supplier in New Jersey."

"New Jersey, L.A., what's the difference? You'll get cost."

And with that, I had still managed to make a healthy and happy profit on my first eBay order, not to mention my shop had gone nationwide overnight — literally: I was hooked.

This is not how it works for everyone's first time, but every serious seller on eBay gets his moment — the first surprise sale, the first hefty profit, the first monthly income statement that competes with his monthly salary at the office — the moment where everything snaps into place and the road to the West opens up right in front of you. It happened to me, possibly the most unsuspecting and cynical eBayer online that night in October 2001. A year later, I was recognized as one of eBay's top sellers, grossing over a million dollars every month with my billiards store. My point to every eBay seminar attendee or reader of mine is, "get in the game and stay in the game and it can happen to you too."

My role as an eBay mentor to thousands evolved from my belief, fortified with the mounting evidence in front of me, that it was possible to replicate my success on eBay. I developed a roadmap for setting up a business on eBay, something which I would have almost killed for back when I decided to get serious about my own eBay business. I realized that my success on eBay was just a launch pad for me to do what I really wanted — to help others find wealth through independence. eBay provides that independence, as well as the foundation to build your wealth-machine. My roadmap helps others use that foundation, and its ever-increasing assortment of tools, to build a solid business with solid earnings.

There is an automatic money-machine hiding on eBay. From your "About Me" page to your "Autoresponders," the key is to use each and every element of the infrastructure provided to its fullest capacity, and then push them one step further and use them in a way that perhaps the eBay developers themselves had not imagined. Sound business strategies coupled with innovative thinking about your selling platform can produce marvelous results. Building and maintaining a smart customer database, tailoring your "store-front," finding unique ways to attract "window shoppers" with audio and video, and increasing opportunities for customers to find related products that might interest them; serious sellers use these issues daily and hundreds more like them. Building wealth on eBay is not something achieved simply by listing a Louis Vuitton purse here and a vintage 1980s "Transformers" figure there — although that could be a good start, but about making the choice to take your seller status to the next level by starting to think like a veritable entrepreneur running a great business. And that business just might be selling Louis Vuitton purses and rare "Transformer" toys — if it works, your bank account will show it.

Knowing how to use the resources at your disposal is key to growing a business on eBay. The good news is the dimensions for buying and selling on eBay have gotten deeper and deeper over the last ten years. For instance, selling one line of products for volume and another for high margin, or selling substitute goods, can hedge your business against downturns in any one particular demand curve.

Likewise, knowing where to get your product, on eBay and elsewhere, is a crucial element to your profit structure. The initial search for saleable merchandise can be a lengthy process of trial and error, or it can be right under your nose and virtually effortless. Either way, product acquisition is an ongoing element of your business. You want to make sure you're on top of the game with your suppliers, whether it's your husband with his classic rock belt buckle image printing facility in the basement or the manager at the local Marshalls that you've negotiated a favorable unsold-items deal with. The situations differ for every seller, but the end goal is the same. Find the product, experiment with it, be flexible, be professional, and you will make money.

I have found that practical guidance in business management, financial management and tax management mixed with what I call "extreme entrepreneurial coaching" produces overwhelmingly positive results for my readers and seminar attendees. Yet, in engaging the tried and tested lessons of successful entrepreneurship, I encourage creativity in approaching the eBay sphere, because there is more than one winning recipe for each registered seller.

The truth is, you don't need an MBA to adopt the established pillars of business education in your venture. You need just enough to be able to bend the lessons to your will so they work for you. And you certainly don't need an MBA to run a successful business, on eBay or otherwise. More important, perhaps, than the exposure to theory is the proper attitude that a successful eBay entrepreneur must have. Don Freda, my mentor and a brilliant leader and businessman would pound something known as the "as-if" principle in my head at every opportunity: "If you think and act as if you are running a successful business, you will be." I, in turn, now do the same with my audience.

There is a lawyer in New York unknowingly and single-handedly setting a cowboy in Western Montana off on his very own personal road to riches. The two have never met, and she's happy as pie. How on Earth is this possible? Because the cowboy just sold a used pair of spurs for ten times what he paid for them to a lawyer that just bought her mechanical engineer husband a bona-fide relic of his rancher fantasy for his 40th birthday. This transaction has planted a seed in the cowboy's mind. He has realized an opportunity to capitalize on what he knows and what he surrounds himself with — the stuff of cowboys, in this case. He has the tools on eBay and a market straight across to Beijing to build a business selling the West to the rest of us. He holds the power in his hands to create an independent source of wealth by choosing the path of the entrepreneur. He never has to work another rodeo show again. This cowboy, Mike Hodgson, is one of many success stories I've been fortunate to witness unfold. There are untold numbers of folks out there like him. If I can get one more pioneer onboard on the road to wealth, then I've succeeded.

Here's some food for thought:
"The cowboy and the lawyer are both happy about this value-adding transaction which eBay has facilitated — or as an economist might say, utility is increased on both ends of the transaction. eBay is all about increasing utility in a world where technology is stretching the boundaries exponentially for buyers and sellers alike. The Earth can't get any bigger, but the networks that connect us to each other have, for all humanly purposes, an infinite array of connections to make. This is nothing less than the mathematical genius of our Universe — within finite systems, there are an infinite number of possible events, each with an infinite array of variations and possibilities therein. In the world of eBay, each buyer is a potential seller and vice-versa, new buyers and sellers enter the arena at every turn, and every transaction increases the overall value of the system. Before I get a red card from Stephen Hawking, let me put it this way: eBay is no fad. It is the natural extension of our human inclination to trade for the means to sustain ourselves. It will evolve and, certainly, it will grow, and in its wake it will be pulling the fortunes of the sturdiest pioneers right behind it."

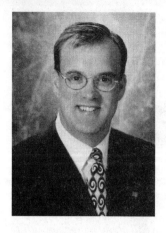

Inspiration To Action From The Warden's Office

How I Went From a Prison Guard to North America's Top Apartment Property Investment Guru

By Darin Garman

As I finish a commercial real estate consulting session with one of my clients, I started to reflect on the path I took in becoming one of America's most sought-after apartment and commercial investment property experts. I am convinced that nothing happens by accident.

I grew up in a single parent household as an only child. We depended on subsidy for most of the things we needed. The first few years of my life my single mom raised me in a small apartment. To compound the problem, my mother — although loving — fought a losing battle with the bottle and chronic alcoholism. We continued to struggle until we moved into a two-bedroom home with my Grandmother, Grandfather and Uncle when I was 8 years old. There I grew up.

It may not come as a surprise to learn that I constantly ran into trouble with the law as an adolescent. Along with a couple of friends of mine, I became a regular at the police station throughout most of my teenage years. A judge placed me on probation during my teenage years, and a friend of mine went to prison.

When I talk to people today that knew me back then, well, they can't believe it. The success I have enjoyed shocks them, especially since the community voted me "least likely to accomplish anything."

As a senior in high school, I started to mature and decided that despite my past, my future lay in my hands and my destiny depended on my choices. Knowing this, I decided I would major in (what else) criminology. My natural athleticism helped me during those years. I was an all-state football player in high school and went on to play college football on scholarship at the Division I-AA level.

I did well in college and got good grades. I worked hard on that criminology degree and graduated in four years.

Upon graduation, I wanted to start my life, and I looked high and low for a great entry-level job in the criminal justice field, but during this time I found out I was colorblind — and had a really bad case of it. Not many law

enforcement agencies wanted someone that had trouble distinguishing between a red getaway car and a green one, so my pickings were pretty slim.

However, I finally found an entrance-level criminology job about six months after graduating college. They didn't even care about my color blindness problem. What was it? **A Prison Guard**!

So, for about three years I worked as a prison guard and oversaw inmate leisure activity programs in the prison. The job was actually not too bad, but I started to come to a scary realization; I really did not want to work in the criminology field, after all. I could not see myself working in this kind of environment for another 30 years, color blind or not.

Then, "IT" happened. Eleven years ago, thanks to Napoleon Hill, I decided to quit my job as a prison guard in Iowa (sounds glamorous, doesn't it) and work in the world of commercial real estate, and more particularly, investment real estate. You know — apartment buildings, office buildings, shopping centers, etc..

Why does Napoleon Hill deserve my thanks?

Well, one day prison administrators found an empty liquor bottle in a garbage can right outside of my office in the prison. Of course, I had no idea how an empty liquor bottle made it inside the prison and into the garbage can outside of my office, but the Warden wanted some answers from me.

As I sat outside of the Wardens office, waiting to be questioned, I spotted a worn-out book on a bookshelf. The title of the book was "Think And Grow Rich." Of course, this is Napoleon Hill's classic.

Anyway, I started reading this book and it made a huge impact on my outlook on life. It had such a strong effect on me that after I read the book, I quit my job at the prison to pursue my burning desire — to work in the world of commercial-investment real estate, specifically with apartment buildings. Why? Why would I do this? Talk about extremes — it's a big leap from prison guard to apartment property investment specialist!

I made that transition because I thought I could do better for myself than working for a salary as a prison guard, and because it interested me. Even though I was a bit "green" and inexperienced, I jumped out of my prison guard job right into the world of investment real estate here in the heartland.

The Difference Was Unbelievable!

I suspected I knew how the world of commercial-investment real estate operated, but you could imagine **my shock** at how quickly this kind of property built the wealth of the investors that decided to invest in it. In other words, the speed with which these investors built their wealth shocked me. And here's the interesting thing: you never hear people talk about this kind of real estate investment — especially here in the heartland!!

Since that time AND over the last 10 years, I've found the ultimate

71

"hands down" real estate investment that no one ever talks about; the way these people keep this information to themselves, is almost like a secret society. The profits that I have on file that these investors have achieved far exceed other typical investments, and I mean — **all** investments.

Where else can you get information on investing in or purchasing apartment buildings or other commercial investment real estate? Its not on CNBC, not on Bloomberg and rarely in the Wall Street Journal; there are a few books out there, but try to find constant accurate information on how to properly and profitably purchase and own apartment and commercial investment properties and you will be looking for a long time. The information just isn't accessible to the average person.

The scarcity of information on the topic contributes to the fact that not many people invest in good profitable apartment properties. Information scarcity on this topic helps make it so lucrative. Most people think that if they invest their money in an apartment property, they will have management and tenant hassles, property damage, tenants that don't pay rent and other problems like vacancies and lawsuits, or they feel that apartment properties are "risky."

In fact, you can invest in great wealth-building apartments and commercial property, have zero management headaches and zero tenant interaction AND have a great return on your money with even greater tax savings. Also, if you research which investment has been among the best and most predictable over the last 30 years — investment real estate tops the list. Is it any wonder that many of the wealthiest own investment real estate? It's not an accident.

My Wealthiest Client's Secrets Revealed ...

I have worked with some of the nation's wealthiest people, assisting them in purchasing, managing and profiting from apartment properties. After 12 years in this business, I have found a common theme among these people.

Top Four Strategies of the Most Successful Apartment Property Investors That I Work With:

1. **They Treat It Like A Business.**
To succeed in the apartment investment world, you need to treat it like a business. Does this mean you work in this business? Does that mean you babysit this business all of the time constantly nurturing it? The answer is NO. You can of course be actively involved in it, but the point is that it requires a higher level of involvement than a CD or mutual fund. This "business" mindset takes me to the second strategy....

2. **Have and Use An Expert.**
By employing an expert, you do not have to take the time to become an expert yourself. By having an expert work for you and oversee your apartment investing and apartment business, you can still generate profits while saving

yourself the time and hassle of having to deal with the day-to-day problems that apartment properties bring. Having an expert "doing it for you" can make you money and still not interfere with your lifestyle.

3. **Don't Take Shortcuts.**
People fail in this business when they try to take shortcuts. These shortcuts ultimately cost thousands, if not tens of thousands of dollars. Some "shortcuts" to avoid include **A.)** Not using an expert. By working with someone that has no proof of expertise, you are looking for trouble. Many of my clients made this mistake at first and wish they had not. **B.)** Being a "cheapskate." Don't get me wrong here; you always want to negotiate the best deal, but don't try to save pennies when dollars are available. For example, on a recent apartment house transaction a client complained about how much the management company charged, even after paying the management company, this investor was earning about a 14 percent return on his money. This was a $2,000,000 property and he thought he could save $210 per month by having a relative manage the property instead of my property management company. Well, he put his relative in charge and he is now getting about a four percent return — besides a lot of other problems. Don't pinch pennies when real money can be made.

4. **Take Action And Invest Some Money In Apartments — Getting Past The Emotional Barrier....**
The biggest problem most of us have is that apartments are not a mainstream kind of investment like CD's, stocks or bonds. Apartments appear to have huge capital investment requirements far beyond the reach of most of us, so we tend to view them as a risky investment. Almost without exception, my most successful clients wish they had invested five- to 10- to 15-years before they did. Now, they view those lost opportunities with remorse. Don't make the same mistake. Get your emotion out of it and do it! You don't have to pour your life savings in it, but in the future you'll be glad you did.

I Discovered Successful Apartment Investment Strategies Could Be Easily Duplicated

But, here's the crucial point — These Investors Simply Did the Opposite Of What 99 percent Of All Other Investors Do!

And then it dawned on me, everyone was putting his or her efforts into the typical investments we all hear about. Most investors ignored apartment properties or commercial investment properties here in Iowa or the Midwest. Most investors concentrated on the wrong investment. In fact, after working with successful apartment investors, I've discovered three easy steps to learning and (more importantly) using these apartment and commercial investment property investment secrets:

1. How to easily locate that "instant profit" apartment property.
2. The secret to profitably managing your apartments and commercial investment property (without all the tenant headaches and management hassles).

73

3. How to sell for a huge profit and legally avoid any capital gains taxes. If you didn't know, investment apartments allow you to defer capital gains legally. You don't have to pay Uncle Sam a dime when you sell, **IF** you know what you're doing.

What you'll discover as an apartment property investor will contradict many things you've been told, taught or schooled regarding investments in real estate.

This is not to try to convince or "sell" you on going out today and buying an apartment property, but, I do want you to think "outside the box" a little. The more you want to build your wealth, the more unorthodox thinking should take place. If a guy like me can start out with nothing, "graduate" to becoming a prison guard and then become one of the most sought-after, apartment property specialists, with ownership in excess of $9,000,000 in apartments and commercial real estate, then so can you — with action.

If you like what you've read ... check this out!

FOOTNOTES

Darin Garman, CCIM is America's "Apartment Specialist" working as a coach, consultant and broker with many of Americas most successful and affluent Apartment and Commercial Investment Property Owners. Darin specializes in placing clients money into high return, high income apartment and commercial properties. Go to www.commercial-investments.com and get your FREE seven-lesson course on "How To Quickly Become An Apartment Or Commercial Property Investment Expert In 5 Minutes Or Less Per Day."

The Entrepreneurial Life — Just Do It!

by Glenn Wilbor

In "Walking with the Wise II," I discussed how to program one's subconscious mind. In short, it involves programming your mind through affirmations, visualizations and empowering questions to create motivation, which creates action and produces results (for more information, refer to "Walking with the Wise II"). In this book, I will discuss focusing on external things in order to create results because both of these are essential in achieving results. By changing our internal representations, we plant the seed that ripens into the life we desire. For example, if you decide you are a runner or you are going to live to be 100, this belief/desire would affect your diet and exercise regimen. Focusing just on the external requires willpower and sacrifice, but focusing on the internal creates motivation — the opposite of willpower. In other words, you want to "do it."

So, after all that explanation, let's focus just on external things you need to do to become an entrepreneur. Becoming an entrepreneur starts more easily than most people think. It consists of being left to your own devices to create income. Once you are out of the "system" aka working for someone else, it is frightening and/or invigorating depending on how good you are. Then, you immediately begin to realize that it's easier to be a small business person when you are young. For example, when you were 10 years old running a lemon aid stand or mowing the lawn, there was no real expense only profit because you 'borrowed" your mom's lemons, and if you were really lazy you used ready-to-pour lemonade, or you took the family mower filled with gas to neighbor's house; there was only upside profits and time invested.

Most of us found this out pretty quickly when our parents cut us off, whether after college, high school or after we turned 30 that we all have expenses. We have to eat, provide a roof over our heads, wear clothes, use electricity and we certainly can't be without cable. And don't forget entrepreneurs' biggest single expense — TAXES. While everyone has these expenses, they now create a baseline that the entrepreneur must exceed every month to survive, which makes working for your self so difficult. The more successful (more income) a person makes in a corporate career, the more difficult it is for that person to become

75

an entrepreneur because the risks are higher. "Successful" people have a higher hurdle to jump by having more expenses. Our culture does not take failure lightly and an entrepreneur risks his or her prestige, credibility, ego, retirement, lifestyle and possibly his or her marriage and family. None of this sounds very appealing, however, many people have this idea that when we succeed, we will start our own businesses. Wow, do they have it wrong. Most people think they are successful when they are making a lot of money and have nice cars and a beautiful home, but really all it is, is more expenses and debt. Even if you do have a million dollars saved, "Why would you risk what took a lifetime to achieve?"

It's easier to become an entrepreneur when you have the least to lose — when you are younger because if you do fail, hardly anyone will notice. You can look at it like this, "you never really had any money anyway," and a hole in your resume for a couple of years is no big deal just after college; you're not married yet therefore, having fewer expenses. Don't get me wrong, people do defy skeptics, the odds and start businesses after successful careers, but they need to position themselves to get out of debt (except maybe mortgage financing) and lower their expenses to increase their chances of success. It's just easier to get started when you have less to lose!

Income and Assets

In our capitalist society, everyone has to meet financial needs. Many people don't realize that this consists of two components: assets and income. Some people will focus entirely on one or the other, however, you need both to be financially independent. Some people think that if they had a million dollars they would be rich, but then after a few years of thinking you're rich your down to $500,000. Others think if they could just make $200,000 or $250,000 they would be set financially, but then they buy new cars and a bigger home to show off that new income, and after paying the IRS on that income, there's nothing left to save. Then there are others who think that if they just get out of debt they would be financially satisfied, but a debt payment is just another expense, and expenses can never get down to zero.

An entrepreneur needs to first focus on creating income, and then focus on the accumulation of income-producing assets, which isn't new cars and large homes. Really, the true definition of wealth is how many months or years you can live without working. Now, some of you are thinking isn't that just assets. Financial planners and the stock brokerage industry have trained Americans to think that you need to accumulate a big pile of money and live off the interest it throws off, but many different asset classes exist that can create residual income **before** you have a big pile of money. In other words, "how much residual income can you earn without working?"

Financial freedom means the ability to have enough saved to live without working, but we know that savings will diminish by the amount we spend every month. Some work hard enough to have enough in order to live off the interest of the savings they accumulate, but most of us will fall short of that, and most will fall short of having enough saved to live on until we die. Don't just focus on the financial markets to earn interest, dividends and/or capital gains for income. Start a business and work every day on hiring and training people to do your "job." By doing this, you have just created passive income (income without working) without getting that pile of money first. Then, you can use your passive income to buy more assets that create more passive income through investment real estate and other businesses. This is how the rich get richer.

Love What You Do

I would like to add a crazy alternative if you are going to create your own job. "Do something you are passionate about and work at it even if you don't need the money!" Think about it, actors, musicians and athletes do it for the act of "doing." Entrepreneurs should also love what they do. Do you think that Bill Gates, Michael Dell or Donald Trump go to work every day just for more money? They love what they do! These guys worked passionately before they got a lot of money out of it. Find something you love so that if you don't get a pile of money from it, at least you live your life doing something you love. Now, I will give you some ideas to create that "pile of money" we're all after.

First Step — It Isn't What You Think!

The easiest way to become an entrepreneur is to get someone else to pay some or all of the business expenses, teach you how to do it, and it would sure help if they also provided the products, wouldn't it. Some people see this opportunity everyday while others don't think it exists. Opportunities like this abound all across the nation on the internet and in your local paper. "Where?" you might ask. In the classified ads under sales! Some of you might be saying, "I want to be an entrepreneur not a 'salesperson.'" I will preach it to you straight, "Every entrepreneur IS a sales person." You want to be an entrepreneur but you don't want to sell. Sounds like a recipe for failure — aka bankruptcy! Now some will say that doctors, lawyers, architects, engineers and accountants can be entrepreneurs. And yes, they can be, but the moment they stop working for a company, they become salespeople. If they don't get clients, they will experience the same results as any entrepreneur — loss of money and/or bankruptcy. Many successful professionals do leave their successful careers, but they leave with something of utmost importance, their client base.

What about all the billionaires? They weren't in sales. They were in high tech, right? Let's look at Bill Gates. He bought MS DOS for $50,000 and sold it for $250 a copy to IBM and every other manufacturer of IBM compatible computers. Steve Jobs cobbled his first computer together from parts and marketed it in a consumer-friendly package. Jobs bought the Macintosh operating system from Xerox and then created the Mac. Larry Ellison, the President of Oracle, sold software before starting his own company. Don't kid yourself, the key to business is sales, which every entrepreneur has to sell to survive.

How do you parlay your average sales job into a profitable business? Well, you could always just buy one, like Ray Kroc did with McDonalds. Kroc worked as a milk shake machine salesman. He had seen hundreds of restaurants

77

and he knew a good one when he saw it. He then applied his selling skills not to hamburgers, but to selling these restaurants to other entrepreneurs. Most successful professionals (doctors, lawyers, accountants and stockbrokers) become entrepreneurs by creating a business using an existing client base that is already loyal to them. They have taken the most valuable part of any company, its clients and the knowledge of how it got them (the marketing strategy). Then, they create a company to supply the product or service directly.

As a new entrepreneur leaving a sales position, the first thing you will expect is 100 percent of the sales or revenue minus the cost of the product (if there is one). With proper planning, you will be making more money working for yourself, not less. Many people I know have taken this strategy and created financial services companies, appraisal companies, mortgage companies, real estate companies, insurance companies, accounting and law firms, home inspection companies and medical supply companies.

Second Step: Creating a Small Business

Everyone's heard the stats about business failure rates; after 11 years, 90 percent of most businesses are no longer in business. This may not always mean failure, but many times successful businesses do shut down after years of making money. Most of these stats fail to account the fact that many of these business owners decide to "cash in their chips" and retire. Sometimes thriving businesses are sold for a lot of money and because there is no existing system in place and the new owner goes under. Sometimes, new owners lack leadership or sales skills or they drive away key people. My experience is, if you start a business you know nothing about then failure is inevitable such as the retired cop starting a coffee shop. These sorts of things can cause businesses to fail. If you buy a business such as, sales, marketing, leadership and financial savvy (income vs. assets and investing and leverage), then you could fail. In starting a business, many people focus way too much on the product. If the product were everything, McDonald's would not exist. Anyone with a barbeque can cook a better burger. You have to have sales to succeed, and then you implement systems to keep those sales coming in.

Most successful entrepreneurs I know came from successful careers with two- to three-years of professional sales experience. They worked as commission salespeople who made a percentage of each sale and simply competed with their former employer by starting their own company. These people provided a product or service to a customer base that was more loyal to them than their former employer. This strategy works in accounting, engineering, law, real estate, medical supplies, autos, mortgages and the financial service industries. These people have little or no risk because they already have the customers, a working marketing strategy, sales experience, and in many cases, they have the product or service already lined up prior to leaving their job. Entrepreneurs in these areas usually start from home or in a small executive suite. Soon they realize they are not getting 100 percent of the revenue because they have this thing called "expenses." After a year or so, they realize they could make more money by adding on more commission salespeople. They get an office and realize to themselves, "wow I have a real business." Next they realize that the time and energy spent training their salespeople should do more than just cover expenses; they should be making a profit beyond what they make on their own sales. Soon, it takes more time managing the business and they focus less on their "own" sales and more and more on the company sales. At this early stage, entrepreneurs will outsource almost everything except sales. After significant growth, they may realize that the companies they outsource to make a small fortune are not servicing their company alone, and soon they will start to take services "in house" and have paid employees handle things. They may experience turnover and decide to develop not-easily-duplicatable proprietary marketing systems. Then they may develop proprietary products; after all, someone makes money building these things! Then they expand product lines and services to their same customers. The next thing you know, it all looks and runs like a medium-sized business. All this happens with a very organic low-risk expansion and every expansion either creates income or cuts expenses.

I have seen these growth phases in many businesses, including my own mortgage company. Our company decided to buy a building rather than rent since we could develop the real estate in the future. We added real estate services because our existing clients all had real estate and we could offer them that service. In the future, we will expand into financial services for the same reasons. We took our existing real estate holdings and developed them into urban condominiums, and in doing so, we created a real estate development division. We developed a mortgage product line and created a mortgage banking division. Now, we sell our own mortgage products to the general public and offer them wholesale to other mortgage companies to sell. None of these things were risky; they all added revenue or cut costs.

On Leadership

Once you achieve mastery at something, then you can develop leadership. Leadership means charting new territory that you then conquer. This excitement and sense of adventure draws others to you, but if it is not built on a foundation of success (mastery) then you are "the blind leading the blind." Leaders that forge new ground without mastery can come crashing down. We all remember the "Dot Com" bust.

At the most basic level, followers create leaders. Leadership can come from motivating others out of fear, but at its highest level, leadership arises out of idealism — like Gandhi. While not all of us can be Gandhi, we can model his type of leadership, which moved the world from what it was (reality) to what Gandhi envisioned it could be. This sort of vision creates a space which others are drawn to. Entrepreneurs do this, too. The more idealistic your vision, the easier it will be to draw people to your vision. Honesty, integrity, compassion, civility, respect, loyalty and the desire to create a positive difference in the world all should play a role in the creation of your vision — all the things that cynics of society think no longer exist. You want positive, motivated, energized people wanting to make a difference in the world, in other words, idealists. This is how to recruit people to your vision.

79

Rules of Money

Now that I have covered "income," let's go over to the "asset" side. Without the asset side we can become completely unbalanced. I am sure that making $250,000 a year sounds great, but imagine having zero (or just a few thousand) in savings and working 60 hours a week with a $1,500,000 mortgage on your house. This would not fit anyone's definition of wealth. Many entrepreneurs fall into the habit of totally focusing on work to create an income stream. This does not lead to financial freedom — it leads to a heart attack. Every entrepreneur should consider a couple of simple rules about money that most do not follow. The basic rule of depreciation and appreciation maintains that some things go up in value while others do not. Buy things that appreciate. This stems from supply and demand. Things that have a limited supply and growing demand appreciate while those that have a growing supply and falling or steady demand depreciate. Almost all consumer goods depreciate as soon as you buy them. No one would buy a new car if they thought strictly in financial terms, but our emotions get involved. A new model just came out, the car is beautiful, the leather smells just right, the stereo rocks and we buy! Emotions and making sound financial decisions don't go well together.

However, stocks, real estate and businesses appreciate consistently. No one thinks of a used home like a used car, even though they are both used, one appreciates (the house) while the other depreciates (the car). Obviously, homes in better areas go up faster due to supply and demand, and since the population continues to expand, demand for housing almost always goes up even though we build many new houses every year.

Businesses follow a similar course though hard "assets" depreciate year by year (copiers, computers, faxes, furniture). The time and energy it took to build systems, train people, create a product and find customers gives it value. A business with a proven track record of sales lowers the inherent risk and makes it attractive to individuals and other businesses interested in buying that cash flow so it goes up in value. Stocks are company ownership broken into smaller pieces so more people can participate as owners. Stocks tend to be a little more complex than real estate since demand can easily outpace supply (especially when a stock goes up), which causes stocks to get overvalued and start to fall. If you want to build an asset base, start by buying assets. Most people think the only way to build an asset base involves saving in a 401K or an IRA. Just buy assets (business, real estate and stocks) and eventually you will have enough to live off of.

Investing and Leverage

Most people do not understand the "rule 72," which says your rate of return divided by 72 gives you the amount of time your money will take to double. An eight percent return (take 72 divided by 8 = 9) would double your money in nine years. A 12 percent return (72 divided by 12 = 6) would double your money in six years. If properly applied to things that appreciate, you can see that doubling your assets shouldn't take long. People also fail to understand the law of leverage. Most peoples' single biggest asset is their home. The amount of the down payment is usually very small compared to the size of the asset. A homebuyer can make a buy these days with 10 percent or less, meaning if he or she put 10 percent down and the home goes up in value 10 percent, then that homebuyer has doubled his or her investment. Over time, homebuyers end up multiplying their down payment by 10 times. Most people fail to realize this on any other property but their primary residence. Why not have three homes appreciating in value? The rent should cover the mortgage payments. It is not hard to structure financing to achieve positive cash flow/income (rent exceeding the mortgage payments). By implementing the "rule 72" and the rule of leverage you can easily accumulate assets, but most people take equity out of their homes not to buy more assets, but to pay off depreciating consumer items purchased on credit cards or sometimes on ill-conceived "home improvements," neither of which appreciate.

On Credit Cards

I see ads on television everyday that urge homeowners to pay off all their credit card debt with a new home loan (cash out refinance) that has a lower rate. While it might seem like a smart move, using your appreciating assets to pay off depreciating assets, which are not getting out of debt, makes little sense. This is called getting deeper in debt (it's a longer term to pay it off). This is a strategy to turn your appreciating asset into a liability. If you can't live within your means and pay off those credit cards out of your income side, then in a short period of time you'll have those cards maxed out again and you'll be looking to another cash out refinance. You're spending equity in your only asset that's going up in value. This is a formula to consume wealth, not create it.

Why not take an asset (your house) and borrow against it (the concept of leverage) to buy another appreciating asset and let your credit cards stay maxed out. Why borrow from an appreciating asset to pay off liabilities that depreciate. Why not borrow to buy more assets instead of liabilities. It does not take any sizable risk, and it doesn't take a significant investment to acquire a large leveraged asset. Achieving high returns on assets in real estate is not difficult (the stock market is harder). Making a 100 percent return on an investment (10 percent down on a property that appreciates 10 percent) using leverage isn't a matter of "if," but "when." It **will** happen and in the worst case, it takes a little longer than you thought.

Just Do It

Fear prevents most people from following these simple rules. They want to remain in the safety of the herd and be like everyone else. Why and what would people think, or similarly, prevent people from creating wealth. This fear makes them cynical of investments and opportunities. The fear of losing money causes them not to take action. What people really fear is not the loss of an asset (most just waste their money anyway), but fear of ridicule from their spouse, family and friends. We should not derive our self-worth from what other people think of us. Often times, the same people you fear are the ones that ridicule you and they are in no better shape financially themselves. Subconsciously they sabotage your efforts in order to "preserve the status quo."

81

Many believe that to excel in today's society, you need a great education (preferably Ivy League). To go off to work as an investment banker, attorney or doctor at one of the "best" companies, and it is at this point, you will achieve "success" in order to start your own company. Nothing could be further from the truth. Steve Jobs, Bill Gates, Donald Trump, Mark Cuban, Ted Turner and Michael Dell never followed that formula and they are all billionaires.

Take responsibility for your life. Design your life. Install empowering beliefs in your mind through affirmations, visualization and empowering questions. Such affirmations and visualization can take the form of statements: "Anyone can make a difference; I am uniquely special; I deserve success; everything happens for a reason; what goes around comes around; problems just make me stronger and smarter; and (heaven forbid — as politically incorrect as it is) God has a plan for me." Most people fail to believe in anything or anything different because their insecurities won't allow them to face possible failure or ridicule.

And I understand such insecurity. Not until I was driving a Porsche and living in Del Mar, Calif., with an ocean view (outward signs of success), did I feel confident enough to proudly tell people of my self-help library and what I believe in. You now have the tools to succeed in your entrepreneurial efforts. Too often successful entrepreneurs (out of pride) make their achievements sound so difficult; instead of encouraging would-be entrepreneurs, they intimidate them! Everyone in a capitalist country already runs a business, that is, his or her personal financial life. If you run that properly, starting another business should come naturally by using your mind and following these basic rules of success. Really, it's not that difficult. JUST DO IT!

If you like what you've read ... check this out!

FOOTNOTES ♻

*An entrepreneur and real estate developer, **Glenn Wilbor** is the founder and president of California Equities, a real estate brokerage and wholesale/retail mortgage banking firm. Glenn is currently developing three urban condominium developments in downtown San Diego and serves on the board of "Alpha of San Diego," a non-profit organization dedicated to helping people in need empower themselves. Glenn also competes as a tri-athlete and trains continuously. For information on investing in one of his real estate development projects or employment opportunities within his organization, contact Glenn Wilbor at **glenn@californiaequities.com**.*

SECTION II

How To Overcome Obstacles on Your Journey to Prosperity

© 2005 Kim Muslusky

Turn Mistakes Into Re-Takes

by Ted DiBiase

How do you handle the business and personal mistakes you make? Do you blame your mistakes on someone else? Do you sweep them under the rug and pretend they didn't happen? Do you beat yourself up over them? Do you dwell on them so much that it keeps you from moving forward?

Or ... do you analyze your mistakes just enough to see what went wrong so you don't make the same mistake again?

Everyone makes mistakes. Even the most successful people you know or may have heard of make mistakes. In fact, many successful people often make more mistakes than "Joe Average" because they are constantly moving forward with projects and taking risks.

The successful few differ from "Joe Average" in that they not only learn from their mistakes, they also study and learn from the mistakes of others.

Like most people, my life has been full of mistakes. When I was a child, my parents made mistakes. As I got older, I made many mistakes. My employers, friends and relatives all made mistakes. And no, I didn't always learn from my mistakes right away, but praise God, I eventually did, which helped me to become a real honest to goodness rags-to-riches story.

Now if you don't follow pro wrestling, you may not have heard of me. You see, I was a pro wrestler and I played the role of a super mega-rich jerk known as "The Million Dollar Man," Ted DiBiase. I went on to become one of the most famous wrestling characters in history. Millions of people actually believed that I was one of the richest men in the world.

That was over ten years ago, and even though my true-life story has become a best-selling book, many people around the world still believe I am Ted DiBiase, "The Million Dollar Man" — a man born with a platinum spoon in his mouth, who has unlimited money to buy anything and everyone I want. Such a man can pay for mistakes with cash.

My real name *is* Ted DiBiase, and I DID play the role of a pro wrestler,

"The Million Dollar Man." But that's where reality and fiction part ways. As a child, I grew up in the very real world of poverty and broken marriages. After my step dad died when I was only 15, I had to watch my mother give up on life while leaving my grandmother the task of raising me and my two brothers.

We grew up in a small dirt road-town where no one ever expected to amount to anything. I lived as a "Joe Average" person who had to pay for his mistakes by dealing with the consequences they brought. Unlike "The Million Dollar Man," I had no cash to get me out of difficulties.

Without the success principals my step dad taught me before he died, I probably would not have made much out of my life. Let me explain. A highly decorated high school and college athlete, my step dad eventually went on to become a famous pro wrestler. At one point my mother also worked as a pro wrestler, which is how they met.

My dad didn't want me to become a pro wrestler, so he taught me how to set proper goals, and how to discipline my mind and body to accomplish my goals. He also taught me a strong work ethic. My dad saw that I liked football and he helped me develop the skills needed to play. He encouraged me and supported me 100 percent when I told him I wanted to play pro-football.

After my dad died of a heart attack in the wrestling ring, I continued to work toward my goal to play pro-football. I eventually earned a college football scholarship, which got me out of the small town we were living in. Once in college, I saw that I was not going to make it into the pro's as a football player, so I decided to follow in my father's footsteps and become a pro wrestler. Using the success principals my dad taught me, I made it to the top of that industry before eventually retiring with a serious neck injury.

Let's face it, jocks don't have a reputation as the smartest humans on the planet, and professional wrestlers sometimes occupy a special "dumb jock" class all by themselves. So, since I went from football jock to pro wrestler, some would say that I have a double "learning disability." Mistakes are supposed to be a normal part of life for men like me, so it probably could have been easy for me to make excuses for all the mistakes I made.

I must admit at times it was tempting to play the jock to see if I could get out of trouble. And, I probably did use it a few times when I was younger; however, even if you have a learning disability, people still hold you responsible when you do dumb things. So, the jock excuse would not have saved me very often, besides, if I had made excuses instead of learning from my mistakes, I never would have enjoyed the success I am experiencing now.

Today I am a husband, father, Christian minister, life coach, author and professional speaker. I am much older and wiser than my wrestling days. So although I would like to say that I no longer make mistakes, I can't. Unfortunately I still do make mistakes. However, I do several things that help to keep my mistakes to a minimum — or at least help me from repeating them. ...

I continually seek the counsel of my loving wife, Melanie. Like the successful people I mentioned earlier, I continually analyze my mistakes in order not to repeat them. I socialize and hang around other successful people to learn from their experiences, both positive and negative.

I also have a partner/coach, Reggie Cochran, who helps keep me on track. I have a board of advisors for my nonprofit ministry that always look out for my best interest. And I saved the most important for last, I put my deepest trust in God and my Lord and Savior, Jesus. The Bible is my ultimate success book and I read it daily, I encourage you to do the same.

No matter what type of business you're in, whether you're male or female, the basic keys to success remain the same. One of those keys is being able to learn from your mistakes and quickly correct them. My partner Reggie calls this "learning how to turn your mistakes into re-takes."

I strongly encourage you to take the time to think about the last few mistakes you made, and how you reacted to them emotionally. Did your mistakes affect the outcome of the task you were working on when you made them? What did you do (if anything) to correct the mistake? Take a little more time to think about how you could have handled the situation better.

Every one of us in this book has made mistakes. Some of us have made more than others, but we have all learned from our mistakes and now take the time to share our lessons with you. The articles in this book contain information that can change your life. So I encourage you to read this book cover to cover, and then go back and read it again. After you have read it at least twice, share it with someone you care about. If you want more people to bless you, make sure you bless them. I pray that you will experience an abundance of great health, happiness and prosperity. God Bless.

If you like what you've read ... check this out!

FOOTNOTES ۞

*Ted DiBiase is available for Corporate and Christian speaking events as a keynote speaker and trainer. Ted is also available for teleseminars, fundraisers and autograph sessions. For more information visit **www.teddibiase.com.***

If I Can Do It, You Can Do It

By Ginger L. Wishner, LMFT

I was sitting at my desk in fourth grade when Mrs. Cook said, "Ginger, third paragraph." Everyone's eyes were on me. The moment I'd been dreading was here.

Goosebumps erupted on my arms as my fourth-grade-world threatened to implode. My knees shook, my hands trembled. I fumbled and stammered in front of my classmates as I tried to make sense of the words in my book. I couldn't understand the tangle of shapes and sounds that seemed to fall into place so easily for the kids who read before me. I blinked hard enough to bring tears. Then I forced my eyes open and waited for the letters to tell me how to pronounce them correctly.

"Well … Ginger?"

I looked up. "I really have to go to the bathroom ... I'll pee in my pants if I don't." Giggles ensue around me, and I twisted my face to convince the teacher I was in torture. My fingers crossed behind my back, I waited as I watched her eyes fill with that all-too-familiar look of impatience and annoyance.

This humbling moment when I was nine was one of two events that collided to shape my life. The other event was cataclysmic — when my parents woke my brother and me one night to tell us they were "separating," — something that "just wasn't done" at that time.

I was scared and overwhelmed. Things would never be the same for me or for us as a family. I cowered at one end of our overstuffed couch, pulling my knees to my chin to keep my shattered heart inside my chest — I couldn't breathe. This couldn't be happening. What was I supposed to do? I struggled to keep my world from spinning off its axis. There had to be a way to help us — and not just us, but others who were going through something similar. I needed to find a way out of this pain, whatever way that might be.

COPING

As a child I knew I would survive both events. I didn't know how — I just knew I had to. I eventually learned to read words, but details and meaning still

87

eluded me. I couldn't comprehend what the words meant. I understood only the gist of what I read or heard. I refined my ability to distract others from focusing on my inabilities and maneuvered my way through school; "miracles" saving me every day.

My desire to help others grew as I avoided my own problems. My friends labeled me "Susie social helper." My waking hours were consumed by my passion to help and save anyone in need. I began to journal. Putting my secrets down on paper filled me with confidence and gave me a safe place to expose my inner thoughts — I felt like I finally had someone to talk to — out poured my anger about my parents' divorce....

"Dear diary: How could it hurt so much? It's not fair, no one should have to go through this. I need to learn how to help my brother and myself so it doesn't have to hurt all the time. That's what I'll do. Somehow."

My daily battles with normalcy...

"Dear diary: Another good report card. I hate cheating, but what else can I do? Why do I have to be this way? What's wrong with me?"

My confessions ...

"Dear Diary: I am only thirteen and I feel old. Already my life is almost too hard to stand sometimes. Thank God for my friends and their families. Thank God I've found a way to survive all this. I need to stay positive and stick with it no matter what."

And my darkness ...

"Dear Diary: They put me in 'Dummy English' today — so embarrassing. What did I do to deserve this? What am I supposed to do without all my friends? Who's suppose to help me now? It's totally unfair ... but, I guess I'll figure it out."

This was my life:
Avoiding detection.
Hiding my secret.
Acting normal.
Telling no one.

Graduating high school was one of my biggest triumphs. Without knowing how, I had developed enough skills to pass undetected through the academic and social radar. The next challenge would be college. After struggling, however, with the simplest calculations that my courses required, I became overwhelmed by the painful process of learning and hiding — I took some time off. A friend asked if I'd considered majoring in social work.

"What is that? What do they do?" I checked into social work and psychology — it "clicked." I could finally analyze and fix myself while learning a "helping" profession. "If I can just make it through college; this would be incredible."

I did make it. I found unique programs and small universities where I knew I could manage the work, even with my inabilities. I graduated with my Bachelor's degree in Developmental Psychology and Master's degree in Counseling Psychology, leading to state Licensure in Marriage and Family Therapy — an amazing feat for someone still struggling to read, write and comprehend. I began my private practice in 1984, proud that I was able to make a living at something productive, pleased that I was doing what "I was meant to do."

Years later, my therapist and mentor told me, "You are 'debroüillard,' " and wrote out the word phonetically. It means "resourceful" in French.

OPENING NEW DOORS

Into my late 30s, as I shaped my career, I continued to believe that my inabilities stemmed from the trauma of my parents' divorce. My business prospered, my internal world stabilized, and at 40, I felt that I was ready to get married. Yet, as I prepared to walk down the aisle to begin the second half of my life, the fears came back: "What was I thinking? He might find out. How can I have these fears? It will be fine. He's the one. He's perfect for me. Now, I can have a real life after forty hard years of being alone, always dealing with everything by myself and hiding. I deserve it, don't I? I'm being stupid. My business is going well. My clients love me. I'm helping so many people. Life is good. I need to get some sleep and stop worrying. But what if I screw up in front of all those people and ruin the wedding? Stop it. We've rehearsed everything. It will be fine. He's the one. I can put my life in his hands...."

Shortly after we were married, my husband confronted me, insisting that I didn't understand his jokes and often misunderstood what he said. He told me I was using the wrong words to convey my ideas. I was incensed and defensive. We went round and round.

A new client in my practice — the owner of a center for people with learning problems — told me about her work. When she described her adult married students, I realized she was describing ME.

I covertly ordered an information packet from her center, watched the videotape and read the materials. I recognized that I had learning disabilities based on a processing problem: I did not see pictures in my mind when reading, listening or speaking. I had trouble making and understanding the sounds in words and sentences. I had trouble organizing and expressing my thoughts, answers and ideas. I had struggled with personal relationships and employment issues as well.

Shock understates my reaction to the deluge of emotions that flowed through me. With fear, relief and anger, I asked, "How could I not know this? How could I have never learned about learning disorders? How could professors, supervisors or mental health professionals not have known about learning disorders?"

I began anew the process of learning — about myself and hidden learning disabilities. I read everything I could find. I took tests. I traveled around the country to work with specialists. I completed classes and training and everything else you can and cannot imagine so that I could educate and treat myself.

89

SHARING THE KEYS

Today, my passion is educating the world about hidden learning disabilities and their co-mingling with mental health that can result in anxiety, depression, self-esteem, relationship and employment issues. Because of the challenges I faced, I have had to work harder and smarter to succeed in business and life. I know from experience success can be achieved.

Why am I telling you my story? Because I've spent a lifetime pushing through a quagmire of information, doctors and therapists until I found my way to the path of recovery — a path no one person was able to show me. Today, I know that I love myself and my life. Today, the light on my pathway grows brighter because I realize that the work I have done and the knowledge I've gained will benefit others.

My goal is to motivate and educate others about learning disabilities and mental health issues so they can live life fully and be loved without so many struggles.

I am a good therapist because I can empathize with my clients' pain and situations. I offer unique solutions, options and referrals that others don't have. Most importantly, I have honed my intuition to an art because of my (in)abilities. I know that hope and solutions exist even when people think they can't find them. Hidden learning disabilities are more prevalent than we realize, and they keep people from achieving their goals — I want to help turn that around.

There is always a way to open the door. I believe in my heart that, by sharing my story, you will see that my journey's destination has been one of triumph, peace and happiness. Yours can be, too. You must take the first step, but you don't have to take it alone.

Do you or someone you know:
- Have a hard time following and understanding the content of lectures, presentations or complex conversations?
- Struggle to express yourself in meetings or classes?
- Have/had difficulty learning in school?
- Does life seem like hard work, like slugging through mud?

If you answered yes to even one of these questions, go to: **www.adultlearningdisabilities.com** for a Free Report NOW.

If you like what you've read ... check this out!

FOOTNOTES ✆

Ginger L. Wishner has been a Licensed Marriage and Family Therapist for over 20 years. She has a private practice in La Jolla, Calif., specializing in learning disabilities and communication, relationships, anxiety and depression. She also provides individual and couples counseling, along with coaching and consulting.

Applying Success Principles Where They Really Matter: In Your Family

by Phillip Cohen

Standing in the middle of the gravel road, tears welled in my eyes as I gazed upon our beautiful 20-room dream house and the cabinet shop that had been our home business for 17 years. Surrounded by rivers and national forests in Southern Missouri, our well-manicured, idyllic 57 acres was truly the place of our dreams.

I could hear God asking me, "If following me means giving up all this, will you?"

From a place of longing deep inside me I softly replied, "Yes, Lord. It has cost too much to come this far and turn back now."

I might be giving up even more: my beautiful wife of 23 years and nine children, all of whom meant more to me than life itself. The thought of losing them pierced my soul like a knife because I had never known a happy home in my childhood.

The year was 1999. As members of a closed religious sect, we only believed that we were right with God. We weren't permitted to have friends outside the community — including our parents and siblings — because they didn't subscribe to our beliefs, and therefore, could potentially contaminate our faith. Moreover, if I decided to leave the sect, the sect wouldn't let my family leave with me, since they would view me as a heretic and an outcast.

I had been silently wrestling with this issue for more than a year.

The sect offered peace, joy and a happy home life, but it wasn't working for me. For most of my life, I had battled depression and suicidal tendencies. A childhood surrounded by drug and alcohol abuse, emotional abuse and domestic violence left festering wounds on my heart, and I still wrestled with the demons that destroyed my father. Dad was an alcoholic and drug addict who drifted in and out of mental hospitals. In 1972, he deserted Mom and ran off with his business partner's wife, and in 1975, he committed suicide.

All the rules and disciplines of this religious community helped relieve my pain a little, but I still felt miserable inside. My wife and I did everything

91

that supposedly makes for a happy marriage, but deep in our hearts we knew something was wrong.

Standing in that road, I knew it was time to leave. I didn't know where I would go, but I knew I couldn't remain there. I had to find real life at any cost, even if that meant losing my family and everything I owned and living on the streets again as I had done three decades earlier.

I had stood on a road like this before...

In 1970, I lived with my parents and siblings in a nice house in a quiet neighborhood in Coral Gables, Florida. Tropical fruit trees adorned our yards and we had our own swimming pool. My dad gave me a generous allowance and a new fastback sports car. I attended junior college, wore the latest clothes and dated many girls.

I had everything a person could ask for, but I was miserable! So many questions haunted me about life, love and reality. I tried baring my heart to my parents and friends, but they didn't seem interested in life's deeper meaning. Perhaps they feared the cost. Perhaps they thought true happiness was unattainable.

So I left home. My parents blessed me, but said, "You'll outgrow this stage. You'll come back, get an education and work a 9- to 5-job, like everyone else." I never did.

After I left home, I became a hippie and wandered around the country, often wasted on drugs, homeless and broke. I filled hundreds of pages of journals with poetry and the cries of my heart.

1973 found me on a commune in Tennessee, a hippie's haven. We did all the hippie stuff: drugs, sex, 24-hour music, loafing, stealing from others, living on welfare and inheritances — but I was still empty.

Then, in 1974, while alone in the woods, I met Jesus. That was the happiest moment of my life. Wow, I just wanted to love everyone! I apologized to everyone I had ever fallen out with. I repaid everyone I had ever stolen from. My parents thought I had flipped my wig!!

I left the commune and joined the religious sect. But I didn't realize what I had gotten into because for the next 25 years, I slowly died inside. Held there by the fear of God's supposed wrath, I couldn't face what was really happening.

So, here I stood on a lonely country road at another crossroads in life. I didn't know where to turn. I just knew I had to leave.

Gradually, my wife and children began to realize it was time to leave. When we left the sect, practically everyone we knew rejected us. We lost all our friends and needed to start over.

Of course, the rejection hurt, but how can I begin to describe the happiness our family slowly began to experience now that we could explore our real selves?

We were free to fail and make mistakes without fearing the scorn of others. Now we could develop our inner character instead of worrying about how people saw us.

Today, we're free and moving toward our dreams. Mary and I, and all nine children, feel closer to each other than ever before. We tearfully apologized to our parents and siblings, and they received us with open arms. My former lifelong battle with depression has been gone for more than five years.

Perhaps you face a similar crossroad in your life. You've climbed the ladder to success, only to find it's leaning against the wrong wall. Or you've pursued dreams someone else has imposed upon you, or have been afraid to dream because you think good things only happen to other people. I have learned some things that can help you....

Be honest about where you really are, regardless of the cost, or who might disagree with you. The truth sets us free. I've always found this works.

Find out who you really are. Many people never ask life's hard questions about the deeper meaning of life, love, relationships and God. Because of this, multitudes of people live in quiet desperation, outwardly doing happy things, but never asking why they're so miserable inside.

Be honest with your loved ones, no matter how painful the truth is. Reach out to them for help. I apologized to my wife and children for leading them in the wrong direction. I also apologized to our parents and siblings. Meanwhile, the people in the religious cult did all they could to turn my family against me. Don't be afraid to let your family see you weep and agonize for real breakthrough.

Work on your character, not your image. Right after we left the sect, rumors and gossip began flying so fast, we were helpless to stop them. I told my family, "Work on your character, not your image. Then we'll develop the 'true inner gold' that makes life satisfying and attracts high quality people into our lives."

Always live for your highest purposes. Don't waste time holding grudges or rehashing offences and setbacks. Move toward your dreams with all that's in you!

Move forward. If you're not where you know you really want to be in life, or you can't express your real self where you are, wake up and take inventory. You don't always need to know where you're going. Sometimes you just need to go, and believe that although you don't know what you're looking for, you'll know when you find it. As you move toward that distant dream, it will begin moving towards you. You will meet people along the way who will point you in the right direction.

Make sure your dream is all-consuming and so big that you're willing to lose everything else in order to achieve it; so grand that you would rather die than miss your goal. When you're willing to pay that price, you'll experience rewards in the common hours of life, from unexpected places that exceed your wildest dreams.

93

Make sure it works in real life. Many things people teach both in business and religion sounds logical and makes you feel good, but doesn't work in everyday life. Make sure your beliefs work in everyday life. Don't settle for less. Seek and you shall find.

Look for treasures in the darkness. You may be passing through a "dark night of the soul" right now. Don't waste your season of darkness, but search for its treasures. These treasures will become the gifts you can offer others when your season has passed. Refuse to let yourself die inside. The sun will rise again.

Apply success principles where it really matters. How tragic to see multitudes of people pursuing their careers, but failing in their families! Many of the same principles that work in our careers also work in the family. Why not apply them?

Everyone has a cry for a mom, a dad, children and siblings. This cry is so deep that we often create temporary, pretend families with business associates and other organizations just so we can temporarily feel like "family."

The truth is that many families don't need to fail. Everyone wants to feel like they belong to a family, preferably their own family, whether they were born or adopted into it; everyone wants their family to succeed.

"The family that prays together, stays together" really works. But we need to do more than say our prayers. We need to really pray! Talk to God like a close friend who's right here, not as a formal or angry person somewhere far away.

A family makes a great mastermind team. We often meet informally to talk through problems and hold each other accountable. No one knows you as deeply as your family. When there's love and respect, your family can "level" with you and help you build character at the deepest levels.

When the family is succeeding, success feels easy. When tough times come, everything can look impossible — but don't give up! No matter where you're at today, begin right where you are. Past failures become stepping-stones to future success. It's never too late to start. Let's go!

—Phillip Cohen

Endnote: When my father-in-law read my essay for this book, he sent me the following response:

"Excellent job. I would expect writing this made you feel even better about your life choices. You have certainly chosen a challenging road for the next few years and I have no doubt you'll find it as rewarding as the choice in 1999. You have a good writing style, readable, to the point, with the ability to hold the interest of the reader."

Three weeks later, Frank died from a massive stroke. In so many ways, he was the greatest man I ever knew: former top executive for three major corporations, a wonderful dad and grandpa, and a perpetually optimistic person — to think that I turned my back on him for so many years! I'm so thankful I made peace with him before he died. Once again, I want to emphasize that no matter how difficult your family life has been, start moving toward your dreams — today — from right where you're at. I believe you already know at least a couple of things you need to do. Get going! You will never regret it.

If you like what you've read ... check this out!

FOOTNOTES

*Phillip Cohen is founder and president of **Cohen Architectural Woodworking**, a family owned cabinet business in central Missouri that specializes in high quality custom cabinets for hospitals, hotels and a few select businesses. They are rising to become one of the most sought after cabinet shops in their region. You can reach Phillip at **573-265-7070**. Check out their website: **www.cohenwoodworking.com** and get a free copy of, "Seven Costly Mistakes Contractors and Homeowners Make When Purchasing Cabinets."*

*Phillip and his wife Mary help people find emotional and spiritual freedom through becoming honest with themselves. For a complimentary 30 minute coaching call, email Phillip at **phil@phillipcohen.net**.*

"RichMom.com"

Thriving Entrepreneur Freed from the Past so She Could Embrace a Future of Success

by Bridget Copley

The Back Story

If necessity is the mother of invention, then "divorce" may be the mother of all necessities.

At the end of 2001, I filed for divorce. It was a stressful time and when it ended, I was a single-mom with two kids, no job and no recent work experience living in Silicon Valley where the economic situation resembled the Great Depression of the 1930s.

I was scared ... and I was desperate.

Parenting meant everything to me, and I thought if I just "got a job" that I would have to give up my type of parenting. It was a compromise I wasn't willing to make. Still, I knew that I needed to work to support myself. So, I enrolled in a private Masters of Arts program in Psychology, with the dream of becoming a counselor.

What I failed to include in my dream, however, was the cost. I entered the world of student loans and soon realized that I would barely be able to afford the student loan payments each month, even after I got a job as a counselor. This was desperation at a new level.

The Answer Seemed To Be Real Estate. ...

I researched real estate investing, and I went for it. I did not use much of my own money to start. I couldn't, since I had a **very negative net worth.** So, in order to begin the real estate ventures, I had to do a lot more than just learn the "how-tos" of investing. I had to change my whole outlook on my life and on myself.

An **integrated approach to personal and professional success** changed my life — not a real estate investment course. The system I used gave me the confidence to take full advantage of the endless opportunities that exist and equipped me with a "self image" of someone who couldn't fail. I have

now been investing for about 2.5 years. I have turned my financial life from a nightmare into one of abundance, and I get to spend lots of time with my children.

Like many people, I had been limited by low self-esteem. I knew that dwelling on the past and on things that could no longer be changed was unhealthy … and was certainly not conducive to any kind of personal or professional success.

When I started attending educational seminars to support my efforts in real estate, I always felt inferior to the others there.

Things "came to a head" for me at a seminar in Los Angeles. My own inner conflicts seemed to sabotage me as part of my brain tried to absorb new information and learn about real estate, while another part kept busy with affirmations like "I'm good," and "I'm worthy" that the self-help experts recommend during stressful times. Yet, even as I was repeating the affirmations, my negative childhood feelings and the low self-worth, which accompanied those feelings seemed to take a fresh hold on me.

By the end of the day I was **physically and mentally exhausted.** Because of this **internal turmoil,** the seminar experience was really not as fun or productive as I could have made it. What a shame. ...

I realized with startling clarity that although I *wanted* to learn, the warring thoughts in my head — all of them focused on the past — prevented me from achieving my goal. I was so busy trying to ward off the feeling that I was "not good enough" that I couldn't do what I needed to do to make me more than good enough. The conflict kept me from doing what I needed to do to **make me the best.**

Talk about a vicious circle!

This feeling of inferiority became a common theme in my life, and I knew that I had met literally hundreds of people who wanted to stop thinking about the past so they could get on with their lives. In a rut dug deep by backward-looking thoughts and feelings, I was not alone....

Yet, like them, I could not figure out how to do it. I didn't have the skills, the tools or the knowledge to make a change.

Searching for Answers

I guess you could call me an "information junkie." I truly believe that knowledge is power, so I decided to do everything in my power to "get smart." While I boned-up on real estate, I read business motivational books, listened to inspirational CDs and tapes, watched DVD's and videos and attended seminars with some of the world's most successful self-help gurus.

I came away from each experience with something useful, but I knew that there were vital pieces missing.

After my "light-bulb moment" at the L.A. seminar, I went to a trusted

97

advisor with my problem. I explained that part of my mind says one thing positive and part of my mind says another thing negative. I admitted that the negative always won out and I felt awful most of the time.

She gave me the key. She encouraged me to listen to my inner dialogue and identify and acknowledge my feelings — the good ones and the bad. I was shocked. This was exactly the *opposite* of the "common wisdom" of positive thinking … affirmations … and the old "out with the bad air in with the good" philosophy.

At first, I didn't realize what a powerful, useful gift my mentor had shared. In fact, I thought it was too simple, but I decided to have a little faith and I put her words into practice.

I allowed myself to "open up" to feelings formed in childhood and throughout my life, and I examined all the events that brought about my negative feelings. I re-experienced feelings of worthlessness, shame, guilt, intimidation and many more. With the feelings came understanding — a clear picture of the effects of the past on my present and future — and the way that my repressed emotions controlled my life.

But here's what surprised me: "By allowing myself to acknowledge and respect my past feelings of unworthiness, I was able to **stop feeling inferior!**"

Feelings are strong and tough to beat … so don't try! The best way to "get over" our feelings is to **let them be** … and getting over the past is the first and **most critical step in embracing the present and moving towards success in the future.**

Sharing What I Learned

I've gone from being a "desperate housewife" in Silicon Valley to a successful entrepreneur with a thriving real estate business with an incredible "system" that I can use to achieve all my goals, both personal and professional.

With so many chapters written in my own success story (including a "happily ever after" ending), I've decided it is time to "share the wealth." I'm reaching out to people who find themselves today stuck … not due to a lack of talent or desire, but simply because of negative and self-limiting thoughts.

In many ways, RichMom.com is a reflection of my original desire to become a counselor. But now, instead of sharing the sometimes moth-eaten theories of the academic world, I can share my **real-life experiences** and equip my clients with an integrated approach to their life that's been **proven to grow success.**

For young moms, single moms and stay-at-home moms with young and school-age children … and for dads, too … there's much more to life than earning a paycheck. More leisure hours, a passive cash flow that leaves time for

family, a bigger and better retirement "nest egg" and the emotional satisfaction these things bring are what I want for my clients.

RichMom.com and the "recipe for success" it offers can help people change their lives for the better. People can break out of the mold of "a stay-at-home parent" to become "multi-tasking" entrepreneurs — using their talents to raise a business along with a family — and for anyone imprisoned in an unsatisfying or unhealthy relationship, RichMom.com is the key to "breaking out" and finding true joy.

Five Steps to being a "RichMom"

RichMom.com is an **integrated approach to living**. It harnesses the individual powers of mind, body and spirit together to form a single super-potent, super-powerful system. Your "super powers" may not allow you to leap tall buildings at a single bound, but they will allow you to approach life head on and power through any obstacle that stands in your way.

Step #1 — You've Got to Feel It to Heal It
Identify your feelings and analyze the affects they have had on your life. Don't be hard on yourself if you start to see a pattern of negativity. Everyone has "issues" and negative feelings that they would like to get over. Instead of judging yourself harshly, get into the habit of **being empathetic with yourself** and acknowledge that you are human. Accept that **negative feelings will tend to come and go** and their effect on your life decreases with time.

Step #2 — Paint Your Vision with Passion
Don't limit your dreams — think BIG! Let your goals go beyond merely taking care of yourself and your family. Give yourself freedom to ignore the rules. You don't have to follow role models. You don't have to do what "they" say (whoever "they" are). Discover your passion. Identify what you care about in life and your passion will power your success.

Step #3 — Keep the Faith, Baby
You must **believe in yourself**. You may not know how in the beginning; in fact, it's one of the most important issues I cover with my clients. I help them to develop an automatic response system so that every new challenge is met with an "I can do it" positive mindset.

Step #4 — Be A Team Player
Create your dream team of **allies, advisors, coaches, mentors, support** and whatever you need. Humans are social "pack animals." We are not meant to "go it alone." It takes the synergy of people working together to accomplish grand realization. This synergy is another reason that the client-coach relationship is so powerful.

Step #5 — The BIG Step - Do Something!
After all the thinking is done, it's time to **take focused action**. Ask for help. Study the techniques and strategies of people who have done what you'd like

99

to do — experiment, compare and contrast. Keep following up, questioning, researching, and doing whatever you need to do to keep moving forward.

Without this last step nothing gets done.

Finding Your Way

Learning about yourself and your emotions is an exciting, challenging and often a difficult process. There are lots of self-help tools to choose from and many "paths to enlightenment." My philosophy is "what's right for you is what works for you." That's why I provide a variety of ways to access my materials and use them to succeed as I have.

On my Web site, success-oriented visitors, especially the moms and dads struggling with the balance between working and parenting, can select from different media and "delivery systems" to suit their style and needs. I also provide a broad spectrum of learning packages and plan to expand my work to include live seminars and workshops, as well as information-dense teleseminars.

My goal is to help others live lives that go far beyond their wildest dreams, to help them take control of their lives, to teach them (and you) to *live each moment with intention, and to be a "RichMom."*

If you like what you've read ... check this out!

FOOTNOTES

*As president and founder of RichMom.com, **Bridget Copley's** mission is to help other Moms become healthy and wealthy while staying at home and enjoying their families. Go to **www.RichMom.com** to receive your free newsletter, RichMomSecrets.com.*

Writing to the Glory of God

by Marlys Johnsen Norris

Who would ever imagine that a young boy's kidnapping — perpetrated by a rich "society" woman who kept him as her son for over 30 years — would help realize a young girl's "dream" of becoming a writer?

My premise: Absolutely everyone has a significant story to share. My first book "God Moves Mountains, It was a Miracle" reveals the story of an obsessive woman and the trauma she caused our family as she invaded our lives over and over again. Going through that experience, I never dreamt it would ultimately become a book and passionately draw me into my current profession as a published writer. It just goes to show you how much you can accomplish through faith!

Today, many people write their memoirs and poetry as a legacy for their children and their children's children. Many people find reading biographies of their relatives and/or friends an exhilarating experience, and you don't have to be a celebrity or a politician to write yours. I met Phil Silvers, a writer who'd published stories he created and read as bedtime stories to his children years ago. Another writer-friend relates in his World War II memoirs how he miraculously escaped death numerous times. A writer I admire — Doris Eutzler — has written poems as her legacy to her family, relating her life and the events that colored it for over 80 years. Finally, Gary Garison writes skits and plays that move the observers to listen to the voice of God. What's your story? Perhaps you should write it down!

These writers all have amazing stories to tell that reflect the origin and depth of their faith in God. These stories often testify to how God intervened in their lives in times of crisis. Oftentimes, reading someone's biography can help someone somewhere find the courage to fight life's battles. Why wouldn't everyone want their story told? Perhaps you have a story you'd like to tell, but don't know how to go about it or where to start. Let me share something of my own journey to becoming a published writer — hopefully, it will help you on your journey!

Before I published my first book, I joined Sacramento Suburban Writers, hoping to learn more about the craft of writing. The speakers each month stirred the gift within me. In the writing group, I learned about "query letters." Query

101

letters are to a writer what bait is to a fisherman. A writer sends out query letters as "bait," hoping to find a publisher interested in publishing his or her story. In my innocence and inexperience, I kept sending these out one after another, only to receive one rejection after another, day after day. While the rejection letters devastated me, I began to understand that it also contributed to the quality of my writing. With every rejection letter, I took a closer look at my manuscript. Gradually, I learned to make my manuscript more acceptable to editors. While I first wrote about my family occurrences chronologically, I decided that the story might be more suspenseful and interesting if I changed the chronology around and incorporated the occurrences as "flashbacks" further along in the story. I also learned about "hooks" and "conversation." A "hook" is to a writer just what a hook is to a fisherman — you catch something with it. A writer uses a "hook" to grab a reader's attention, which gives him just enough to lure him along for the ride. If you give away the whole story in the beginning, you'll lose the reader. Hooks keep readers interested in finishing your book.

I also learned how to write "dialogue" or "conversation." It isn't always necessary for a writer to always "tell" the story using description of the characters and events. Think of *Shakespeare* or your favorite movie. Most movies and plays depend solely upon dialogue to "show" the viewer the story. I had to keep in mind that for readers to stay "hooked," I needed to entertain them and keep them interested, so I began to incorporate more dialogue, which made reading easier. When I finished the book, it wasn't perfect, but it was better.

Since my book really detailed the amazing things God accomplished in my life and family — and my writing had a decidedly Christian emphasis — I joined the Sacramento Christian Writers. This group seemed to really meet my needs as a writer: each week I would come away with helpful materials, useful information and lots of encouragement from the other members.

Many writing groups take the summer off, but I wanted to continue meeting with someone. Writing, rewriting and editing my story became my passion — I couldn't stop working on it. If you're like me, it's not easy to write alone, day after day without any helpful feedback. Receiving input from other writers and editors helped me immensely, and I would recommend to anyone who struggles with the process of writing (which is clearly "work" by anyone's definition), to join a writer's group. I began to talk with a couple other women interested in starting a writing group in our church. We met and talked about the possibility, and decided to name our new group "Sonrise Christian Writers." Only one of us had been published before, but we decided that we wanted to help other writers who wanted to learn to write. I began to recycle information that I received from Sacramento Christian Writer's Group and share it with the writers from my church. We decided we would meet once a month in various homes and promote our group by having our meetings printed in the Sunday bulletin. We made up the following mission statement for our goal:

". . . to support other Christian writers in our church and community. To encourage, uplift, share and help one another to reach success, and to endeavor as Christian writers to glorify God and reflect His Love."

Published writers gave short lessons to the members on how to improve

their writing and their chances of getting published. The members sought to emphasize Christian principles and values in an easily understandable manner. We gave each member a "writing assignment," which consisted of a topic and a prompt. Each member would then write 300 words on that topic and share it at our next meeting. Some of the topics included bereavement, honesty, eternity, personal responsibility toward others and other similar things. At each meeting, we would share what we were working on and we used our "cumulative knowledge" to help each other we compiled files on writing query letters and proposals, how to publish, where to publish and we also created critique forms that we used to critique each other's work.

Still having more to learn, I continued to edit and rewrite the book until I felt comfortable with my manuscript. Even experienced writers need feedback; I didn't yet consider myself an "experienced writer," so I enlisted the help of friends and family in critiquing my work. Be careful who you ask to read your work! You need something of a thick-skin to hear people's criticisms, so asking your friends and families (as I did) might not always be a good idea. First of all, make sure the person you ask is literate (well-read, that is). Try to get as many opinions as possible. If several of your readers say similar things about your work, there's a chance that what they're saying is true. Take such criticisms to heart. It's tough, I know, but your story or manuscript will be better for it. Writing, like life, is a learning process, and sometimes growth hurts. But just as pruning a tree brings forth new fruit, so will criticism improve your work.

Writing's not only about criticism and revision. It's also about learning how to use technology and the technological innovation to your advantage, which can be exhilarating (if you're technologically savvy) or exhausting (if you're not). One of the writers in our group had used a Print on Demand (POD) printer and was about to publish his second book. I decided to give it a try. My writer-friend was very helpful, but learning this process exhausted me and took longer than expected. Publishing any book, no matter how simple it appears, quickly becomes an involved process that requires a lot of patience.

I began to chronicle the story of my family, concentrating on a curious event that changed the course of all of our lives forever — my brother's kidnapping by a very wealthy actress/society woman — and the traumatic events following the kidnapping. Although the event seriously interrupted our lives, the outcome relates the miracle-working power of God in our lives, and particularly in the life of my family. I related it all from memory, and many of my readers have told me how suspenseful they found it — in fact, many told me they read it in one sitting!

When I finally felt finished with the writing, I mailed my manuscript off to the publisher with a sigh of relief, however, with the relief came a wave of anticipation and impatience — I wanted to see my book in print!!! My book, "God Moves Mountains, It was a Miracle!" recounts my brother's kidnapping and the way in which God miraculously reunited us after 37 years of separation. Writing this book helped heal me, gave me great insights into my character and personality, and gave me a chance to try and do something I wasn't sure I could accomplish. I

103

truly believe that writing helps people explore areas of their life where pain has existed. Dealing with them honestly enables the healing power of God to touch their lives and heal — inexpensive psychological help!

With my first book *"God Moves Mountains, It was a Miracle"* (ISBN 1-4107-0010-0 1st Books Publishers) behind me, I decided to focus on a new book *"Recipes for a Happier Marriage."* In "Recipes" I recount the amazing events God accomplished in my 44-year marriage. I asked my Sunday School teacher Joe Baginski, if he might like to add to what I had already written and he agreed. Joe's contributions to the book as a Social and Marriage Counselor made the book even better. The book focuses on the power of the Word of God to restore lost love in our marriages. I mailed the manuscript to my former Pastor, Drell Butler (of Mt. Vernon, Washington), Pat Boone (yes, him) and my present Pastor to read. I asked for their comments for the cover of the book, if they enjoyed it. When we received their encouragement and responses, we included them on the back cover of *"Recipes for a Happier Marriage."* When I received the first copy of the book, I jumped for joy and ordered my first 100 copies. My husband and I both felt that we had really accomplished something significant by helping couples in marital trouble, as well as young couples just beginning to adjust to marriage.

When I began to market the book, an acquaintance suggested that I join the Sacramento Publishers and Authors, and submit the book to their yearly contest. *"Recipes for a Happier Marriage"* (ISBN 1-57921-639-0 Pleasant Word Publishers) **won "BEST CHRISTIAN BOOK FOR 2003-04" from Northern California Publishers and Author's.** Northern California Publishers and Authors acknowledged us at a special awards dinner with a lovely framed plaque and special gold stickers to apply to each book. Success at last!

I've continued to write and publish in 2005. I just published another book called "Defining Moments" (ISBN 9-7809-939802 Heavenly Bound Book Publishers). "Defining Moments" includes my personal devotions along with testimony of how much God has accomplished in my life. Do you have a defining moment in your life? If so, I'd love for you to share it with me. You'll find my contact info at the end of this article.

My fourth published book entitled "Short Stories for the Family" (ISBN 1-4184-7752-4 1st Books Publishers) includes:

- **A Norwegian Love Story** — A story that incorporates ideas from my grandparents history together.
- **A Miracle Called Grace** — A mother tries to find just the right toy at Christmas for her little girl.
- **It Just Feels Good!** — A woman struggles with temptation.
- **Airport Romance** — A chance meeting in an airport leads a couple to find their "soul mates."
- **Two Sailors and a Girl** — A girl writes a "Dear John letter" to her boyfriend, but the boyfriend finds a new love and marries. The old boyfriend's buddy checks in with this old girlfriend and has some stories to tell.

If **I** can do it, so can **you**. I never thought I'd write one book, much less

www.mentorsmagazine.com

four! While I continue to write about the love, grace and mercy afforded me daily by my Lord, and to recount all He has done in my life these 30-plus years, I know I'm not the only one out there with a story to tell. We all have stories. Every person out there should write a book, even if they never decide to publish it. Your kids — no matter how disinterested or egotistical they might seem — will jump at the chance to read your story someday. I continue to encourage new writers to explore the gift of writing within them.

If you like what you've read ... check this out!

FOOTNOTES ✝

*Writing continually teaches me new things, and for me, it has evolved into the process of becoming a publisher. We call our company **Heavenly Bound Book Publishing**. Visit our Web site for more information on buying any of my books, or requesting any of my **Free Brochures**. **The Beginner's Writing Brochure** helps give direction to the novice writer, or the **Sonrise Christian Writer's Brochure** gives ideas on starting your own group.*

*Web page: **www.heavenlyboundpublishers.com***
*E-mail: **Marlysj@sbcglobal.net***

or you may write me at:

Heavenly Bound Book Publishers
*Attn: **Marlys***
P.O. Box 5144
Fair Oaks, California 95628
*or call **1-916-961-0575***

"Staying Up, Up, Up, in a Down, Down World"

by Zig Ziglar

Psychiatrist Alfred Adler said that hope is the foundational quality of all change. It is also the great activator. People without hope take action to realize their dreams. People without hope are often so discouraged, they feel incapable of doing anything significant. Good news: hope and help are available.

Persistence Pays

The March 16, 1998 issue of "USA Today" featured an article about dieting in America. It seems that after 20 years of diet, exercise, miracle potions, and a host of gimmicks, the American people have concluded that losing weight is a lost cause for them. They take it off and put it back on. They are unhappy losing the weight, depriving themselves of their favorite foods, and then feeling guilty because they regain the weight. There's a major trend among millions of Americans who are saying, "To heck with it! I'm going to eat what I want and just suffer the consequences, but I'm not going to be miserable about it."

That's an unfortunate approach. But I understand why they feel that way because for many years I was on that roller coaster. A quarter-of-a-century ago I decided to lose weight one a gradual basis, and in a 10-month period of eating sensibly and exercising regularly, I lost 37 pounds. I averaged losing 1 9-10 ounces per day.

I'll bet you just said to yourself (if you have a weight problem), "I could do that."

Most attempts at weight loss are undermined by unrealistic promises made about a "revolutionary" new approach or product that "will take weight off permanently and you won't feel hungry." The real answer is a change of lifestyle, a combination of eating sensibly and exercising regularly. Benefits are enormous. On November 24, 1999, at age 73, I stayed on the treadmill at the Aerobics Center more than two minutes longer than I was able to stay at age 45, when I weighed 200 pounds and was terribly out of shape. I have a resting heart rate of 47, my cholesterol level was described by Dr. Larry Gibbons, the examining physician, as "perfect" at 156, and my blood pressure is 110/60. Those are the readings typical of a much younger man. And my enthusiasm for life grows every day.

A Formula for Success

Over the years I've come to realize that some specifics help you enjoy success in each area of your life. You start with the right mental attitude, and I speak of more than positive thinking. Attitude is not everything, but it is the beginning point for success. With the right mental attitude you will recognize that you need to learn specific skills. A positive-thinking doctor, without the necessary education, would not be successful and would have to bury many of his mistakes. The right attitude plus the right skill makes a substantial difference. When you add to that the right philosophy, namely that you can have everything in life you want if you will just help enough other people get what they want, which turns things from being self-centered to a secularized version of the golden rule, then success draws even closer.

To this you might add the right direction. You must have a balanced goals program that encompasses all areas of your life. The final key to the success formula is character because all long-term success is character based. This is true in the home, on the job, and in the community. Success and winning relationships are built on trust, and without character, how can there be trust?

Character also produces endurance and persistence when the going gets tough, and life truly is and endurance race, not a sprint. When you follow this simple formula, which over time has proved to be true, you will discover success in all areas of your life because you will have the wherewithal to handle whatever comes your way.

Why I Will Succeed

Charles Surasky said some nice things about one of my books and gave me permission to use his comments in a book or column. This writing was produced at the request of the managing partner of a West Coast legal practice and was a significant part of a larger project:

- I will succeed because I am a winner.
- I will succeed because every lesson I've learned has prepared me for this challenge.
- I will succeed because I want to succeed and because people believe in me and trust me.
- I will succeed because success will help me to grow into a bigger and better person.
- I will succeed because I know what I must do.
- I will succeed because my family is the foundation of my success.
- I will succeed because success is the most important legacy I can bequeath to my children.
- I will succeed because my wife and I are inseparable, unstoppable and uniquely talented.

107

- I will succeed because I've faced opportunities before and I have triumphed.
- I will succeed because success is a birthright I inherited from my parents and my ancestors.
- I will succeed because I've always wanted to expand the range of challenges in my life.
- I will succeed because I have family, friends and acquaintances who want to — and will — help me.
- I will succeed because I am young, healthy and dynamic.
- I will succeed because my plan for success is flexible and my thirst for success is unquenchable.
- I will succeed.

Surasky covered some poignant thoughts, and I noticed that he included no "if-only's" or "I plan to's" or "I'm a'gonna do's." If all of us borrowed the concepts identified here, more of us would experience greater success.

Questions Are the Answer

For centuries knowledgeable people have recognized that successful leaders have a talent for asking the right questions to get the information they need. They are probing, penetrating, thought-provoking questions that force the other person to think. Doing this enables the leader to bring out the best in that individual.

As individuals, we need to ask ourselves penetrating questions because questions force us to explore our thinking. For example, do you believe your doubts and doubt your beliefs? John L. Mason asks that penetrating question in his book, "Ask," and it really forces you to think. Are you optimistic or pessimistic? Do you lean toward the cynical, or are you open-minded, giving the other person benefit of the doubt? Do you question everything just to be questioning, or are you intellectually curious, really interested in the answer?

Are you preparing yourself for the future, or are you simply waiting for the future? Do you know more about your profession, your family, and yourself today than you did yesterday? What new information or task have you learned? Are you waiting for the future to just happen, or are you taking steps to make certain your future is going to be what you can make it? Do you let your past teach you, or do you let it beat you? Do you recognize that the other person has a point of view and it could well be right, or do you stubbornly push ahead with the iron-clad belief that you've got to the answer and refuse to be confused by any compelling evidence that there is a possibility you could be wrong?

Questions really are the answer, and if you ask enough honest ones, you'll end up with a happier, healthier, more fulfilled life.

Life Is an Attitude

Ron Heagy is an outstanding author, speaker, and counselor who has his master's degree in a social counseling. He is also a mouth painter and has sold more than a thousand pictures. He has been happily married since 1992 to a loving and beautiful wife.

To see Ron is an inspiration. To listen to him is an encouragement. To read him is educational. He developed all his skills and accomplished all these objectives after he broke his neck in a surfing accident that left him a quadriplegic. Today his most outstanding characteristic is his tremendously good attitude. Meeting him and looking into his eyes, watching his video, and reading his book, "Life Is an Attitude," are inspiring experiences. As he expresses it, "Attitudes are contagious. Is yours worth catching?"

Before the accident Ron was an outstanding high school athlete who had a scholarship to play football at Oregon State University. He was injured on the day before his eighteenth birthday. One day he could bench-press three hundred pounds; the next day he couldn't life a finger. In the early days following the accident, Ron was heartbroken, angry, and bitter, and he held more a than a few parties as he grieved his losses.

Fortunately for Ron, his mother, and upbeat woman who loves him deeply, encouraged him to develop his other talents and abilities, and suggested that he become a painter.

Eventually he could lift his voice and his paintbrush with his mouth. Now Ron travels the country encouraging people to use what they have to help others have a better life. Ron's accomplishments are an inspiration to all of us. Take Ron Heagy's approach, and you will be more, do more, and have more of what life has to offer.

If you like what you've read ... check this out!

FOOTNOTES

Zig Ziglar, one of the most sought-after motivational speakers in the country, delivers his message of humor, hope, and enthusiasm to audiences throughout the world. He is chairman of Zig Ziglar Corporation, whose mission is to equip people to more fully utilize their physical, mental, and spiritual resources.

Bestselling books by Ziglar include "See You at the Top," which has sold more than 1.5 million copies worldwide, "Over the Top," "Raising Positive Kids in a Negative World," "Something to Smile About," and "Confessions of a Grieving Christian."

Article excerpts reprinted from the book, "STAYING UP, UP, UP IN A DOWN, DOWN WORLD" by Publisher Thomas Nelson, Inc., Copyright © 2000 by the Zig Ziglar Corporation. All rights reserved. Used here by permission.

Molding a Millionaire Mindset

by Kathy Kennebrook

More people are becoming millionaires today than ever before. Unlike a generation ago when most millionaires inherited their money, most of the recent millionaires made their millions themselves. So, what makes these wealthy entrepreneurs so different?

Along the road to wealth, I heard many success stories similar to my own, and one theme seems to stand out. Most of the millionaires I met gained their wealth by trial and error, constant motion and the pursuit of a dream that would change their lives forever. They were also willing to take a risk.

My Story

Certainly, I'm no different than most Americans. I grew up on Long Island in New York where my father usually worked two jobs just to make ends meet. My mother stayed home to raise my older brother and me. After high school I spent the next 12 years in the banking industry before realizing I really hated punching a time clock. I awoke one morning, went to work and quit my job without any idea of what I was going to do next. My first marriage had recently ended and I was raising my daughter pretty much on my own. It was a financial struggle to make ends meet and I worked all kinds of jobs just to stay afloat.

Two years later I remarried and together we raised our two children. My husband has a son from his previous marriage, and so we became a much smaller version of the "Brady Bunch." For the next nine years I worked in sales, logging thousands of miles each year on my vehicle. Since I worked commission sales, my pay structure was simple: if I didn't work, I didn't get paid. My husband worked in a "mom and pop" auto parts store and took second jobs whenever we needed extra money.

I tried to keep our bills paid current (most of the time) since I always worried about not making enough money through mere commissions. We almost never had extra money to do the things we really wanted to do. Like most Americans, we were just making ends meet. I would try to put some money in an untouched savings account just in case of an emergency, particularly since neither of us had health insurance coverage. I knew there had to be an alternative to the way we were living, but I just didn't know how to create a better lifestyle for us. Soon, my husband got a better job and the family finally had benefits, but I knew this just wasn't what I wanted on a long-term basis.

I'd always dreamed of an early retirement. This was especially poignant for me since my dad passed away from a heart attack two days after he retired at age 65. I just had to figure out how to come up with long-term passive income if I wanted to accomplish the goal of early retirement.

I'd always been interested in real estate, and I was lucky enough to own a modest "fixer upper" so I understood the concept of appreciation with my little fixer upper going up in value year after just one year. After staying up late one night watching an infomercial on how to buy houses with no money down, I decided to find out more about the real estate business.

I Took the Plunge

I began this life-changing business by going to local real estate clubs and seminars where I dragged my husband along, kicking and screaming. Fortunately, he finally came around to my way of thinking. Yes ladies, there is hope! Fueled by my new-found determination, I began to formulate my plan to be financially free. I realized that my desire to succeed was greater than my fear of failure, or the financial risks I thought were involved. I learned that in order to get ahead, I had to tame the fear monster and not let anyone or anything stand in the way of my success.

Initially, my plan was to buy houses, fix them up, and resell them for a profit. It sounded a lot like another job, but at least I would be my own boss. I would be able to control my own destiny, or so I thought. If there were bumps in the road, I found every one of them! I quickly began to see that my conservative attitude about money and real estate wasn't the way to financial freedom. I needed to take the big step!!

I'd read about people making huge amounts of money in the real estate business and I wanted a piece of that action, too. I started surrounding myself with like-minded people who were making more money than I was in real estate. I began to emulate what they were doing and this provided a constant source of positive energy for me. I learned to avoid the negative people in my life who either couldn't or wouldn't support my goals and plans. I also discovered that the more education I got in the real estate business, the more money I began to make.

How I Did It

I discovered several things along my path to financial wealth. I had to change my attitude about myself and about those around me. Most of all, I had to commit to the dream! After I bought my first house, I stood up in a real estate club meeting and committed to doing ten more house deals before the year ended. I knew that if I said it out loud in front of a group of about 200 friends and peers, I would do what I needed to do to avoid the embarrassment that would come with not fulfilling my public commitment. For my real estate business to succeed I needed to stay committed, to push harder and to finalize more and bigger deals. This became even more important after I left my job; when there is no "boss" to tell you what to do each day; it can be hard to stay focused.

By the way, I ended up doing a total of 15 real estate deals that first year. Each year since, I've honed my real estate business by learning more and developing systems to make things run automatically, this way, I have more time to do more deals and make more money.

What I Learned

I've learned some truths along the way that kept me moving forward to accomplish deal after deal:

• **Get the minutia out of your life.** By minutia, I mean anything that holds you back from attaining your goals and dreams. In my life, minutia also included excuses. There was always another reason not to get started.

Set specific boundaries and learn how to say "No" when necessary. I kept a log of my daily activities, which helped me quickly see how much "stuff" I did that was a waste of time and energy. Find someone else to do those unproductive activities like mowing the lawn or cleaning the pool.

Turn off the television. Resist the urge to choose pleasurable endeavors over forward motion. You can choose success over failure. I now tape my favorite programs, pick the time I want to watch them (which best accommodates my money-making schedule) and fast forward past the commercials.

Create systems or use systems others have created to help you move forward more quickly and efficiently. As my business grew, I created systems for finding motivated sellers and for buying and selling houses more quickly. I created another system by putting my "dream team" in place to handle all the details required to do my marketing, put my deals together and get them closed. I built teams to handle all the bookkeeping and other mundane tasks my business required. Check out my Web site at **Marketingmagiclady.com** for free information on building systems in your business.

• **Set specific goals for yourself.** Create a written list of short term and long term goals and hang them where you can look at them everyday. Include both business and personal goals. These are written affirmations. Without focus and direction, how will you ever know what you've accomplished or where you're going?

Commit to whatever it is you want to do both verbally and in writing. I find nothing holds me more accountable than telling people exactly what it is I plan to do. Don't feel like you need to excuse or justify your goals or dreams to anyone. Do something toward your goal every single day! Nothing will make you grow more quickly.

• **Figure out the "Why."** Take the time to figure out what the "why" is for you. Why do you want to achieve this goal? What do you want your future to look like?

Once that "why" becomes real and tangible to you, you'll do whatever is necessary to make it happen. The "why" for me was that I wanted to be able to retire before I turned 40 years old so I would have more time to pursue the things I love to do. I even made specific lists of what those things were, and now I'm working my way through that list because I was able to stop living paycheck to paycheck.

• **See Your Dream.** Do what those around you will not. Be willing to take a risk, be willing to do things differently than those who have come before you. Learn to think like a millionaire and program yourself to be rich. More than a change in lifestyle, you need to embrace a total mindset. I know of one person who wrote himself a check for a million dollars and placed it in his wallet to cash in the future. He eventually reached that goal.

Say the words, "I am a millionaire, the money just hasn't been deposited in my bank account yet." This is verbal affirmation of your goal and desire. You must redefine your beliefs before you can become who you want to be. Begin to visualize what you want your future to look like and move toward that reality.

• **Find a mentor.** Find a person who already is where you want to be, and who will hold you accountable. Don't take advice from anyone making less money than you are, or who hasn't already attained the goals you've set for yourself. You can go through a coaching program, or find someone to guide you through a local club or association.

My mentor helped me with many things, one of which was to help me prioritize critical steps to grow my business. He created deadlines that kept me moving in a positive, forward motion. He was a sounding board when I had problems I didn't know how to solve. He gave me positive input, which helped me grow. He helped me stay focused and offered guidance when I needed it. He also took years off my learning curve since he'd already "been there, done that."

• **Educate Yourself.** Read everything you can get your hands on regarding your passion. I bought or borrowed every book or tape I could find regarding the real estate business. I went to every seminar available. I always picked up some new tidbit of information that made me money.

The learning process never ends. You can always implement new ideas. Join organizations within your niche market. Continue to hone the skills you need to succeed. The more I learned, the more I earned!

• **Create Credibility.** Become the expert at whatever it is you want to do. People naturally want to work with someone they perceive to be an expert in their field. I became an expert in the real estate business by finding solutions for people who needed to sell their homes quickly, and making them feel like I was there to help. I have a philosophy: If I can't create a "win-win" solution, I won't do the deal.

Become the person your customers want to contact whenever their situation requires your product or service. You can create credibility for yourself in a variety of ways. Let people know what it is you do. Hold free classes for example at the library, or your local clubs and associations. You can write and

113

submit articles to your local papers. Participate in local radio shows. Many radio programs are looking for talk radio guests on all sorts of topics; become known as the best at what you do.

Create a credibility kit that includes testimonials from satisfied customers, copies of ads or articles you have written, a color business card with your photo and a page telling "your story" including your philosophy or business ethic.

• **Make a choice.** Dare to step outside of the box and be different. Be outrageous! You are where you are today because of choices you have made. Are you where you truly want to be? If not, why not?

Self-made millionaires made a conscious choice to do things differently than most everyone else. You can choose to do something, or you can choose to do nothing. But doing nothing doesn't net a positive result. The decision to be wealthy lies in your hands. You can wake up tomorrow with a different, life-changing perspective. The decision is yours. Success requires a plan and a mindset of commitment. Decide if you're willing to pay the price, whatever that price may be.

Take the information you already have and build on it. If you wait until you know everything, or the timing is perfect, you'll never act. It might be too late. Choose to take those first steps now and the rest will work itself out as you go.

Surround yourself with like-minded people who will support you and keep you moving forward. If you hang out with enough people who make more money than you do, some of that money is bound to start "sticking" to you, too. Most of my friends and family thought I was a little crazy to want to go into the real estate business and become wealthy. Most of them have only known the concept of working all their lives for a paycheck. What I wanted to do was totally foreign to them, so they didn't support it — but I did it anyway. I made the conscious decision to be different.

Knowing that I won't have to depend on children, social security or a job gives me a sense of freedom you can't imagine unless you've experienced it. I've worked hard for other people and companies and helped them make money all my life; now the money I make is mine. If you think you can't change your attitude about money or the opportunity to be wealthy, believe me you can, no matter how old you are. You just have to make the choice to be wealthy and free. It's a decision to have a millionaire mindset.

I always had the confidence that I could be financially free. Once I did it, I found out it wasn't nearly as hard as I thought it would be. I finally discovered that I could build a business I could systemize that continues to throw off cash, even when I'm sleeping.

I found myself ready to put together a system to teach others how to do the same thing. I've trained thousands of people throughout the country how to build a successful real estate business and to find all the motivated sellers they need to make the deals. For more information on finding motivated sellers for your real estate business, visit me at **Attractmotivatedsellers.com**.

If you like what you've read ... check this out!

FOOTNOTES ❸

*Kathy Kennebrook is a speaker, author and real estate entrepreneur. This 4'11" grandmother is the country's leading Real Estate Marketing expert on finding motivated sellers using direct mail. She has been actively investing in real estate since 1999, and is known throughout the United States and Canada as the **Marketing Magic Lady**. She publishes free weekly articles for real estate investors at her website **attractmotivatedsellers.com**. Nothing excites Kathy more than teaching others to attain the level of success she has. She currently authors "Marketing Magic-How To Find Motivated Sellers" and "Marketing Magic Spanish Upgrade." Visit her at **Marketingmagiclady.com** for a free CD on marketing to find motivated sellers.*

Live The Life You Have Imagined

by Lynn Shepherd

"If you advance confidently in the direction of your dreams and endeavor to live the life you have imagined, you will meet with success unexpected in these common hours." — Henry David Thoreau

Hitting Bottom

A favorite getaway destination for my husband and I is the scenic Hocking Hills area. However, with its sandstone caverns, ledges and waterfalls, its beauty can be hazardous. Always mindful of the possibility of falling, I use caution in the steps I take.

My husband and I had experienced a wonderful day hiking in the Hills. By the time we returned to our cabin, nightfall had arrived; it was very dark. Although, it would have been wise to leave on a night-light in case either of us should have to navigate the unfamiliar surroundings at night, we didn't. I found myself groping down the dark hallway to the bathroom and fumbling around for the light switch to no avail. Remembering I had to step down to enter the room, I gingerly felt for firm footing before easing myself down. I started to walk, and then it happened — I stepped down into nothingness! I had forgotten the second step.

The seconds it took to hit the floor seemed like an eternity. After losing my balance, I scrambled to hold onto anything that would prevent my fall, and fall I did — directly on my hip. Then, my head hit the wall and my arm hit the cabinet. Amazingly, I had lodged myself between the sink and the commode. So, there I sat, with nothing broken but a bruised ego. I started to laugh; hitting bottom had definitely taken on a new meaning.

Isn't that just like life? Life happens when we least expect it. Falling while hiking would have been expected, but in the safety of the cabin?

As I sat there trying to get my bearings, I realized the profound life lesson that had been so difficult for me to grasp and accept years ago could also apply here.

Hitting bottom means new beginnings. It doesn't matter whether you invited this change into your life or it just happened, this unfamiliar territory becomes your new reality. The next chapter in your life has arrived. It's all about how we choose to respond to each circumstance that molds our lives.

The Blame Game

I could have chosen to play the Blame Game.
- It's the park's fault. Why in the world did they build a cabin with steps in the bathroom? And why couldn't they put the light switch in the right position?
- It's my husband's fault. He should have been more considerate and left the light on before *he* went to bed.
- It's my fault. Why did I make such a bad choice? After all, if I had just turned on a different light or remembered there were *two* steps, I wouldn't be in this predicament.

Hindsight is perfect, isn't it?

Blame solves nothing. From the time Adam blamed Eve for eating the apple, we still try to shift responsibility to others.

I can blame whomever I choose — as long as I want. It is not going to change my circumstances.

Until I decide to get up, I am still going to be sitting on the floor, alone, in the darkness.

Every situation that occurs in our life requires a choice that will impact not only our lives, but the lives of those around us. It may be of little consequence or of vital importance. It may be a conscious response or an unconscious reaction. But a choice *will* be made. There is wisdom in knowing when it's appropriate to accept life and when to *take control*.

Genuine freedom occurs when you take responsibility. If you are response-*able*, you control the direction of your life. That freedom of responsibility means that you don't have to continue living a life that doesn't serve you. The perception of others or your present circumstances won't limit you. You are in control. When you change your perspective, you will literally change your life. Only self-limiting beliefs will continue to hold you back. You can live the life you have imagined. Believe.

Life Lessons

It's funny how the lessons of life seem to be repeated until you understand them well enough to share your wisdom with others. I had experienced the "fall" before under different circumstances.

I had entered my "second Act" with an identity crisis. I was 44 years old and had no idea who I was. Within the span of a few short years, my entire life had been turned upside down.

117

My long-term marriage ended, and with it, the lifestyle that had previously defined me. Everything I loved had revolved around my family and the home we shared; family gatherings, country living, and raising horses — gone.

Not only was my marriage over, my children were young adults and starting lives of their own. I was feeling very much alone and didn't quite know who I was anymore. The comfort of family and familiarity was suddenly and irretrievably gone.

I had always defined myself as a wife, mother and homemaker. I worked outside the home, but it was just a job and it didn't really define me. Then, all that changed.

Suddenly, work was all I had — and work I did; six days a week, 10 hours a day. By all outward appearances, I experienced success, built a beautiful home and had a great income, but I didn't feel at peace with myself.

The Prayer of Serenity had been my mantra for years: *"God grant me the serenity to accept the things I cannot change, the courage to change the things I can, and the wisdom to know the difference."*

It was "the courage to change" that created a stumbling block for me. The fear of "what ifs" — those possible unforeseen circumstances — controlled my life.

After years of internal turmoil, I hit bottom. Just like my experience in the Hills, I scrambled to find something to hold on to. Only this time, I tried to hold onto a life that didn't exist. I found myself lodged between the woman I used to be and the woman I was now. It didn't matter that everyone perceived me as successful because in my mind, I was living someone else's life. I was alone, in the darkness, not knowing who I was — I had a choice.

I decided to get up.

I trusted and accepted that God had a greater plan for my life than I could have ever imagined. It was time to begin my journey of self-discovery. I needed to connect with the person I was now so that I might fully experience and enjoy my new reality. I didn't want to just survive the rest of my life, I wanted to thrive, to live a life of abundance.

The Journey Within

Wanting to do something and knowing *how* to do it are two very different things. To change my life, I realized I had to understand who I was now and how I wanted to live the rest of my life. I had spent a lifetime making a living and now I want to spend the rest of my life making a difference.

Shifting my perspective, I realized my entire life had been perfect. Every experience, good or bad, has created the person I am today. Don't get me wrong,

www.mentorsmagazine.com

there are many lessons I would have preferred not to learn, but in hindsight, each one has contributed to my personal growth. I am a culmination of life experiences and this is my gift to share.

Becoming aware of my values and what I wanted, helped build the foundation on which all my decisions rested. Presented with choices, I immediately knew these choices would help or hinder my journey to living a life of abundance. **This same process can be applied to the choices you make about your career, your relationships, your money or your health.**

Are you ready to live the life you have imagined? I can tell you from personal experience, it is possible. This process will help guide you through whatever new chapter of life you might be experiencing.

Build the Foundation

The opportunities for living a life of fulfillment, meaning and connection surround us. Each of us has our own vision of what that life looks like. Your foundation becomes solid when you reflect, define and master the following four areas of your life:

Security: When you know who you are, what you want, and have a plan to get there, you will feel secure about your future. Take time to reflect on vital core values.

Wisdom: Take time to discern the difference between truth and expectations; information and knowledge.

Alignment: Align your core values with your way of life. Incorporate those values into both your personal and business relationships.

Navigation: Develop action strategies to propel you forward. Define what success means to you and recognize the obstacles that you must overcome. Decide in advance how you will deal with them.

Power Tools

At some point, we've all been skeptical about the use of power tools. Just look at technology. Although, it can help us improve our efficiency in the long term, the learning curve can be intimidating. In building your personal foundation, you will need a set of power tools. You are building something of importance — your future.

The Power of Connections

We network to find *the* influential person who will connect us to the right people and the right opportunities. Look in the mirror, the most powerful connection you will ever make is the one you make with yourself. Once you become aware of whom you are, what you are passionate about, and how you can

119

share that gift with others, the world and all it has to offer will open its arms and connect with you.

No other relationship can or will dramatically influence your life. When you program your internal compass for success, you will feel secure about the direction of your life. You will know you have made wise decisions based on your priorities. You will have aligned your way of living with your values. Your belief in yourself will either propel you to success or stifle your growth.

Power of Choice

You are a culmination of every life choice you have made. Each decision comes with a price. You will either pay with your time, your emotions, your health, or your money — choose wisely.

Power of Acceptance

Life is perfect. Accept yourself despite your imperfections and past mistakes. Every experience, good or bad, has created the person you are today. That is your unique gift to share.

Accept your freedom of responsibility and end the "blame game."

Power of Action

Understand nothing happens without action. You can be busy without moving forward. Design specific measurable steps of action. Be committed to the process and the perseverance it will take when things don't quite go the way you had hoped. Act as if you are already the person you want to be — begin.

Power of Achievement

Keep track of success stories. Write them down. Create an achievement journal with imagery that vividly shows your progress. Make it tangible. Revisiting your accomplishments will remind you of past successes when you feel stuck.

Power of Commitment

Eliminate the word "try" from your vocabulary. If you are standing and someone asks you to sit, you either do it or you don't. There is no "trying." Your level of commitment will determine the success or failure of your vision. Don't give up.

With a committed heart, we can transform lives — especially our own.

There is magic in the power of choice. Choose to find your voice and " ... *live the life you have imagined*." You can become a powerful instrument of change when you " ... *advance confidently in the direction of your dream* ..."

Are you ready?

Women of Wealth

SECURITY ~ WISDOM ~ ALIGNMENT ~ NAVIGATION

If you like what you've read ... check this out!

FOOTNOTES ♛

*Clarity. Answers. Empowerment. Created by Certified Financial Planner®, speaker, author, and life coach **Lynn Shepherd**, Women of Wealth helps women in transition open their eyes to the power of possibilities! True wealth is so much more than money. Free mini-course available at **www.WowLifePlanning.com**. Enter Code: Wise05*

Success at Home

by John Blackwell, Ph. D.

I was with a group of people last week and we were all asked to share a joyous occasion in our lives. I said, "I have three. The first is that our son, David, is graduating from Arizona State University with a degree in Global Business. The second is that our daughter, Jaime, is graduating from University of San Diego Law School, and the third is that my wife, Nancy, and I are taking Jaime and David off of the payroll!"

Needless to say, the first two exceed the third in order of importance. Our children's graduations gave us a great opportunity to reflect on how Nancy and I did in our roles as parents. I haven't been successful at everything I've done, but in the parenting department, I feel pretty good. I tried to achieve a satisfying level of success at home. Our kids feel that Nancy and I did well with them.

Parenting involves a lot of improvisation. We can all read how-to manuals, and many of them contain helpful guidance. Still, as parents, we are all amateurs. There's no such thing as "turning pro." As a parent, no one offers you multi-million dollar contracts or signing bonuses. And it's up to us to report to camp.

When Jaime and David graduated, I sat down and asked, What worked? What did I try to do consistently that helped our kids the most? Here's what I came up with.

#1 Create a Sunny Climate

I'm not talking here about southern exposure, or extensive thermostat use. I'm talking about the emotional climate of a home. I was amazed at how much the climate in our home affected all us occupants — it mattered to everyone. One of the most important things I learned was that I bore a huge responsibility for the climate of our home. My moods, my tone of voice and my intensity affected everyone. When I was intense, gloomy and withdrawn, our home felt like a dreary winter day.

Then one day, I woke up. I realized that I could change the climate in our home — for the better. I lowered my intensity, I began to smile, started softening my voice and complimenting everyone. I tried to convey to Nancy, Jaime and David their importance to me. Within a week, our home felt like a warm summer day.

Nancy and I tried to create a climate in which our kids could tell the truth without fear. Jaime and David needed to know that there would be no negative consequences for telling the truth. Nancy and I never expressed shock and dismay over what Jaime and David told us. They knew that they could safely share anything and everything with us; as a result, they didn't keep secrets from us. We were all free to dialogue, learn and grow together as a family.

I'm not suggesting that the weather is never bad in our home. But together, we ensure that gloomy moodiness doesn't last too long. No matter what the weather is outdoors, it can be spring and summertime inside. This way, everyone can feel comfortable with each other and begin to grow and thrive. As a family, we found the climate to be essential to our success as a family.

#2 Treat the Kids Like Adults

When David was in the eighth grade, one of his teachers asked, "Why are you so mature?" After pausing, David said to his teacher, "I guess it's because my parents always treated me like an adult."

I don't mean that we tried to get the kids to grow up too fast. But I don't mean that we held them back, either. From the get-go, we tried to deliver the kids successfully into adulthood. This meant teaching them to function as adults in every way possible and appropriate to their age. We never held back their growth. We never tried to push them too hard or to give them too much to do, but we allowed and encouraged them to grow up. We did not wait until they were 18 years old to start treating them as adults. We started early — when they were in elementary school.

Nancy and I welcomed our children's presence when discussing important issues. We tried to resist the temptation to be over-protective by sending them out of the room when we were talking about sensitive "adult" matters. In other words, Nancy and I tried not to say, "You run along and play now. We're going to have a little grown-up talk." We included the kids, and we did so for one important reason: To teach them something about what's involved in trying to think like an adult, act like an adult and to resolve issues as an adult. If Nancy and I didn't include them when discussing important or difficult issues, from whom would they learn? This doesn't mean that we included them in every single sensitive conversation, but it does mean that we welcomed them far more often than not.

#3 Confer Trustworthiness

This goes hand-in-glove with treating the kids like adults. Successful parenting requires that we cultivate the capacity for trustworthiness within our children. Nancy and I accomplished this by trusting Jaime and David. Our trusting them gave the gift of trustworthiness. They rose to the occasion. For example, when Nancy and I left town for the weekend, we would leave our ATM

123

card with our teenage children. They knew that they could use the card in an emergency. Yes, they both knew our PINs. They still do. Not once did they use our ATM card. Not once did they take advantage of us. Why? Because they knew that we trusted them.

Our trusting them conferred trustworthiness. It's a paradox, but we found that the more we trusted them, the more they became trustworthy. The opposite — to demand that the kids earn our trust — doesn't work. When our kids have to earn our trust, this puts them in a defensive position and provokes a sense of hopelessness. If the hopelessness becomes acute, it can turn to despair. Despair is debilitating. Not once did Nancy and I require that Jaime and David earn our trust. We gave them our trust from the outset. Their trustworthiness followed.

#4 Don't Punish; Teach!

When our children were quite young, Nancy and I punished them only rarely. When David and Jaime became older children and teenagers, we never punished them. Instead, we tried to teach them. We tried to show them a better way, and we tried to do so with lots of love and affirmation.

I'm not a big fan of punishment as a strategy for parenting. I don't think it honors our children's dignity. We humans grow primarily through learning. We found it better to act as mentors than as dog trainers or law enforcement officers.

If Jaime or David did something wrong, we tried to show them a better way. We did this with words, and we tried to do this with actions. We'd help them to think things through. If we didn't have an immediate answer or solution to their behavior, we made them partners in the search for an answer. Sometimes several possibilities presented themselves.

A teaching/mentoring approach meant simply that we made our children our allies. Human growth is a process, and growth involves all of us working together — playing on the same team. Nancy and I wanted to never alienate Jaime and David. This meant that we never tried to treat them as adversaries; that only provokes a climate of adversity. We wanted to communicate as a family that we're all pulling for each other: we're on the same team.

Perhaps most important, we celebrated their successes — all of them — and in turn, they also celebrated ours. To this day, Jaime and David celebrate the good job that Nancy and I try to do as parents.

#5 Take Responsibility

Over the years, I have needed to change lots of things about myself. I am a work in progress. I imagine that's true of all of us.

There was a time when I was quite depressed. My depression affected everyone. I didn't always make the best decisions. I wished others would take responsibility for me. Then there came a point when I began to realize that I needed to take responsibility for me. I began to reflect. I didn't like the way I felt, or the way I was acting. Neither did my family or friends. It wasn't fair to them.

I needed help. This was tough to admit to myself, let alone to others. I needed the attention of a physician and I needed some counseling. With their help, I was able to make changes — both to myself and to my relationships.

It turns out that my embarrassment over needing help was needless. My family saw me admitting my mistakes and trying to take responsibility. They liked that. It inspired them. Not only did they support me in my efforts, but they gave me tons of encouragement.

Perhaps most important, my taking responsibility set an example. It gave permission for each member of our family to take responsibility, knowing that they would get full support from the rest of us.

From the beginning, Nancy and I regarded our family as a great treasure. We wanted to succeed with each other, and we wanted to succeed together. We weren't big on rules, but we did find that these five strategies helped us find our way. Nancy, Jaime, Dave and I believe that our family is one of our greatest sources of satisfaction and meaning. The rewards cannot be measured, but they can sure be felt!

If you like what you've read ... check this out!

FOOTNOTES ☜

How is your family? Are you in tune with your spouse and children? Entrepreneurs notoriously seem to have difficulties somewhere in their family life. John is a celebrated author, speaker, retreat leader and professor in mentoring entrepreneurs, and has helped many regain their family health. He has created a questionnaire as a FREE diagnostic of your unique family relationship situation. Help is here for you right now so go to www.familiesthatthrive.com and fill out the questionnaire. John will get back with you for a FREE one hour consultation to help you regain your most important asset.

"The Money Book for the Young, Fabulous, & Broke"

by Suze Orman

L isten, I know dealing with the responsibility of money, especially a lack of money, may not necessarily by high on your list of priorities. But something motivated you and brought you to this page, so in some way you are telling yourself it's time to start dealing with your financial life. It's time to make some changes.

BROKE IS not opening your credit card bills because you're so terrified to see what you owe and have no way of paying. So instead, you get hit with the late fee and finance charges.

BROKE IS counting every coin in your change jar as well as scrounging under the sofa cushions in a desperate attempt to find the dough to cover your bounced check and the $25 fee your bank is going to slap on you.

BROKE IS not having one penny saved, even though you have a good job. If your car breaks down, so will you. You don't have the money for repairs, but you need the wheels to get to work.

This is by no means an exhaustive list. I'm sure if we all met up, we could have a great time seeing who has the best "Broke is" story. But even though your specific stories may differ, you all want the same thing. You want to fix your situation so you are no longer broke.

Give Yourself Credit

Check your expectations at the door before you read any further. You're probably expecting me to jump all over you about how evil credit card debt is, and what a financial hole you are digging for yourself if you run a high credit card balance. Don't sell me short.

Let's make sure we are on the same page here. This isn't some free pass to blindly pile on debt. Don't you dare try to twist this around in your head and interpret my advice as a ticket to live a party-hardy lifestyle courtesy of your credit cards. That is not what I am suggesting. If you think you are entitled to use your credit cards for blowout vacations, a closetful of expensive clothes, and going out four times a week, you are financially deranged.

While you are starting out in your career, I think it is perfectly reasonable to lean on your card for monthly living expenses, but you are to keep those charges to less than 1 percent of your annual gross income. For example, if you make $30,000, I don't want you to use your card for more than $300 in monthly living expenses. After two years, that would mean you have charged $7,200 on your credit cards. That's the upper limit of what I think is "safe" for you to take on, given your current earnings. My thinking is that within a few years, your career should be picking up some steam, and you can stop adding to your card debt. And I don't want you to get cowed into thinking that the balance is so big that you will never wrestle it to the ground. Committing to a plan where you add $50- to $100-a-month to your required monthly payment will shave down your balance a lot faster than you would imagine.

Save Up

Your salary is on the rise, yet your bank account isn't. You're doing better, but it's still tough to make ends meet. Your salary has finally started making a noticeable climb, but it seems that the more you make, the more you spend. And you're not really sure where it's all going.

I know the feeling. When I became a stockbroker after seven years of waitressing, I was finally making real money. At the age of thirty, my annual income shot up from $5,000 to more than $50,000 within one year. I was on Easy Street, right? If only. The crazy thing was that I had more debt when I was making $50,000 than I did when I was pulling in $5,000 as a waitress. The next year, I was making $100,000, and I still wasn't getting ahead. Oh, sure, I looked like I was doing great: my wardrobe got a serious upgrade; I had better furnishings; my lunches had moved from Taco Bell to pricey restaurants with tablecloths; I went from a fouteen-year-old, beat-up car that I owned outright to a brand-new one (which I financed); and my weekends were a lot of fun, courtesy of my friends Mr. Visa and Mr. MasterCard. My income was a lot bigger, but my bank account had more holes than a sieve. Whatever came in went out even more quickly. I got trapped into thinking that because I was earning more, I could afford to have more debt; at one point, my credit card balance broke the six-figure mark and I was paying 21 percent interest. I was more broke than ever.

Think that's odd for a financial advisor? Give me a break. I was just like most people who finally had money. Rather than act responsibly with my newfound cash flow, I felt I was entitled to make up for lost time by eating out every night, hitting the clubs, taking nice vacations, and filling my life with whatever gadgets I wanted. I thought picking up the tab was a great way to impress people; so what that I couldn't really afford to do it? In the end, I had to learn the hard way that success is not solely about making more money. It is about knowing where the money you make is going.

Sweat the Small Stuff

I need you to indulge me for a sec on this one. You've probably already heard a lot of the "small" savings tips I am about to run through, but my guess is that you haven't really given them a fair shake. So please just take a look and size up if scaling back on just one or two of these items could save you $25 or more a month.

127

- Wait an extra week or two to get your hair cut. Switch from a six-week cycle to an eight-week cycle, and you cut out two appointments a year. Same goes for hair coloring and manicures — skip the polish and they last longer.

- Wash more, dry clean less. I'm not talking about the office wear that you must dry-clean, but what about all the other clothes that end up at the cleaner just because it is more convenient?

- Drink economically. Okay, you're out with your buds and you order a $10 martini. Two, in fact. That's $20 before tip. How about some wine or beer instead? You can cut the bar tab in half. Or, better still, head across the street to the old-school bar with the rock-bottom prices. It's the company that makes the evening, not the décor.

- Brown-bag it. Try it one or two days a week. Rather than spending $10 to $15 at lunch places near your office, bring your lunch to work.

- Go public. This if for those of you in big cities. Yes, taxis are most convenient. They are also a huge cash drain. Taking a cab should be treated as a special occasion or reserved for when it's really the only safe alternative to public transportation.

Investing Made Easy

This section is called Investing Made Easy, because I truly believe that it can be. The so-called "money experts" just want you to think it is hard. It's a head game; if they can convince you that you don't have the aptitude or training to manage your money, then you will seek out their advice. They make a living off your fear of handling your own money.

But I am here to tell you that in most cases, you don't need them. No one will ever care more about your money than you will. You can lean on others for help, but ultimately you must take full responsibility for every money move you make. The most important lesson that I want you to learn is that brokers — or "financial advisers," as they like to call themselves these days — can be some of the most well-intentioned people in the world, but many (not all) are nothing more than salespeople who have been trained to sell you investments. Many financial advisors will offer you free financial advice, because they count on getting paid when you actually buy the investment they suggest. However, there is a breed of planners I love. They are called fee-based advisors. Rather than living off your commissions, they charge you a flat fee for basic services, or to manage your assets. They make no money off commission, so they have no incentive to suggest that you buy something that really doesn't make sense for you.

Saving vs. Investing

It's all about risk. When you've got a short time frame, which is anything less than five years, you can't afford the risk that your money could lose value and won't have time to rebound before you need it. Let me explain. Let's say you had an investment that went from $100 to $50; a 50 percent decline. Guess how much you need to gain to get back to break-even?

A. 25 percent   B. 50 percent   OR   C. 100 percent

I'm afraid it's C. You lost 50 percent, but it's going to take a 100 percent gain from $50 back to $100. That'll take some time, my friend. And that's actually a pretty mild example, compared to the real-life experience many investors suffered just a few years ago. A popular index of tech stocks fell from 78 percent from its March 2000 high through its October 2002 low. It will take more than a 350 percent gain fro the index to just get back to where it was in March 2000; that works out to about a 7.8 percent average annual gain. Yikes. If you had invested in that index to finance a home down payment, you'd be renting for a whole lot longer. You get my point. Stocks and mutual funds are not the right investment for short-term goals.

Summing it Up

There's a saying that's important for you to hear. It goes: People first. Then money. Then Things. So what's it mean? The nature of money is that it will come and go in your life. And the last time I checked, there's no way you can take a penny of it with you when you finally exit this world. I can also promise you that when you are on your deathbed, you are not going to be thinking about how great you life would have been if only you had bought that latest and greatest car, plasma TV, or fabulous outfit you always wanted.

There's a lot more to life. And the first person you need to focus on — to truly value — is yourself. If you were motivated enough to read this, I know you have what it takes to master your career and your finances. You just need to give yourself time to put your plan into action.

If you like what you've read ... check this out!
FOOTNOTES ⚘

Suze Orman is the author of four consecutive "New York Times" bestsellers, "The 9 Steps to Financial Freedom"; "The Courage to Be Rich"; "The Road to Wealth; and The Laws of Money, The Lessons of Life;" and the national bestseller "You've Earned It, Don't Lose It and Suze Orman's Financial Guidebook." The host of her own national award-winning CNBC-TV show, she is a contributing editor to "O, The Oprah Magazine" and is the featured writer on Yahoo! Personal Finance with her biweekly, "Money Matters" series. The 2003 PBS special inspired by "The Laws of Money, The Lessons of Life," earned her an Emmy Award.

A Certified Financial Planner Professional ®, Orman directed the Suze Orman Financial Group from 1987-1997, served as Vice-President-Investments for Prudential Bache Securities from 1983-1987 and from 1980-983, was an account executive at Merrill Lynch. In 2003 she was inducted into the Books for Better Life Awards' Hall of Fame, in recognition of her ongoing contributions to the field of self-improvement. A highly sought-after public speaker worldwide, she lives in south Florida. Visit her at www.suzeorman.com

Article excerpts reprinted from the book, "SUZE ORMAN, THE MONEY BOOK FOR THE YOUNG FABULOUS & BROKE" by Riverhead books. Published by the Penguin Group. Copyright © 2005 by Suze Orman, A Trustee of the Suze Orman Revocable Trust. Used here by permission.

How to Become a People Magnet — keys to increasing your sales, client retention, referrals, company morale and more!

by Dani Johnson

I grew up in an abusive, drug-afflicted home, and my father told me my whole life that I was fat, ugly and a good for nothing. I had no dreams, no goals, no self-esteem — nothing. So, when I was first exposed to the business world, I did not believe I could succeed. After six months of failure, a mentor taught me some key principles that turned things around — what a blessing! Then, I got married. My new husband drained my bank account to $2.03 and left me with $35k in credit card debt: I became homeless and lived in my car! Starting all over again, I became a millionaire within two short years by the age of 23.

I'd like to share with you some of the foundational key skills I learned early on, and have since taught tens of thousands of other entrepreneurs through our coaching programs and live seminars. By putting these skills into practice, you should notice an immediate change in the results you are getting and you will change into a people magnet that others want to follow. Learning and consistently applying these simple skills will increase your sales, client retention, referrals, company morale and loyalty. If you sell for a living, this formula below will change your closing ratios dramatically. If you are married or have kids, these simple steps can turn around any relationship on a dime or make a good relationship great!

Smile!

Ninety-three percent of communication is non-verbal. Smiling changes your non-verbal communication with others. Look around you — very few people smile. Doing so will make you stand out from the crowd! Smiling also shows that you're confident in who you are and what you have to offer. Smiling builds curiosity! People will wonder what you have and what you must know that puts that smile on your face. Smiling relaxes others, and smiling can immediately change the energy in a room. It will attract others to you and make them want what you have. Smiling will give you a competitive edge in your business and in your market with your customers. Make sure you smile while talking on the phone; I'm not kidding, this is SO important. Smiling on the phone has raised people's closing ratios by more than 50 percent — smiling changes your posture.

Smiling says, "I know where I'm going," even if you don't. It's says "I'm excited, I have energy! And I'm going with or without you!" If you feel you don't have something to smile about, just look around you. You don't have to look far to find someone else worse off than you. While I was homeless and living out of my car, I searched for one positive thing I could focus on. For me, it was the fact that I was homeless in Hawaii. I told myself, "Most people save for a lifetime to visit Hawaii. I'm also blessed I'm not homeless in Oakland, Calif., where it's cold at Christmas time." That one thought changed my focus, gave me something to smile about, and began to turn my situation around. During the next 10 hours of work in my business, I made $2000, which got me out of my car and into an apartment.

Be yourself — not an amateur sales person.

It's very important to be yourself. If you're yourself, then your guard is down and guess what, so is the other person's! You want to build a relationship with the person you talk with, and this is what we call "friends first." I learned this many years ago when I get on the phone being myself. My whole goal was to build a friendship with the person on the other end of the phone. I started my conversation off in a very friendly way which built the trust right away. If you are trusted then they're going to do business with you. If you're being yourself, the prospect or client can tell. Come on, we all know when someone is being fake or putting up a front — everyone appreciates people who are real. You don't appreciate people who are not real and/or are trying to deceive you. You don't appreciate slick "snake oil type" salespeople. In fact, I recently got an e-mail from a gentleman that had attended all the top sales trainings and seminars. He said, "I am no longer a slimy slick salesperson! I have done terrible in sales for 26 years," and here, he just got it. When he absolutely understood that he was not an amateur salesperson, he learned how to be himself and after building relationships, his closing ratios skyrocketed!

Encourage sincerely.

Develop the habit of sincerely encouraging your prospects, clients, employees, friends and family members. When you first meet someone, find something to encourage them on. Be sincere, don't flatter. Most people go months without someone else showing any interest in them — be that person who encourages and appreciates them and you'll have an instant friend who trusts you. I built my business by trying to be a positive and encouraging influence on every person I came in contact with. You can always point out something in the other person that is good. I don't care who it is. If your heart is in the right place, this is simple and it makes an impact on everyone around you. With a prospect, begins a relationship, which can move them from just a "short term sale" to a long term referring "client."

Ask questions.

Learn to become a good interviewer. Use the acronym F.O.R.M. to find a person's needs, strengths and goals. Ask them about their family (F), where

131

they live or grew up, if they have any kids, if they are married, etc.. Ask about their occupation (O) or what they do for a living. Ask what they like about it and what they don't like. Ask about what they do for fun or recreation (R). And finally, offer a message (M) or solution to their needs or goals. You can use this formula to get to know someone and discover what motivates them as well as what they are dissatisfied with in their life. Practice this with clients, employees, friends and family until it becomes second nature and a habit. You'll be amazed at what you'll learn about the people you have known for years. You'll also realize how easy it is to misjudge others, but most importantly you'll discover the easiest fastest way to motivate others to action by helping them get what they want. Truly listen to people when you talk with them. Don't just think about what you are going to say next. Make eye contact and repeat back to them their needs, strengths and goals. This works beautifully for problem solving, resolving personal issues, and even discovering their personality to make sure you are maximizing their strengths.

Speak to their personality.

Learn how to identify and speak to each of the four primary personality groups. *Rubies* are generally motivated by challenge, money and being the best. *Emeralds* like to have all the facts before making a decision. *Safires* are motivated by fun and being part of the team and *Pearls* are motivated by a cause and helping others. Learn how to focus on the other person's strengths and put them in positions that allow them to excel. If you are in sales, learn how your product or service meets the needs and motives of each group and target your message to the person you are working with. Don't make the mistake of talking only about what gets you excited or what's important to you. The other person may not even care! Talk about what gets them excited and now you have their attention! Listening and asking questions is how you find out what motivates the other person. An organization can maximize this by having people work in areas that capitalize on their strengths and key competencies. The organization that does this will far surpass their competitors. Go to **www.danijohnson.com/wiseinfo** to learn how to further develop all of these skills!

Be a winner NOT a whiner.

Don't just complain or talk about your problems because no one else really cares. They just care about their own problems, and whether or not you can help solve them! Whatever you focus on, you will excel at and you become more of what you focus on. So, complaining about the problem will only make it bigger and seem insurmountable. Focusing on the solution and taking steps toward that solution solves problems in the quickest way possible. When I lived in my car I had every reason in the book to complain, whine, murmur and blame, and for several weeks, I did that and it didn't contribute to finding a solution. When I stopped nursing my problem, cursing my problem, and rehearsing my problem — and I started looking for one good thing that I could focus on and taking steps toward that solution — I went on to make my first million. So be a winner, not a whiner!

Offer a solution.

When working with people, help them take their next step toward their goal. If you can help others get what they want, you will always have what you want. So think in terms of what does my prospect, my client, my spouse, my kids, my boss, my employee want? Then figure out a way to make that happen. Since we have built our lives on this principle, we have never needed anything. The author of this principle is faithful and He always comes through!

Have faith.

After surviving an abusive father, a husband who drained my bank account, maxing out my credit cards and living in my car as a homeless person (as well as countless other trials), I know one thing beyond a shadow of a doubt: If you don't fight the trial, the person, the circumstances, the issue, the pain, the suffering — and you just put your faith and your trust in God and move forward — you will always come out better on the other side of the trial! Don't freak out the next time a bomb drops on your life — just have faith and say, "Okay I know something good is going to come out of this one. What do I need to learn out of this so that I can be better next time?" The bombs will drop, this is for certain, but how we deal with the bombs and the circumstances those detonations cause, determines our success in every area of our lives. Know that God allows us to go through trials to build our character and get our attention on Him! He wants us to succeed, but our success is not just for our glory, it's for His and to be used to help others!

Lastly. ...

You may be saying, "Dani, there's nothing new here that I didn't already know or hear before." My question to you is, "Are you practicing it?" It's one thing to "know" something (know about something), however, it's quite another to put that knowledge into practice. Do you practice it consistently, daily? If not, why? What is stopping you? For many people, the issue is a matter of the heart. You have to be willing to drop your ego and get over your own insecurities and issues in order to focus on others first. The key to attracting people and positively influencing them depends upon the realization that you are NOT the issue! If you want long term success and peace of mind, you must have a clean heart with pure motives. This is extremely difficult to do on your own; for me, it took prayer and humbly turning towards Christ for help — and it's still something I work on continually. Anyone can learn some techniques and use them to manipulate people. However, if your heart is pure and you truly have that other person's best interest in mind, and you learn to serve others first, then you are sowing a good seed. Do that, and there is no level of success you cannot attain — your influence with others will be positive and eternal!

133

If you like what you've read ... check this out!

FOOTNOTES

Dani Johnson A dynamic speaker and trainer who went from living out of her car with $2.03 to her name to earning her first million in two short years by the age of 23, Dani Johnson also founded "Call To Freedom International," a Christian-based business and personal development company. Dani's training seminars have helped many earn six- and seven-figure incomes and become debt-free. Dani regularly coaches successful entrepreneurs on prospecting, closing, presentation skills, leadership, team development and personal achievement. Dani's passionate about helping people break through barriers that prevent them from experiencing true freedom emotionally, mentally, physically, spiritually and financially.

*For FREE "Walking With The Wise" business and personal coaching, or for upcoming live Dani Johnson events, visit **www.danijohnson.com/wiseinfo** or call* **209-463-5210**

SECTION III

The Way You Think Will
Determine Your Life

© 2005 Kim Muslusky

"Rich Dad Poor Dad"

by Robert T. Kiyosaki with
Sharon L. Lechter, CPA

I had two fathers, a rich one and a poor one. One was highly educated and intelligent; he had a Ph.D. and completed four years of undergraduate work in less than two years. He then went on to Stanford University, the University of Chicago, and Northwestern University to do his advanced studies, all on full financial scholarships. The other father never finished the eighth grade.

Both men were successful in their careers, working hard all their lives. Both earned substantial incomes. Yet one struggled financially all his life. The other would become one of the richest men in Hawaii. One died, leaving tens of millions of dollars to his family, charities and his church. The other left bills to be paid.

Both men were strong, charismatic and influential. Both men offered me advice, but they did not advise the same things. Both men believed strongly in education but did not recommend the same course of study.

If I had only one dad, I would have had to accept or reject his advice. Having two dads advising me offered me the choice of contrasting points of view; one of a rich man and one of a poor man.

Instead of simply accepting or rejecting one or the other, I found myself thinking more, comparing and then choosing for myself.

The problem was, the rich man was not rich yet and the poor man was not yet poor. Both were just starting out on their careers, and both were struggling with money and families, but they had very different points of view about the subject of money.

For example, one dad would say, "The love of money is the root of all evil." The other, "The lack of money is the root of all evil."

www.mentorsmagazine.com

As a young boy, having two strong fathers both influencing me was difficult. I wanted to be a good son and listen, but the two fathers did not say the same things. The contrast in their points of view, particularly where money was concerned, was so extreme that I grew curious and intrigued. I began to start thinking for long periods of time about what each was saying.

Much of my private time was spent reflecting, asking myself questions such as, "Why does he say that?" and then asking the same question of the other dad's statement. IT would have been much easier to simply say, "Yeah, he's right," "I agree with that," or to simply reject the point of view by saying, "The old man doesn't know what he's talking about." Instead, having two dads whom I loved forced me to think and ultimately choose a way of thinking for myself. As a process, choosing for myself turned out to be much more valuable in the long run, rather than simply accepting or rejecting a single point of view.

One of the reasons the rich get richer, the poor get poorer, and the middle class struggles in debt is because the subject of money is taught at home, not in school. Most of us learn about money from our parents. So, what can a poor parent tell their child about money? They simply say, "Stay in school and study hard." The child may graduate with excellent grades but with a poor person's financial programming and mind-set. It was learned while the child was young.

Money is not taught in schools. Schools focus on scholastic and professional skills, but not on financial skills. This explains how smart bankers, doctors and accountants who earned excellent grades in school may still struggle financially all of their lives. Our staggering national debt is due in large part to highly educated politicians and government officials making financial decisions with little or no training on the subject of money.

I often look ahead to the new millennium and wonder what will happen when we have millions of people who will need financial and medical assistance. They will be dependent on their families or the government for financial support. What will happen when Medicare and Social Security run out of money? How will a nation survive if teaching children about money continues to be left to parents — most of whom will be, or already are, poor?

Because I had two influential fathers, I learned from both of them. I had to think about each dad's advice, and in doing so, I gained valuable insight into the power and effect of each one's thoughts on life. For example, one dad had a habit of saying, "I can't afford it." The other dad forbade those words to be used. He insisted I say, "How can I afford it?" One is a statement, and the other is a question. One lets you off the hook, and the other forces you to think. My soon-to-be-rich dad would explain that by automatically saying the words "I can't afford it," your brain stops working. By asking the question "How can I afford it?" your brain is put to work. He did not mean buy everything you wanted. He was fanatical about exercising your mind. The most powerful computer in the world. "My brain gets stronger every day because I exercise it. The stronger it gets, the more money I can make." He believed that automatically saying "I can't afford it" was a sign of mental laziness.

Although both dads worked hard, I noticed that one dad had a habit of

www.mentorsmagazine.com

putting his brain to sleep when it came to money matters, and the other had a habit of exercising his brain. The long-term result was that one dad grew stronger financially and the other grew weaker. It is not much different from a person who goes to the gym to exercise on a regular basis versus someone who sits on the couch watching television. Proper physical exercise increases your chances for wealth. Laziness decreases both health and wealth.

My two dads had opposing attitudes in thought. One dad thought that the rich should pay more in taxes to take care of those less fortunate. The other said, "Taxes punish those who produce and reward those who don't produce."

One dad recommended, "Study hard so you can find a good company to work for." The other recommended, "Study hard so you can find a good company to buy."

One dad said, "The reason I'm not rich is because I have you kids." The other said, "The reason I must be rich is because I have you kids."

One encouraged talking about money and business at the dinner table. The other forbade the subject of money to be discussed over a meal.

One said, "When it comes to money, play it safe, don't take risks." The other said, "Learn to manage risk."

One believed, "Our home is our largest investment and our greatest asset." The other believed, "My house is a liability, and if your house is your largest investment, you're in trouble."

Both dads paid their bills on time, yet one paid his bills first while the other paid his bills last.

One dad believed in a company or the government taking care of him and his needs. He was always concerned about pay raises, retirement plans, medical benefits, sick leave, vacation days, and other perks. He was impressed with two of his uncles who joined the military and earned a retirement and entitlement package for life after 20 years of active service. He loved the idea of medical benefits and PX privileges the military provided its retirees. He also loved the tenure system available through the university. The idea of job protection for life and job benefits seemed more important, at times, than the job. He would often say, "I've worked hard for the government, and I'm entitled to these benefits."

The other believed in total financial self-reliance. He spoke out against the "entitlement" mentality and how it was creating weak and financially needy people. He was emphatic about being financially competent.

One dad struggled to save a few dollars. The other simply created investments.

One dad taught me how to write an impressive resume so I could find a good job. The other taught me how to write strong business and financial plans so I could create jobs.

Being a product of two strong dads allowed me the luxury of observing the effect different thoughts have on one's life. I noticed that people really do shape their life through their thoughts.

For example, my poor dad always said, "I'll never be rich." And that prophesy became reality. My rich dad, on the other hand, always referred to himself as rich. He would say things like, "I'm a rich man, and rich people don't do this." Even when he was flat broke after a major financial setback, he continued to refer to himself as a rich man. He would cover himself by saying, "There is a difference between being poor and being broke. Broke is temporary, and poor is eternal."

My poor dad would also say, "I'm not interested in money," or "Money doesn't matter." My rich dad always said, "Money is power."

The power of our thoughts may never be measured or appreciated, but it became obvious to me as a young boy to be aware of my thoughts and how I expressed myself. I noticed that my poor dad was not poor because of the amount of money he earned, which is significant, but because of his thoughts and actions. As a young boy, having two fathers, I became acutely aware of being careful which thoughts I chose to adopt as my own. Whom should I listen to — my rich dad or my poor dad?

Although both men had tremendous respect for education and learning, they disagreed in what they thought was important to learn. One wanted me to study hard, earn a degree and get a good job to work for money. He wanted me to study to become a professional: an attorney or an accountant or to go to business school for my MBA. The other encouraged me to study to be rich, to understand how money works and to learn how to have it work for me. "I don't work for money!" were words he would repeat over and over, "Money works for me!"

At the age of nine, I decided to listen to and learn from my rich dad about money. In doing so, I chose not to listen to my poor dad, even though he was the one with all the college degrees.

If you like what you've read ... check this out!

FOOTNOTES ()

The article excerpt above is from the "New York Times Bestseller" list "RICH DAD, POOR DAD" and is a true story on the lessons that Robert Kiyosaki, the author, learned from his two "Dads." One Dad, a Ph. D and Superintendent of Education never had enough money at the end of the month and died broke. His other Dad dropped out of school at age 13 and went on to become one of the wealthiest men in Hawaii. In "RICH DAD, POOR DAD," Robert explains how to make your money work hard for you instead of you working hard for money. It is available through your local bookstores. You can learn more by visiting www.richdad.com

Prosperity Consciousness

Money is Simply a Symbol of Energy

by Lee Milteer

How many times have you thought to yourself, if I only had more money all my problems would be solved? "In truth," money usually has very little to do with your level of personal happiness. In and of itself, money possesses no value. Here is a thought for you: money is just small piece of green paper with dead notables on it. It's not the money! It's how you use it that determines it's true worth.

Pay close attention: It is very important to realize money for what it really is — just a tool — no more and no less. Money is simply a symbol of energy. Just as your lights turn on when you hit the electric switch, just as your car gets you from one location to another, money is simply a financial tool that, when used correctly, can assist you in reaching your goals.

The bottom line is that true abundance is not about how much money you have, but how you feel about what money you do have.

Let's begin by defining wealth. It is not just money because having more money alone will not always bring you happiness. Wealth is being at peace with yourself and feeling fulfilled in what you do. It is enjoying and appreciating your life, your family and your career. Money is only one form of abundance. There are many forms of abundance in our lives: love, happiness, friendship, good health, vitality and joy. These things are true blessings and that is what true prosperity is about. Do you wake up in the morning and feel happy, feel loved, feel you have a future to look toward? You are a wealthy person.

Everyone is interconnected by one energy source. Jung called it the collective unconscious. Still others call it spirit or the grace of God; whatever name you use, the connection is there. Prosperity means integration with the "God Source" in all things. The "God Source" is unlimited so everything is unlimited. If everything is unlimited, so is wealth and prosperity in your life.

True "prosperity consciousness" is simply increasing the level of awareness about your ability to create prosperity that enables you to create more self-confidence, self-trust and self-esteem. These new empowering traits will help you generate and create wealth and financial security plus all the other aspects of wealth.

Ralph Waldo Emerson described prosperity as the law of compensation whereby like attracts like, meaning that what you radiate out in your thoughts, feelings, mental pictures and words, you also attract into your life. Your beliefs about money will determine how you relate to it and how you spend it. If you see the world as having unlimited resources, which it does, then you tend to feel more relaxed about money. You know you can earn it or attract it whenever you need it, if you're willing to do whatever it takes.

Conversely, if you think you can only receive money by working extremely hard, through toil and sweat, then that is exactly what you'll end up doing. Why not make life a little easier for yourselves? Why exhaust yourselves with so much toil and sweat when you could apply your mental capacities and achieve even more?

Great teachers have taught us over history that we can learn to create our destiny through our thoughts. We can use our thought energy rather than physical effort to produce results that go beyond anything we will be able to create with just physical effort alone.

You must open your mind to the perception that creating wealth and abundance has a lot to do with internal decisions and external knowledge, and little to do with the state of the national economy. We must rise above the popular belief that it is necessary to be affected by the economy. Abundance is a mind-set, not an external condition that controls your destiny. God has filled the earth with good things for us to enjoy and use. You can claim the abundance you so richly deserve because there are no limits to what we can create with these unlimited resources around us.

Think about the definition of the word **"prosper"** — to flourish, succeed and thrive, to experience favorable results to get what you want out of life. The truth is that we are where we are in our life at this moment because of our past programming.

You Must Be Responsible for Your Wealth

You must start to take action to create whatever you want out of life. Be kind to yourself, and allow yourself to build your confidence by simply taking small steps in the direction of your goals. Try something new every single day. It's very interesting to note that changing just a few small actions or habits in your life will compound itself. In a few months, these changes can produce dramatic results in your professional and personal life.

You may have thought that just being lucky, working hard or investing wisely would create wealth. These things certainly can assist you in becoming more prosperous, however, there is a little-known secret about how to create success. The secret is that you must focus on what you want to occur in your life instead of what you don't want to occur. Whatever you focus on is what you

141

will get. Remember, energy follows thought. Pay attention to this one folks! The more you focus on being poor, the poorer you will become. The more you focus on and picture and talk about abundance, the more elements of abundance will be attracted to you.

To attract great prosperity into your life you must pay attention to the quality of information you put into your computer — your brain. It truly is your success mechanism. For "prosperity consciousness" to work, pay even closer attention to your self-talk because it is your self-talk that guides you to live in "poverty consciousness" or "prosperity consciousness." The decision is up to you. Your success depends on the caliber of information you allow in your environment and brain.

In life, your success will depend on your self-talk as well as your spoken word. You must also replace those thoughts that do not serve you. Instead of saying, "I don't have enough money," replace this with "I have an abundance of money." Our positive thoughts are more powerful than our negative ones, so remember that you can reprogram your computer with your thoughts.

Obviously, your intention is to create abundance and prosperity to obtain the things you want in your life. By using affirmations you will actually be reprogramming your "subconscious mind" to accept these new thoughts as reality. As you imprint this information on your mind, it begins to create changes in your life to match this new inner reality.

Your goal is to focus on the new reality you want to create for yourself. Take on the spirit of creating something new rather than changing or resisting what is now. You do have the power to create a new destiny for yourself by giving yourself permission to go for what you want. Ignore reality and BELIEVE that what you want is true right now. Create the feeling you want to experience so that your subconscious mind knows what to imprint. Whatever we think about ourselves and our abilities on a consistent basis will determine how successful and prosperous we become.

Here are some examples of affirmations that you can use to feel more prosperous:

Prosperity Thoughts
• I am in this world to experience and enjoy success.
• I have every natural right to be wealthy and successful.
• I am confident of my talent to create success.
• I am enthusiastic and confident.
• I choose to be prosperous.
• I love myself more and more daily.
• I have the energy, resources and time to be successful and prosperous.
• I am more intelligent every day, in every way.
• I think of new creative ways to attract money.
• I am powerful and confident, and that attracts to me the right people and the right situations.

- I am willing to be powerful and successful.
- I have valuable contributions.
- I reinforce my successes as I correct my errors.

Enjoy Your Successes

Isn't it interesting how most people look ahead to the next mountain peak in life, without ever taking the time to appreciate the heights they just conquered? When you have a successful day you should celebrate! When you celebrate your successes you are training your subconscious mind to create more awareness of your success, which will help aim you in those directions.

By appreciating and acknowledging your successes, you will not only enjoy them more, but you will have more energy and confidence to create even more success, abundance and prosperity for your future. All of our energy will create some type of result. If we focus on remembering the feelings of mastery in the various areas of our lives, those feelings will actually imprint on our computer and help us create success for the future. Remember, your thoughts create your beliefs, and your beliefs create your reality.

Evidence Book

It is important to track your successes and acknowledge your efforts in achieving goals. I suggest that you create an "evidence book." This book is a tool to help you feel in control and powerful in your life. For this fun project, invest in a large, inexpensive photo album and fill it with all your past successes, such as pictures, awards, articles about yourself, and letters of congratulation, sales contest mementos and graphic charts of your top sales records. This is not a brag book to show other people — it is a tool that is only for you. Let it remind you just how successful you really are.

I studied salespeople and found that salespeople who review their successes before they go out to make sales calls tend to have more sales that day. You might want to create a ritual every morning before you go into the world that you go through your "evidence book" to reinforce your beliefs that you have the skills, talent, knowledge and persistence to be successful in whatever you want to accomplish. When you take just three- to five-minutes a day to remember how great you felt when you met your goals, you guarantee that, no matter what challenges come your way, you have the resources to handle it. After all, the evidence is right there before you in your "evidence book!"

I have personally used this confidence boosting technique for many years. Even today, when I have a bad day or I have made a mistake or failed at something, I still take the time to go back over my "evidence books" of the past. I have them lined up in my personal office, so that anytime I need a boost, I can easily pull them out and acknowledge my hard work, my devotion and my tenacity. There is nothing that can give you more motivation than acknowledging the success you've already enjoyed.

As a side note, since you are the role models for your children, you might

143

want to start a different kind of "evidence book" called a "victory book" for each of your children. Every time they get a good report card or do something that they are proud of, please take the time to record that achievement in your child's book. This is a wonderful way of creating confidence. Next time your child comes home fearful about not being able to do something, you can pull out their "victory book" and remind them how they were successful in the past.

This one tool will build self-confidence for you. Remember, what you focus on expands. Any message you give your subconscious mind regularly will imprint and start to become part of your comfort zone and part of your perceptions of yourself. Since you are a self-fulfilling prophecy, it behooves you to do as many things as possible to create a prosperous new personal image of yourself. In closing, I would like to encourage you to value yourself to create the prosperity that you so deserve in life by first giving yourself permission to change your mind and when you do that you will change your life. Your point-of-power in this life is right this minute; do something now that will create a rich future for yourself!

This is an excerpt from the book: "Spiritual Power Tools for Successful Selling" written by Lee Milteer and Published by Hampton Roads Publishing in 2005.

If you like what you've read ... check this out!

FOOTNOTES ()

Lee Milteer is a human potential speaker and productivity coach for the Millionaire Mindset Coaching Program. She is the author of the books: "Reach Your Career Dreams," "Feel and Grow Rich, Success Is an Inside Job" and "Spiritual Power Tools for Successful Selling." Lee also has educational audio and video programs. Lee is available for limited speaking engagements. For more information go to www.milteer.com

Lee Milteer Inc.,
P.O. Box 5653, Virginia Beach, VA 23471
Call: (757) 460-1818
Fax: (757) 460-3675
www.milteer.com

What Would Your Life Be Like If You Were Truly Able To Influence Your Destiny?

by Joe Syverson

WARNING: DO NOT READ *this chapter if you are not seeking change, as reading this information may very well result in a paradigm shift in your belief system, and ultimately change your perception of life.*

First let me start off by Honoring, Respecting, and Congratulating YOU on your decision TO IMPROVE THE QUALITY OF YOUR LIFE! If you are reading this information, then I know that you are a seeker — someone who is curious about finding new perceptions and strategies that will empower you and the people around you. You must truly care about becoming a better you, and your action here and now is proof of that. Appreciate yourself, as I appreciate you for representing the five percent of the population of the world truly seeking improvement in their lives and lifestyles; most importantly, you either realize or are beginning to realize that you play a very large part in the overall quality of your life.

As you sit in your chair and read this information, allow your mind to absorb my short story of how I "woke up" to the truth behind influencing a person's destiny. *Realize you now are in a position to receive something you may have heard before, but did not realize the importance of. The quality of our life is not a result of "What we have heard, or even What we Know," it is a direct result of "What we feel is IMPORTANT that we DECIDE to LIVE BY!"*

Having Outstanding Mentors and undergoing a "Baptism by Fire" proved indispensable IN LEARNING THE LIFE LESSONS REQUIRED TO ACHIEVE SUCCESS. By committing to self-reinvention, seeking honest feedback from my mentors, and staying in the game of Free Enterprise through incredible challenges, I was able to turn my dreams into reality.

Just four years ago I lived in fear and constant worry, I had nearly $100,000 in unsecured debt, I possessed next to no cash and survived on Top Ramen noodle soup. Now at age 28, I attract over a million dollars a year through my business ventures. Most importantly, I love my life and my family more than the day before. So, whenever you see me... it is absolutely the best day of my life!

The Day I Woke Up to The Truth...

5:47 A.M. BEEP! BEEP! BEEP! I reach over and hit the snooze button

145

on my annoying $6 alarm clock. One minute later, BEEP! BEEP! BEEP! I reached over, pulled my alarm clock out of the wall and whipped it across the room where it shattered on the floor. As I sat up and rubbed the sleep out of my eyes, I thought to myself, "Great, another beautiful day of no shows and professional people pleasers telling me they don't have the money or some other lame excuse why they can't get started with me." I laid back down for a few minutes.

A little over an hour later I woke up. "Shoot! What time is it, honey?" I asked my wife. She said, " I don't know; Where is the clock?" I sprang out of bed and ran out to the living room, kitchen, home, office, dining room, and looked at the clock in there. "7:15! Oh man, am I going to be late! I have someone showing up at 8:00 at the office!" I shouted. I got dressed in two minutes, brushed my teeth, and hustled out to the car. I got out to the car and as I backed out of the driveway, I realized that the gas gauge "empty" light was on. "Great, Just Great!" I dug through my pockets and pulled up nothing but lint. I dashed back into the house yelling, "Hey Honey, do you have any money?" My wife replied, "No Joe, the debit card and credit card declined on me yesterday and we just ran out of Credit Card Checks!" "Oh just wonderful," I said angrily.

Just then I realized how broke I really was. Not only was my gas tank and my bank account empty, but now I felt empty. If you have ever felt empty, disappointed, frustrated or powerless, then you know how I felt. It seemed like no matter how hard I worked, I just kept going backwards. Two steps forward, four steps back. I was literally working 80 hours per week at a Network Marketing office for the last 10 months, a 100 percent commission business. I was putting in my time, going through the numbers, following the system and doing what my mentors asked of me. I modeled the advertisements, the scripts, and the actions of successful people, yet success eluded me. The day I started, I thought I would be making about $100,000 a year; instead, I found myself financially devastated, and (frightfully) closing in on $100,000 in unsecured credit card debt.

As I was thinking these thoughts, and thinking about my baby (due in four months), I heard my wife Mary's loving voice from the other room (the only other room) say, "Joe-dig in the couch and you will find some change for gas."

I jumped onto the couch, and went digging for change between the cushions. AS I stood up, I counted the change… $1.85… and I thought, "Hey, what if today is different? Maybe — just maybe — something great will happen for me today. I REFUSE to GIVE UP… I WILL MAKE IT THROUGH TODAY somehow, some way!"

As negative as my thinking became at times, and as angry and disappointed as I became, my wife Mary always encouraged me, and her voice would ring in my head, saying, "NEVER GIVE UP!"

At 8:23 a.m., after a grueling 45 minute drive in my 1991 Beat Up, Dirty White Pontiac Grand Am, weaving in and out of six lanes of slow moving San Diego Traffic, I finally made it to the office.

As the big office door opened just before I got to it, I lifted my head and

noticed one of my main mentors, a beautiful blonde woman that went from making $15,000 a year as a preschool teacher to a professional direct sales business coach making over a million dollars a year in just a few years time! I surely respected her and what she had accomplished.

My face went flush red as I made eye contact with her. I must have looked like a deer stuck in the head lights as her eyes pierced me right to my soul. "Hello Joe, How are you doing today?"

"Not bad — just in a hurry, I have to meet a prospect!" I walked by her quickly hoping she wouldn't talk to me. I walked past the "Fortune" and "Forbes" plaques on the wall, focused on making it to my desk at the end of the hall, and then I heard... "Hey Joe, can I have a word with you?" "Oh no," I thought as my heart shot up into my throat, and my palms instantly started getting sweaty...I turned around to face her. "We need to have a quick chat," she replied.

Her office door swung shut. "Gulp." I swallowed as I sat down in her office. It was just the two of us. She sat down at her desk, and looked across at me and through me at the same time, and said, "Joe, Do YOU WANT TO KNOW WHY YOU ARE BROKE ?"

My eyes began to get watery, although somehow I contained the tears — time stopped. Thoughts came rushing at me which I didn't voice...I don't have good credit, I don't have good prospects, I don't have rich parents that could help finance my business, I don't have a good image because I am wearing cheap suits and a cheap car, and I am unlucky... and life is not fair and... and then she asked again, a little louder this time...

"DO YOU REALLY WANT TO KNOW WHY YOU ARE BROKE ? ? ?"

"Ummm ... OK, " I said, sounding intimidated and frightened. She didn't scare me, and her opinion of me didn't even matter that much to me, but change, and the need to change, DID scare me. In my gut I could feel a change coming, and it was about time.

"DO YOU REALLY want to KNOW WHY you're analyzing the numbers, taking a lot of action, investing money in advertising, and still going backwards after 10 months !!!???"

I said with certainty, "Yes, I want to know." Even though I knew it would be hard to hear, I knew somehow that this was the answer to my prayers and those of my wife as well.

"You're broke because YOUR CONTRADICTIVE THINKING has MADE YOU BROKE!"

"To win the outer game in life, and create wealth and abundance, you must first master the inner game. Your inner game consists of your belief systems, internal dialogue and what you choose to focus on at any given moment. This is also known as your psychology. Wealth is psychological."

147

I was thinking to myself, Wow, could this really be it? My mindset is fairly good (I assumed). There has to be more to why I am broke than....

"Your consistency and discipline to contact large numbers of prospects has been very good, but action alone will not get you to your 'promised land.' As long as you keep crippling yourself with contradictive thinking, you will forever be like a fish trying to swim upstream."

"What do you mean 'contradictive thinking?' " I asked.

"You have heard about positive thinking and negative thinking ... it is much more accurate to say 'contradictive thinking' from my opinion. Contradictive thinking means that you spend more time renting out space in your mind, and giving energy through your mental focus to ideas, thoughts and beliefs that oppose what you really want to achieve. I know what thoughts dominate your mind by looking at your results. If you are not getting the results that you want in life, it always boils down to one of two areas: 'Either you are NOT creating compounding because you are not giving a consistent and focused effort for a reasonable period of time, OR you are NOT vibrating at a place mentally and emotionally to attract the proper resources to attain the results you seek.' "

"Wait, I understand the first part of what you said...about creating compounding through consistent actions, and I know that I am doing that, but I'm a little fuzzy about 'vibrating at a place mentally and emotionally to ... ,' " I mumbled.

She jumped in and delivered it to me straight, "Let me give you a picture of what I am explaining to you now. First, science proves that what we believe to be solid matter, this desk, our body, this furniture is not really solid at all, it is only our limited perception that perceives it as solid. All matter and all things are composed of elemental particles (like protons, electrons and photons), which really have no mass at all. In fact, to give you an illustration to help you understand this: picture a baseball in the middle of a stadium with golf balls around the outside of the stadium, spinning around the baseball in the center. Now, remove the stadium from the picture, and what you have is a lot of space and an accurate understanding of how much space is between the particles. The electrons spin around the nucleus at such a fast rate that when millions of particles come together it looks like matter, but really everything is moving, and everything is vibrating, including us. Our thoughts, our beliefs, our mind, our bodies are vibrating. We are vibrational beings that attract to our reality people, places and circumstances that vibrate at the same frequency (speed) as we do.

This is important because of one universal law that governs our reality. This universal law is proven by physics, is absolutely real, and operates in your life, even in your ignorance of it. It is called the Law of Attraction. It means that, which is like unto itself is drawn, or anything of the same 'frequency of vibration' is drawn together through an attractive magnetic force. So, you see that whatever you focus on or think about begins to vibrate, and after about 17 seconds or more, an emotion will get created in your body that is a result of what you thought about. Your consistent thoughts and emotions send out powerful vibrations into the world, and you tune into everything else on the same station or frequency.

Picture your body as a radio tuner: depending on what you think about and how you feel most of the time, you create what I call "your core vibration" or "your most-listened-to radio station" on the radio of life. Joe — when you think things with poor internal dialogue — like I'm broke, I'm not good enough, life is unfair, I am unlucky, etc. — that type of thinking creates a vibration on a lower frequency. For example, let's say you are vibrating on 88.9 FM. You want better prospects for your business, so you want to listen to rock music, but 88.9 FM only plays country, and only has prospects that have excuses and are not ready to change. If you want better prospects, better opportunities, a better team, better friends, better circumstances, realize first that they are on station 101.3 FM. You won't find Rock Music on a Country Station because it defies law.

You have to Tune into Success by tuning yourself at your core. You begin the process by asking yourself much more often how you feel, for how you feel is where you are vibrating. If you don't feel empowered at this moment or any moment, then YOU NOW MUST REALIZE that it is only because you are FOCUSING ON SOMETHING CONTRADICTORY to what you want or *focusing on the lack of something in your life*. It is at this moment that you must catch yourself and interrupt your habitual pattern of contradictive thinking. You have to say. ...

'WAIT, I HAVE A CHOICE!

I CAN CHOOSE and I MUST CHOOSE to focus only on thoughts that make me feel good.

Anything less, and I am creating future pain for myself because I am tuning into a station of music I do not like.'

The Art of Influencing your Destiny hinges on being present moment-to-moment with what you are focusing on, and BEING COMMITTED TO ALWAYS CHOOSING THE BEST THOUGHT THAT YOU HAVE ACCESS TO at that moment.

"OK, so I have to get better at controlling what I focus on. How do I do that?" I asked.

Learning to control your focus is like driving a vehicle, and to drive a vehicle properly takes constant focused supervision. I call this, Being Present. You look down for too long dialing on your cell phone, or looking for the right CD and BAM! You smack into something, and now you have pain. If you want to avoid the self-inflicted pain that your mind will cause you IF unsupervised, then you have to be present with your mind and realize your mind is not YOU, but simply a tool to go and get information for you. If you do not supervise it, it starts focusing on something painful; if you allow it to run on, it will develop momentum. Instead of letting your mind control you, you must control your mind.

All of us to varying degrees have conversations "going on or running on" in our mind. This conversation is a process of questions and answers going back in forth in our mind that I refer to as "internal dialogue." We don't very often stop to pay attention to our own "internal dialogue," or notice that all of

149

this internal conversation stems from simply a handful of questions that we ask ourselves out of habit.

Having an awareness of this internal dialogue, and the questions that create it helps prevent us from crashing. It is this internal dialogue, or these internal questions that we ask. ..."

I piped in, "You mean questions like ... , 'How come I don't have better prospects? How come this had to happen to me? How come I seem to have bad luck? How come I don't have? ... '"

"Exactly," She interrupted me. "These questions Hook the Mind. They steer your mind down different pathways in your brain. The questions that are in your internal dialogue, or the questions you consciously ask yourself or questions others ask of you ... questions are the steering wheel to your mind.

The Science behind Influencing your Destiny relies on YOU TAKING BACK CONTROL OF THE STEERING WHEEL OF YOUR LIFE, *by developing the discipline to* BE MORE PRESENT with YOUR INTERNAL DIALOGUE, and by *asking yourself questions that incur empowering answers* and therefore an empowering focus all the time, questions like:

- What am I grateful for and what can I appreciate right now in my life?
- What are the best feelings or thoughts I have access to right now?
- What am I becoming excited about today and in my future?
- How can I be even more of a leader and role model in my family/ friendships?
- What did I positively learn from this challenge that will allow me to contribute to other's lives?
- How can I enjoy the process while still doing what is necessary to attain the result I seek?

"WOW... thank you. Here I thought that I felt the way I did because of my life circumstances. Now I know that it's not my life circumstances that create how I feel, but merely the focus of my mind. Thoughts don't choose me, I choose them and What I focus on, I will feel. If I change my focus to the life circumstances in my life that are improving, or what the positive future aspects will be, then I am turning the dial up to a higher frequency, right?"

"You're getting it. Just remember, every disempowering thought you entertain turns the dial back the other direction to the lower frequency. Remember to 'kill the monster while it is little' by asking yourself an empowering question quickly to interrupt any pattern of disempowering thinking before it grows."

"I feel like a weight has been lifted off my shoulders now as I realize that it only creates more pain for me if I think about my problems. I now know that I have a GREAT responsibility I never really knew existed. I AM responsible for what I think and how I feel, all the time, no exceptions. How I feel is basically

how I am vibrating and how everything in life is coming to me. Therefore there is nothing more important to me than how I feel. From this day forward I now decide that I will choose to focus only on thoughts that make me feel good, and I will do my best when I am not feeling good to change my focus by asking myself an empowering question!" I exclaimed, truly transformed.

Let me leave you with this final reminder to sum it all up:

"Whatever you think about is literally like planning a future event. When you are worrying, you are planning ... when you are excited, you are planning. The 10 million dollar question is ... , '**What are you planning** ?' "

If you like what you've read ... check this out!

FOOTNOTES ☙

*An outstanding husband and Father of two, **Joe Syverson** is also a sought after Public Speaker & Trainer, Personal Success Coach, and the Owner of a Premier Internet Lead Generation Company. His passion lies in teaching entrepreneurs how to rewire their mindset, and become power persuaders through his online and offline "Influence Mastery Seminars."*

*Join Him Every Wednesday Night for a FREE Teleseminar, and get FREE ACCESS to 40-plus Hours of MP3 Training Audios by visiting **www.InfluenceMastery.net** Today! "Triple your Sales, in half the time you invest now!"*

*For a FREE Personal Coaching Consultation, visit **www.abroaderperspective.com***

*For a FREE SAMPLE of our Real Time Telephone Interviewed Leads for your Home Business visit **www.freshinterviews.com** — and let us know you own a copy of this book.*

Making Intention Your Reality

by Dr. Wayne W. Dyer

Below are 10 ways to practice fulfilling your intention to live your life on purpose from this day forward:

Step 1: Affirm that in an intelligent system, no one shows up by accident, including you. The universal mind of intention is responsible for all of creation. It knows what it's doing. You came from that mind, and you're infinitely connected to it. There's meaning in your existence, and you have the capacity to live from a perspective of purpose. The first step is to know that you're here on purpose. This is not the same as knowing what you're supposed to do. Throughout your life, what you do will change and shift. In fact, the changes can occur from hour to hour in each day of your life. Your purpose is not about what you do, it's about your beingness, that place within you from which your thoughts emerge. This is why you're called a *human being* rather than a *human doing*! Affirm in your own words, both in writing and in your thoughts, that you are here on purpose, and intend to live from this awareness at all times.

Step 2: Seize every opportunity, no matter how small, to give your life away in service. Get your ego out of your intention to live a life of purpose. Whatever it is that you want to do in life, make the primary motivation for your effort something or somebody other than your desire for gratification or reward.

The irony here is that your personal rewards will multiply when you're focused on giving rather than receiving. Fall in love with what you're doing, and let that love come from the deep, inner-dwelling place of Spirit. Then sell the feeling of love, enthusiasm, and joy generated by your efforts. If your purpose is felt by being Supermom, then put your energy and inner drive into those children. If it's felt writing poetry or straightening teeth, then get your ego out of the way and do what you love doing. Do it from the perspective of making a difference for someone or for some cause, and let the universe handle the details of your personal rewards. Live your purpose doing what you do with pure love — then you'll co-create with the power of the universal mind of intention, which is ultimately responsible for all of creation.

Step 3: Align your purpose with the field of intention. This is the

most important thing you can do to fulfill your intentions. Being aligned with the universal field means having faith that your Creator knows why you're here, even if you don't. It means surrendering the little mind to the big mind, and remembering that your purpose will be revealed in the same way that *you* were revealed. Purpose, too, is birthed from creativeness, kindness, love, and receptivity to an endlessly abundant world. Keep this connection pure, and you'll be guided in all of your actions.

It's not fatalism to say that *if it's meant to be, then it can't be stopped.* This is having faith in the power of intention, which originated you and is within you. When you're aligned with your originating Source, then this same Source will aid you in creating the life of your choice. Then, what happens feels exactly as if it was meant to be. And that's because it is! You always have a choice in how to align yourself. If you stay focused on making demands on the universe, you'll feel as if demands are being placed on you in your life. Stay focused on lovingly asking, *How may I use my innate talents and desire to serve?* and the universe will respond with the identical energy by asking you, *How may I serve you?*

Step 4: Ignore what anyone else tells you about your purpose. Regardless of what anyone might say to you, the truth about your feeling purposeful is that only *you* can know it, and if you don't feel it in that inner place where a burning desire resides, it isn't your purpose. Your relatives and friends may attempt to convince you that what *they* feel is *your* destiny. They may see talents that they think will help you make a great living, or they may want you to follow in their footsteps because they think you'll be happy doing what they've done for a lifetime. Your skill at mathematics or decorating or fixing electronic equipment might indicate a high aptitude for a given pursuit — but in the end, if you don't feel it, nothing can make it resonate with you.

Your purpose is between you and your Source, and the closer you get to what that field of intention looks and acts like, the more you'll know that you're being purposefully guided. You might have zero measurable aptitudes and skills in a given area, yet feel inwardly drawn to doing it. Forget the aptitude-test results, forget the absence of skills or know-how, and most important, ignore the opinions of others and *listen to your heart.*

Step 5: Remember that the all-creating field of intention will work on your behalf. Albert Einstein is credited with saying that the most important decision we ever make is whether we believe we live in a friendly universe or a hostile universe. It's imperative that you know that the all-creating field of intention is friendly and will work with you as long as you see it that way. The universe supports life; it flows freely to all and is endlessly abundant. Why choose to look at it in any other way? All of the problems we face are created by our belief that we're separate from God and each other, leading us to be in a state of conflict. This state of conflict creates a counterforce causing millions of humans to be confused about their purpose. Know that the universe is always willing to work with you on your behalf, and that you're always in a friendly, rather than hostile, world.

Step 6: Study and replicate the lives of people who've known their

153

purpose. Whom do you admire the most? I urge you to read biographies of these people and explore how they lived and what motivated them to stay on purpose when obstacles surfaced. I've always been fascinated by Saul of Tarsus (later called St. Paul), whose letters and teachings became the source of a major portion of the New Testament. Taylor Caldwell wrote a definitive fictional account of St. Paul's life called "Great Lion of God," which inspired me enormously. I was also deeply touched by the purposeful manner in which St. Francis of Assisi lived his life as exemplified in the novel "St. Francis," by Nikos Kazantzakis. I make it a point to use my free time to read about people who are models for purposeful living, and I encourage you to do the same.

Step 7: Act as if you're living the life you were intended to live, even if you feel confused about this thing called purpose. Invite into your life every day whatever it might be that makes you feel closer to God and brings you a sense of joy. View the events you consider obstacles as perfect opportunities to test your resolve and find your purpose. Treat everything from a broken fingernail an illness to the loss of a job to a geographical move as an opportunity to get away from your familiar routine and move to purpose. By acting as if you're on purpose and treating the hurdles as friendly reminders to trust in what you feel deeply within you, you'll be fulfilling your own intention to be a purposeful person.

Step 8: Meditate to stay on purpose. Use the technique of Japa, and focus your inner attention on asking your Source to guide you in fulfilling your destiny. This letter from Matthew McQuaid describes the exciting results of meditating to stay on purpose:

Dear Dr. Dyer,

My wife, Michelle, is pregnant by a miracle-a miracle manifest from Spirit using all of your suggestions. For five years, Michelle and I were challenged by infertility. You name it, we tried it. None of the expensive and sophisticated treatments worked. The doctors had given up. Our own faith was tested over and over with each failed treatment cycle. Our doctor managed to freeze embryos from earlier cycles of treatment. Throughout the years, over 50 embryos had been transferred to Michelle's uterus. The odds of a frozen embryo successfully initiating pregnancy in our case were close to zero. As you know, zero is a word not found in the spiritual vocabulary. One precious frozen embryo, surviving minus 250 degrees for six months, has taken up a new home in Michelle's womb. She is now in her second trimester.

Okay, "So what," you might say. "I get letters like this every day. However, this letter contains proof of God. A tiny drop of protoplasm, as you have so eloquently written on many occasions, a physical mass of cells alive with the future pull of a human being, turned on in a laboratory, then turned off in a freezer. All molecular motion and biochemical processes halted, suspended. Yet, the essence of being was there prior to freezing. Where did the spiritual essence go while frozen? The cells were turned on, then turned off, but the spiritual essence had to prevail despite the physical state of the cells. The frequency of vibration of the frozen cells was low, but the vibrational frequency of its spirit must be beyond measure. The essence of the being had to reside outside of the physical plane or mass of cells.

It couldn't go anywhere except to the realm of spirit, where it waited. It waited to thaw and manifest into a being it always has been. I hope you find this story as compelling as I do, as nothing less than a miracle. An example of spirit in body, rather then a body with a spirit.

And now for the million-dollar question. Could this one embryo survive such hostile frozen conditions and still manifest because I practiced the Japa mediation? Just because I opened my mouth and said, "Aaaahhh"? I had a knowing, no question about it. Japa meditation and surrendering to infinite patience are daily practices. During my quiet moments, I can smell this baby. Michelle will thank me for my conviction and faith during the dark times. I praise your work for guiding me. Thank you. Now, nothing is impossible for me. When I compare what I have manifested now in Michelle's womb to anything else I might desire, the process is without effort. After you truly surrender, everything you could ever want just seems to show up, right on schedule. The next amazing manifestation will be to help other infertile couples realize their dreams. Somehow, I will help those who feel there is no hope.

> *Sincerely,*
> *Matthew McQuaid*

Many people have written to me about their success with staying on purpose through the practice of Japa meditation. I'm deeply touched by the power of intention when I read about people who use Japa to help achieve a pregnancy, which they felt was their divine mission. I particularly like Matthew's decision to use this experience to help other infertile couples.

Step 9: Keep your thoughts and feelings in harmony with your actions. The surest way to realize your purpose is to eliminate any conflict or dissonance that exists between what you're thinking and feeling and how you're living your days. If you're in disharmony, you activate ego-dominated attitudes of fear of failure, or disappointing others, which distance you from your purpose. Your actions need to be in harmony with your thoughts. Trust in those thoughts that harmonize, and be willing to act upon them. Refuse to see yourself as inauthentic or cowardly, because those thoughts will keep you from acting on what you know you were meant to be. Take daily steps to bring your thoughts and feeling of your grand heroic mission into harmony with both your daily activities and of course, with that ever-present field of intention. Being in harmony with God's will is the highest state of purpose you can attain.

Step 10: Stay in a state of gratitude. Be thankful for even being able to contemplate your purpose. Be thankful for the wonderful gift of being able to serve humanity, your planet, and your God. Be thankful for the seeming roadblocks to your purpose. Remember, as Gandhi reminded us: "Divine guidance often comes when the horizon is the blackest." Look at the entire kaleidoscope of your life, including all of the people who have crossed your path. See all of the jobs, successes, apparent failures, possessions, losses, wins — everything — from a perspective of gratitude. You're here for a reason; this is the key to feeling purposeful. Be grateful for the opportunity to live your life purposefully in tune with the will of the Source of all. That's a lot to be grateful for.

155

It seems to me that searching for our purpose is like searching for happiness. There's no way to happiness; happiness *is* the way. And so it is with living your life on purpose. It's not something you find; it's how you live your life serving others, and bringing purpose to everything you do. That's precisely how you fulfill the intention that is the title of this chapter. When you're living your life from purpose, you're dwelling in love. When you're not dwelling in love, you're off purpose. This is true for individuals, institutions, business, and our governments as well. When a government gouges its citizens with excessive fees for any service, they're off purpose. When a government pursues violence as a means for resolving disputes, it's off purpose regardless of how it justifies its actions. When businesses overcharge, cheat, or manipulate in the name of profit-making, they're off purpose. When religions permit prejudice and hatred or mistreat their parishioners, they're off purpose. And it's true for you as well.

Your goal in accessing the power of intention is to return to your Source and live from that awareness, replicating the very actions of intention itself. That Source is love. Therefore, the quickest method for understanding and living your purpose is to ask yourself if you're thinking in loving ways. Do your thoughts flow from a Source of love within you? Are you acting on those loving thoughts? If the answers are yes and yes, then you're on a purpose. I can say no more!

If you like what you've read ... check this out!

FOOTNOTES ♻

Wayne W. Dyer, Ph.D., is an internationally renowned author and speaker in the field of self-development. He is the author of more than 20 books, has created many audios, CDs, and videos; and has appeared on thousands of television and radio programs. Four of his books, including "Manifest Your Destiny," "Wisdom of the Ages," "There's a Spiritual Solution to Every Problem," and the "New York Times Bestseller" "10 Secrets for Success and Inner Peace," were featured as National Public Television specials; and the book, "The Power of Intention," has been showcased there as well. Dyer holds a doctorate in educational counseling from Wayne State University and was an associate professor at St. John's University in New York. Visit his website at: www.DrWayneDyer.com

People Pay For Ideas And Solutions ... The BETTER The Idea, The Bigger The Paycheck!!

by Stu McLaren

As an entrepreneur, your future depends on creating great ideas all day and everyday. The world needs big ideas, small ideas, ideas that make money, solve problems, bring people closer together and keep relationships fun and electrifying!

People Pay For Ideas And Solutions

Whether you are looking for more customers, ideas for your marketing or exciting press coverage, generating fresh, unique ideas is vital for every entrepreneur. The quality of these ideas will determine your success.

The Better The Idea, The Bigger The Paycheck

As you can probably tell by my picture, I am younger than most of the AMAZING contributors in this book. But my youth forced me to take a different approach to business as an entrepreneur.

I didn't have the money, I didn't have the experience, and I certainly didn't have the contacts. Therefore, I had to learn how to use my creativity — a skill that can overcome all three of the obstacles I just mentioned.

That's why I am FIRED UP!!

This is a skill that any entrepreneur can learn, and a skill that every entrepreneur should learn. If you want your results quicker, easier and cheaper, you need to learn how to generate creative solutions for your business.

The Good News — Times are Tough

Yes, that is good news!!

People are always going to have problems.

Competition can steal your market share with a revolutionary idea. Customers can lose interest in your products or services. An interoffice divorce

157

can split your staff into friends and foes. A natural disaster can change the way you do business forever. The point is, we just don't know what can or will happen.

This is good news for the creative entrepreneur because people will always want solutions to their problems.

So How Do You Think Creatively?

Thanks for asking.

The creative thinker follows a definite set of rules in order to increase his or her odds of success.

The word "rules" brings an implied set of restrictions. In the case of the creative thinker, these rules actually set you free. By following these creative guidelines, your mind can soar beyond your ordinary day-to-day viewpoints, and jump into a world of imagination and creation.

Research from the renowned creativity hotspot "The Eureka Ranch" confirmed an earlier study published in the "Harvard Business Review." If your ideas differ dramatically from the status quo, then they actually have a higher probability of success in the marketplace — by over 350 percent!

The More Radical Your Ideas, The More Dramatic Your Success.

To develop ideas that stand out, you need to think differently. These simple rules will guide you through that process.

1)   There are NO rules!!
The best ideas flow when your thoughts don't recognize boundaries or restrictions. Realize that anything is possible, and your great ideas will shake the world. Your thoughts should defy mundane, common, ordinary thoughts, and should redefine the word "possible." Stretch your thoughts to new levels. No limitations! As Cole Porter said, "Anything goes!" Forget about financial restrictions (lack of dough) or lack of time. Forget about rules!!

2)   Respect the CATERPILLARS
Ideas, when they first occur, aren't full-blown polished products. In the beginning they're ugly caterpillars, but in the end they could transform into beautiful butterflies. Phrases like "that'll never work," "it's not reasonable" or "only in a million years" stifle your creative environment. No idea is a bad idea. Give your ideas a chance. Defer judgment on all ideas until the end.

3)   Go where no one has gone before
Like "Captain Kirk and the Starship Enterprise," let your mind go numb to reality. In order to create fresh, new, eye-opening ideas you need to push the envelope of your imagination and creativity. What has never been done

158

before in your industry? Think B.O., BIG and Original!! You may not know all the details to turn your idea into reality, and that's OK. Ideas first, details second.

4) Go BIG or go home
Major league baseball fans remember great players like Mark McGwire, Barry Bonds and Reggie Jackson for one thing — homeruns. However, you'll also notice that these players (if you look at their stats) also struck out a lot!! In regards to strikeouts, Mark McGwire is 20th all-time, Barry Bonds 10th and Reggie Jackson is first. The lesson here is not to fear failure. Without trial and effort, your "strikeout" is guaranteed. On the other hand, if you swing, you might just hit it outta the park. Swing "lots," and swing for the fences!!

The same principle applies to creativity, "You need to strive for 'LOTS' of raw ideas. Greg A. Stevens and James Burley confirmed this concept in their May-June 1997 "Research Technology Management" review of the results of 10 major venture capital firms. They found it takes roughly 3,000 raw ideas or 125 formal projects to generate one success.

Swing for the fences and go big — we are looking for quantity, not quality. Quality will naturally come with quantity.

5) Let Loose
Having fun throughout the creative process naturally sparks an infusion of ideas. Let go of any worries, inhibitions or timidity. Without fun, there's no enthusiasm. Without enthusiasm, there's no energy. Without energy, people live their lives in fear and regret of "what could have been." Let go of your fears and have a good time — it doesn't have to be hard work if you don't want it to be!!

STIMULI

With the rules in hand, it's now time to create. Use exercises to help push your thinking (you can find a bunch of them for free at www.creativethinkingonline. com).

Throughout my presentations and workshops I use plenty of whacky pictures, words, toys, magazines, music and food. I want to engage your senses!!

Generating ideas means more than making connections or associations between ideas that have never been made before. The secret ingredient is gathering and surrounding yourself with rich sources of STIMULI.

Picture a long line of dominos all lined up one after the other. It winds itself around the corner, on objects and up your stairs.

In order to set off this HUGE chain reaction, a little nudge is needed on the first domino. Then, as the first one falls, every domino after that falls in a beautiful display of "chain reaction."

159

The creative process works the same way. A piece of stimuli acts as the first domino, which sets off a chain reaction of idea associations and creations. Stimuli helps nudge your brain to start creating.

Stimuli can take many forms from sights, sounds and scents to competitor products, customer feedback and firsthand experiences. The creative thinker views the world as a playground in which everything acts as some type of creative stimuli. Knowing this, you can see why some people generate ideas no matter what the circumstances.

You can find all kinds of stimuli that will get your mind rolling by going to www.stimulicity.com.

Creativity in Action — One Quick Exercise

Put on some music. If it's been a rough day, put on something that will get your energy going. In fact, put on your favorite song and let loose with your best karaoke effort!!

Then define your challenge in one sentence. What do you want to generate ideas for? Put the challenge at the top of a fresh sheet of paper.

Now grab a picture from your favorite magazine. Start looking at the pictures and write down your immediate thoughts, observations, reactions or impressions about what you see.

What does the picture remind you of?

How does it make you feel?

What are the characteristics of the people or objects in your picture? Are they big, small, hairy, plump, juicy, smooth, energetic or colorful?

How might you use what's in the picture to solve your challenge?

What is completely opposite to what you see in the picture? How can that help you solve your challenge?

Who does the picture remind you of and how can they help you with this challenge?

Now, listen to the music that you have playing in the background. What does it remind you of? How can you use music to solve your challenge? What kind of music would you use?

The picture lends itself to the creation of one idea reaction after another. Let your mind wander and write EVERYTHING down!!

People mistakenly don't write their ideas down. By writing your ideas down, you can sometimes set off another idea reaction.

The effectiveness of this process multiplies when you add some brainstorming buddies. As you come up with an idea, say it out loud. By doing this, you might trigger an idea in someone else.

Always, Always, Always, Keep The Momentum Going.

If the ideas start slowing down, you need to grab another picture. When you have enough raw ideas, stop writing and start combining. Sort through your ideas and see if you can combine any together. Often times you can make a single idea much juicier by introducing it to a few other smaller ideas.

Once you tap into the resources that you already have around you, creating comes easily. But **you need to be deliberate** when you want unique ideas. Generating ideas is a process. Trying to brainstorm without the engaging influence of stimuli will decrease your odds of success, as will violating any of the creativity rules. Follow the rules, go through the process and watch the magic happen!!

If you like what you've read ... check this out!

FOOTNOTES ✦

Stu McLaren works with entrepreneurs who want fresh, creative ideas that make life easier and put money in the bank. He has presented his creativity material to audiences all across North America and he continues to coach people through his *live* trainings. Visit www.ideasforentrepreneurs.com to grab a free CD entitled "Idea Power: Taking Ideas From Concept To Cash."

To contact Stu, visit:
www.myideaguy.com
www.ideaseminar.com
www.ideasforentrepreneurs.com

Your Money Blueprint

by T. Harv Eker

Have you heard of people who have "blown up" financially? Have you noticed how some people have a lot of money and then lose it, or they have opportunities that start well but then go south on them? On the outside it looks like bad luck, a downturn in the economy, a lousy partner or perhaps other extenuating circumstances. On the inside, however, it's another matter. That's why if you come into big money when you're not ready for it on the inside, the chances are your wealth will be short-lived and you will lose it.

The vast majority of people simply do not have the internal capacity to create and hold on to large amounts of money and the increased challenges that accompany more money and success. This, my friends, is the primary reason they don't have much money. Now you know the real cause.

Lottery winners offer the perfect example of this. Research has shown again and again, regardless of the size of their winnings, most lottery winners eventually return to their original financial state — the amount they can comfortably handle.

On the other hand, the opposite occurs for self-made millionaires. Notice when self-made millionaires lose their money, they usually have it back within a relatively short time. Donald Trump is a good example. Trump had billions, lost everything, and then a couple of years later, got it all back again and more.

Why does this phenomenon occur? Because even though some self-made millionaires may lose their money, they never lose the most important ingredient to their success: their millionaire mind. Of course, in "Donald's" case, it's his "billionaire" mind. Do you realize Donald Trump could never be just a millionaire. If Donald Trump had a net worth of only $1 million, "How do you think he'd feel about his financial success?" Most people would agree that he'd probably feel broke — like a financial failure!

That's because Donald Trump has set his financial "thermostat" for billions, not millions. Most people set their financial thermostats for generating thousands, not millions of dollars; some people set their financial "thermostats" for generating hundreds, and not even thousands; and some people set their financial thermostats for below zero. They're frickin' freezing and they don't know why!

Most people do not reach their full potential. Most people aren't successful. Research shows that 80 percent of the populace will never experience financial freedom, and 80 percent will never experience true happiness.

The reason is simple. Most people are unconscious. They are a little "asleep at the wheel." They work and think on a superficial level of life — based only on what they can see — they live strictly in the visible world.

The Roots Create the Fruits

Imagine a tree. Let's suppose this tree represents the tree of life. This tree bears fruit. In life, our fruits are called our results. So we look at the fruits (our results) and we don't like them; there aren't enough of them, they're too small, or they don't taste good.

So, what do we tend to do? Most of us put even more attention and focus on the fruits — our results. But it's the seeds and the roots that create those fruits.

It's what's under the ground that creates what's above the ground. It's what's invisible that creates what's visible. So what does that mean? It means that if you want to change the fruits, you will first have to change the roots. If you want to change the visible, you must first change the invisible. In my experience, what you cannot see in this world is far more powerful than anything that you can see.

The Four Quadrants

One of the most important things you can ever understand is that we do not live on only one plane of existence. We live in at least four different realms at once. These four quadrants include the physical world, the mental world, the emotional world and the spiritual world.

Most people never realize that the physical realm is merely a "printout" of the other three. Money is a result, wealth is a result, health is a result, illness is a result, your weight is a result. We live in a world of cause and effect.

Have you ever heard someone assert that a lack of money was a bit of a problem? Now hear this: A lack of money is never, ever, ever a problem. A lack of money is merely a symptom of what is going on underneath. The only way to change your "outer" world is to first change your "inner" world.

Whatever results you're getting, be they rich or poor, good or bad, positive or negative, always remember that your outer world simply reflects your inner world. If things aren't going well in your outer life, it's because things aren't going well in your inner life. It's that simple.

163

What Is Your Money Blueprint and How Is It Formed?

Whether I'm appearing on radio or television, I'm well known for making the following statement: "Give me five minutes and I can predict your financial future for the rest of your life."

How? In a short conversation, I can identify what's called your money and success "blueprint." Each of us has a personal money and success blueprint already embedded in our subconscious mind, and this blueprint, more than anything and everything else combined, will determine your financial destiny.

What is a money blueprint? As an analogy, let's consider the blueprint for a house, which is a preset plan or design for that particular home. In the same way, your money blueprint is simply your preset program or way of being in relation to money.

I want to introduce you to an extremely important formula. It determines how you create your reality and wealth. Many of the most respected teachers in the field of human potential have used this formula as a foundation for their teachings. Called the Process of Manifestation, it goes like this:

$$T > F > A = R$$

Your financial blueprint consists of a combination of your Thoughts, Feelings, and Actions as they lead to your Results in the arena of money.

So how is your money blueprint formed? The answer is simple. Your financial blueprint consists primarily of the information or "programming" you received in the past, and especially as a young child.

Who were the primary sources of this programming or conditioning? For most people, the list includes parents, siblings, friends, authority figures, teachers, religious leaders, media and your culture to name a few.

Every child learns how to think about and act in relation to money. The same holds true for you, for me, for everyone. You learned how to think and act when it comes to money. These teachings become your conditioning, which becomes automatic responses that run you for the rest of your life. Unless, of course, you intercede and revise your mind's money files. This is exactly what we do for thousands of people each year, on a deeper and more permanent level at the Millionaire Mind Intensive Seminar.

So What Is Your Money Blueprint Set For?

Now, it's time to answer the "million-dollar" question, "What is your current money and success blueprint, and what results is it subconsciously moving you toward? Are you set for success, mediocrity, or financial failure? Are you programmed for struggle or for ease around money? Are you set for working hard for your money or working in balance?"

Are you conditioned for having a consistent income or an inconsistent income? You know the scoop: "First you have it, then you don't, then you have it, then you don't." It always appears as though the reasons for these drastic fluctuations come from the outside world. For instance: "I got a great-paying job, but then the company folded. Then, I started my own business and things were booming, but the market dried up. My next business was doing super, but then my partner left, etc.." Don't be fooled, this is your blueprint at work.

Are you set for having a high income, a moderate income, or a low income? Did you know there are actual dollar amounts for which many of us are programmed? Are you set for earning $20,000 to $30,000 a year; $40,000 to $60,000; $75,000 to $100,000; $150,000 to $200,000; $250,000 a year or more?

Are you programmed for saving money or for spending money? Are you programmed for managing your money well or mismanaging it?

Are you set for picking winning investments or picking losers? You might wonder, "How could whether or not I make money in the stock market or in real estate be part of my blueprint?" Simple. Who picks the stock or the property? You do. Who picks when you buy it? You do. Who picks when you sell it? You do. I guess you've got something to do with the equation.

If you are a salesperson and your blueprint is set for earning $50,000 a year and somehow you make a huge sale that makes you $90,000 that year, either the sale will cancel or if you do end up with $90,000, get ready for a crummy year to follow to make up for it and bring you back to the level of your financial blueprint.

On the other hand, if you're set for earning $50,000 and you've been in a slump for a couple of years, don't worry, you'll get it all back. You have to, it's the subconscious law of the mind and money. Someone in this position would probably walk across the street, get hit by a bus, and end up with exactly $50,000 a year in insurance! It's simple: one way or another, if you're set for $50,000 a year, eventually that's what you'll get.

So again, how can you tell what your money blueprint is set for? One of the most obvious ways is to look at your results. Look at your bank account. Look at your income. Look at your net worth. Look at your success with investments. Look at your business success. Look at whether you're a spender or a saver. Look at whether you manage money well. Look at how consistent or inconsistent you are. Look at how hard you work for your money. Look at your relationships that involve money.

Is money a struggle or does it come to you easily? Do you own a business or do you have a job? Do you stick with one business or job for a long time or do you jump around a lot?

Your blueprint is like a thermostat. If the temperature in the room is

165

seventy-two degrees, chances are good that the thermostat is set for seventy-two degrees. Now here's where it gets interesting. Is it possible that because the window is open and it is cold outside, the temperature in the room can drop to sixty-five degrees? Of course, but what will eventually happen? The thermostat will kick in and bring the temperature back to seventy-two.

Also, is it possible that because the window is open and it's hot outside, the temperature in the room can go up to seventy-seven degrees? Sure it could, but what will eventually happen? The thermostat will kick in and bring the temperature back to seventy-two.

The only way to permanently change the temperature in the room is to reset the thermostat. In the same way, the only way to change your level of financial success "permanently" is to reset your financial thermostat, otherwise known as your "money blueprint."

You can try anything and everything else you want. You can develop your knowledge in business, in marketing, in sales, in negotiations and in management. You can become an expert in real estate or the stock market. All of these are tremendous "tools," but in the end, without an inner "tool box" that is big enough and strong enough for you to create and hold on to large amounts of money, all the tools in the world will be useless to you.

Once again, it's simple arithmetic: "Your income can grow only to the extent that you do."

Fortunately or unfortunately, your personal money and success blueprint will tend to stay with you for the rest of your life — unless you identify and change it. And this is exactly what we will continue to do with you at the "Millionaire Mind Intensive" seminar.

"SECRETS OF THE MILLIONAIRE MIND: Mastering the Inner Game of Wealth," by T. Harv Eker (HarperBusiness/March 1, 2005), is a phenomenon in the publishing industry, hitting #1 on the "NY Times Bestseller" list and several other national lists, its first week it went on sale.

If you like what you've read ... check this out!

FOOTNOTES ✿

*Success guru **T. Harv Eker** is the president of **Peak Potentials Training**, one of the largest personal success seminar businesses in North America. He regularly fills convention halls with upwards of 2,000 people with his **"Millionaire Mind Intensive"** seminar and other programs. Harv has taught more than a quarter of a million people "to think rich to get rich" through his seminars. He is now reaching an extensive new audience with his bestselling book.*

T. Harv Eker's Three-Day Millionaire Mind Intensive Seminar Free!
Right now when you purchase "Secrets of the Millionaire Mind," T. Harv Eker is offering scholarships for you and a family member to attend the three-day event as his complimentary guests. That is a total value of $2,590 — for free!

*You can purchase the book at any local or online bookstore, or call Peak Potentials toll free at 1-888-623-7424. Please quote Reference # **191922** when you register for the **Millionaire Mind Intensive Seminar** and receive a FREE bonus gift! To receive your 2 FREE tickets to the Millionaire Mind Intensive Seminar, go to the website listed in your book.*

167

Leading Us Past Our Financial Limits

by Laurie H. Davis

For 15 years of my early working life, I was a classroom teacher. I became a teacher as a result of my early environment and conditioning, which programmed me to believe that the best thing I could do for myself — as a young woman in the 60s — was to become a professional. At that time, the most popular career choices for women included teacher, nurse or secretary. None of those professions appealed to me. I wanted to be a businesswoman.

As I write these words, I have been a businesswoman now for 20 years. Owning my own business has challenged yet rewarded me all at the same time. I have been rich and poor more often than anyone I know to date. Perhaps you can relate. I have asked myself many times, "How can someone with so much have so little?" Sound familiar?

This question set me on my quest to stabilize myself and begin working on consistent wealth building. I made some drastic changes in the way I perceived money and how it is used to magnify situations.

What I mean is that a lack of money is like a magnifying glass: when we have none, all of our other challenges appear bigger than they really are. When we have money, problems seem smaller because money actually CAN solve many of our challenges. Let me share an example, the computer crashes and breaks down, but you need it to earn a living. You have no money to get it fixed. The challenge is not the broken computer that you just threw out the window, it's that you have no cash to get it fixed or buy a new one. We become paralyzed without money. If you have a healthy cash flow, a broken computer is not a problem. A lack of money functions like a magnifying glass.

In 2004, I decided that I would personally sell $1 million worth of product for my company, even though I had a team out there promoting and selling as well; I believe in leading by example. I thought that if I can show the team that this is truly possible, it will break any negative beliefs that might prevent us from achieving this goal. As the owner of the business, I had to make some new decisions, prioritize and go to work. This whole exercise has now developed into a program I teach called, "Leading Us Past Our Financial Limits." I lived it first, recorded what happened and here it is for you. I call it my personal list of 10 essential behaviors in earning your first million.

First, I examined my negative beliefs about money that had been instilled in me during adolescence. Many of our parents and grandparents suffered through the Great Depression of the 30s and many of those financial fears from that sad time have been passed on. I made a list of what "Mom and Dad" taught me about money. It was a very short list, and contained no real solid information about how to become wealthy. School was a similar experience. I then made a list of all the beliefs I held about money. That list scared me as well! I encourage you to make these lists and see what you come up with in regards to your financial education. I had to change and let go of negative beliefs and replace them with positive ones that would propel me toward my goal of selling $1 million worth of product ranging in price from $20,000 to $25,000.

This exercise helped me to discover whether or not I operated from a place of poverty or prosperity. We can have millions of dollars in the bank and still operate from a poverty mentality.

Here are some characteristics of what I call a "Poverty Mentality;" Is this you?
 ____ have a fear of lack
 ____ resents spending
 ____ hoards money and other things — pack rat
 ____ bitter, resentful
 ____ non-charitable
 ____ has a low self-esteem
 ____ money is the only security base

Prosperity Mentality, is this you?
 ____ understands needs will be met
 ____ uses money as a tool to build
 ____ shares/generous to others
 ____ enjoys what money can provide
 ____ understands that you are your best resource
 ____ has high self-esteem
 ____ confident/loves life

I realized that my financial education had been nonexistent, and that I operated mostly from a place of poverty. So, I started by evaluating the past, and in so doing, I was able to change my future.

Secondly, I had to change my mindset. I got a fire burning in my belly that I could actually pull this off! I had to create within myself a desire for wealth. I had already made decisions that prevented me from becoming wealthy. My career choice, teaching, had already set me up for poverty. Poor financial choices (as a result of ignorance) also limited my financial horizons. I proceeded to make a list of 10 decisions I had made that had prevented me from becoming wealthy.

What appeared on the paper amazed me. Try it and you will see for yourself those things preventing you from becoming wealthy. "People," "career choices," "poor spending habits," "not taking advantage of investment opportunities" — all these showed up on my list. I then removed all limiting factors in order to do what I knew I could do.

I made posters, I announced it, I dreamt it and I became empowered to make this happen, regardless of what anybody said or did. That burning desire became greater than all the fears and personal limitations I put on myself.

Third, I had to get organized. I had to evaluate how I spent my 24-hour-a-day deposit into my time bank. What a realization that was! I always considered myself productive and had attended many great time management classes; even so, there was lots of cleaning up to do. Many behaviors were not moving me closer to selling anything, let alone earning my million dollars! I had to decide which of my behaviors were million-dollar producing and what items simply wasted my time.

So, I prioritized and scheduled how much time each day would be spent on my goal. That changed everything right there!

Fourth, I examined the spiritual side of money. I believe money is a physical tool that has spiritual properties when it is used to support others, build projects and be spent philanthropically. Embracing this is difficult since most of our "financial programming" relies on negative experiences and propaganda like the idea that in order to be rich, you have to be doing something illegal like selling drugs or robbing banks, etc.. The universal law of sowing and reaping made a strong impression on me. I realized I would have to be willing to give away no less than 10 percent of the money to support something besides myself. Once I made that decision, it strengthened my chances of reaching my goal by 1000 percent.

I had just become more generous than ever before.

The fifth behavior, I had to change involved my environment! I had to surround myself with like-minded people who could support me in the pursuit of my goal. Sometimes to do that you have to leave home. You can always return to a hero's welcome when you succeed. Travel also broadens one's perspective on the world and how you fit into the scheme of things. It's also important to hear from others about how they achieved their goals by reading books like the one you are enjoying right now. We do not need to reinvent the wheel; others have gone before us and some actually WANT to share the information with you. Go on a trip, take a vacation, travel to a conference and keep your eye on the target!! When was the last time you got out of "dodge?"

For my sixth change in behavior, I started getting up earlier. I decided if I wanted to achieve my goals, sleeping would not help me get there. I became a member of my own 5 a.m. club. By getting up just one hour earlier, I actually created six more working hours per week in the quiet of my home.

Did you know that the creative juices flow best between 3 a.m. to 6 a.m. after four- to five-hours of good rest? When the mind is rested, great ideas come forth. I keep a steno pad on my night table to record those thoughts. The average person has six one-million-dollar ideas a year! Since I am a morning person anyway, I only had to fine tune this behavior.

Number seven has been the most challenging. Associations and relationships had to change. A study followed a group of Harvard graduates with the same level of education, similar family background, same career choices and same age for 25 years. At the end of that time frame, only a small percentage felt happy with their lives, their families, their careers, etc.. What separated the successful from the unsuccessful?

It was the people they chose for friends and associates.

I had to take a hard look at my friends and associates and determine who was truly interested in helping me achieve my goals. Sadly, I have to say that some of my family members weren't supportive. Synergy is created when like-minded people move in the same direction.

I had to let some dear people go and build new relationships with the people who truly cared about me. Some of these people I had never met, but they have since become part of my team. Associations matter if you are to achieve your financial goals. How many millionaires do you have personal contact with who can mentor you? I had to get some new friends.

The eighth behavior I changed was to become a great student. Luckily, I like to learn new things. We all possess great capacities for learning. Information is critical to make high-end productive decisions about all aspects of our life. We must receive that information from people who have experience and credibility to draw from. Many people out there want to tell us how to live our lives, but unless they have the experience to back it up, I do not take instruction. I take offence when a financial planner (for example) comes to my home to advise me on how to invest or manage my money when everything about him indicates that he cannot even balance his own check book!

I am a life long learner. I know the minute I stop learning, I will spiral down and lose the desire to accomplish anything else in life. Keep on learning! No one has ever "arrived" when it comes to knowledge.

Behavior number nine also comes easy for me. I had to be willing to fail, mess up and make a proper fool of myself. By advertising what I wanted to do, I gained support, but I also risked ridicule and rejection if it did not work out. Three basic fears block us from action: rejection, change and a fear of failure/success. I propose that most of us have a greater fear of success than failure. We are used to messing up, but many of us have not had long stretches of success, so this is the unknown! We fear the unknown.

171

I had to overcome any fragments of fear I had about rejection and appearing foolish in the eyes of my family, friends and associates. I let that go because the desire to achieve the million-dollar mark in sales excited me more each day; I decided that whatever fears I had needed to go.

Finally, the tenth and final behavior is "I needed to embrace." Now that I am an entrepreneur, I get to pick what I do, where I go, what I earn and how I spend my time, etc..

I created a survey based on my experience over the past 20 years as a self-employed business owner.

"Wanna Be A Millionaire Survey"

1. I dream big.	**T**	**F**
2. I take risks.	**T**	**F**
3. I can make decisions.	**T**	**F**
4. I am fearless.	**T**	**F**
5. I have millionaire friends to mentor me.	**T**	**F**
6. I need to become financially free.	**T**	**F**
7. I take action on my millionaire ideas.	**T**	**F**
8. I am willing to study and learn more.	**T**	**F**
9. I need to make changes.	**T**	**F**
10. I have a money goal in place.	**T**	**F**

As an ENTREPRENEUR I have the freedom to create multiple streams of income — this is what I do. Make a list of all the ways you have to generate money. It will amaze you!

These ideas that I have presented I actually have practiced in my business. Their greatest strength is their practicality, and they don't cost a cent to implement! The greatest gift you can give yourself is the gift of the time you have and how you conduct yourself 24 hours a day.

I encourage you to give them a try, and I know the results will surprise you. Like a great cake recipe that cannot fail, so it goes when you put these basic ingredients together. You will have a foolproof plan to get the financial results you need to realize your financial goals.

If you like what you've read ... check this out!

FOOTNOTES ♻

Laurie H. Davis created the acclaimed PEP™ Process, the most powerful tool on the planet to accelerate change in any area of your life — for adults, teens and/ or young children. To book your free one-hour online experience of this process, contact us immediately at 1-866-361-6702, or at laurie@lauriehdavis.com. To download your free double CD "10 Ways to Grow Your Business," visit us at www.worldwellbeing.com.

Ancient Greek STILL Coaching Salespeople ... After 2405 Years!

... Being A Successful Entrepreneur or Business Owner is Synonymous With Sales!

by Michael Oliver

Allow me to explain, sales & selling is really all about communicating and connecting with other people. To me, it's even more than that. It's about understanding people and creating long-term relationships.

Selling is an essential skill for an entrepreneur or business owner — and selling also helps in your personal life — but many would-be entrepreneurs feel uncomfortable with the whole idea of selling.

They equate success in sales with pushy, overly-persuasive and manipulative tactics — behaving like the proverbial "door-to-door salesman." It turns most people off — even salespeople!

I once felt that way about sales myself until I discovered an alternative results-oriented process focused on a mutually beneficial conclusion.

I found I could succeed in sales and get all the results I wanted without having to say or do ANYTHING that made either myself or my clients feel uncomfortable! The best part is that I didn't have to resort to using "persuasive closing" and "objection handling techniques" that turns most people off.

I'll share with you my story of how I discovered how to become incredibly successful in sales, without fear, anxiety or the loss of any of my friends!

From There To Here

When I entered the world of selling in 1979, I learned persuasion techniques, manipulative phrases and sales strategies designed to make me successful. I bought all the books on closing, objection handling and how to negotiate to win.

Within a year, I could handle up to seven objections and continually "bridge to a close." It seemed like I had learned well — the money flowed!

173

But, there was just one problem. Despite my apparent success, I felt uncomfortable. Instinctively, I constantly resisted using the conventional selling techniques I had learned ... even though they seemed to work.

It all felt so contradictory, even adversarial. On the one hand, I learned that selling was "the noble art of meeting needs and helping people solve their problems," and on the other, my teachers taught me how to ask manipulative questions to close the sale, and if a client might offer any resistance — how to "handle" their objections.

So what was it? The noble art of service, or the black art of coercion?

This inner conflict started showing daily. I became reticent and I did what many salespeople do — I dragged my feet and met my quota in the last 10 days of the month instead of the first 10 days!

Every time I made a call, I felt like a soldier going to war. It was me against them. The fear of objections and rejection made my life stressful.

For the life of me, I could not understand why there should be any resistance at all **if we met someone's needs correctly in the first place! It made no sense!**

Why was the tension there? Though, I didn't know it at the time, I felt discomfort because I treated people in a way that I would NOT like to be treated myself.

However, I stuck with it because "it" was all that I knew; I really wanted to hold on to the relative freedom and the money that being an independent salesperson gave me. But I paid a price. The adversarial approach of those sales techniques required me to manipulate people to make a sale, which tormented my soul.

Seeing others who appeared totally comfortable at using the conventional approach just added to my dilemma. I felt there must be something wrong with ME if I couldn't accept the techniques as easily as they could.

You might know someone else who feels the same way.

My Search For The Ideal Solution

To resolve these conflicts, I sought advice from people who had a successful track record in sales and sales management.

However, whenever I brought these issues up, I got answers like: "It goes with the territory. That's the way selling is. Rejection is just part of the sales process. Every 'no' gets you closer to 'yes.' It's a numbers game."

My head could understand that, but my heart couldn't, so I continued searching. I read everything I could about selling, especially new approaches. I learned a form of "counselor selling," a method based on asking structured questions.

It helped a little, but it still focused on "closing that sale" and treating people as a means to an end.

The continuing anxiety and discomfort really started to affect my performance. Rather than face the fear of going out and finding new customers or making follow-up calls, I would find other things to do.

Something had to give!

A 2 A.M. Wake Up Call!

One morning I awoke at 2 A.M. — I had questions!

What if I really believed that idea about focusing on, and serving the other person first? What if I let go of my personal agenda and guided them through a process of discovery without using "manipulation" to try and get a sale every time?

However, did I believe it so much I was prepared to completely give up the manipulative approach and really listen to and understand what my prospective client was saying? Was I really prepared to let the sale go if I determined my solution could not meet their needs? What if I was prepared to suggest an alternative solution if I knew one existed ... even if I personally couldn't provide it? I decided to let it happen and went back to sleep.

It Happened!

Two months passed before my resolution was tested. The time was long enough for me to have consciously forgotten it, yet subconsciously it was sitting there, like water under the ground, waiting for the right moment to become a spring.

While sitting opposite of a prospective client I stared those "2 A.M." questions and resolutions in the face.

We had come to a point in the conversation where I realized my solution was OK, but it was not what the client was looking for. I also realized, I was facing my own shadow.

The devil on my right shoulder urged me to go for the sale saying, *"A little bit of persuasive talk here and there and it's in the bag. Remember your responsibility to your company and to your family, go on, GO for it."* On my left shoulder another voice said very quietly in a sing-song voice, *"Remember your commitment to yourself."*

175

It was hard. Years of ingrained habits and experience don't just go away. I went with the "2 A.M." commitment and said I didn't feel I had the right solution. When asked to explain why, I gave the reason based on what I had heard.

And then, the first of two extraordinary things happened. My potential client leaned forward, agreed with me, thanked me for my open mind, and asked what he could do to adjust the company's criteria so as to use my solution!

I was astounded! The inner conflict bounced back, grounded from years of habitual use. The two opposing voices sprung up again, one wanting to grab the opportunity, the other reminding me of my commitment. It was a massive internal struggle. I stayed with the "2 A.M." commitment and stated again that based on what he had told me, my solution was not going to satisfy them. I then suggested another company and left!

The second extraordinary thing was how my action returned in abundance. It came back in the form of two large contracts from people I had not approached before. One of them — an unsolicited referral given by the very person I could not help — astounded me! By letting go of the outcome, my income actually increased!

My comfort level, my self-esteem AND my inner peace had all taken a quantum leap! So did my understanding that other forces were now working for me rather than against me.

How I Discovered The Magic and Power of Dialogue

What happened that day was a breakthrough!

I discovered that by *detaching* or *letting go* of the outcome *I could increase my income!*

But it wasn't the whole solution.

I realized that if I was to truly serve my clients, I had to intimately understand their real problems without regard to my own welfare. It was about finding the problems behind the problems! And they would only tell me if they trusted me.

How could I gain their deep trust?

I found that asking structured questions had a remarkable affect — people opened up more and would volunteer information to me. However, I still went into meetings with my list of "pre-prepared" questions, which steered the client toward my solution. So, while they opened up, I got mostly factual answers and resistance because they could sense my agenda of "getting the sale."

Once more, I decided to let go and I asked questions with the intent to really

understand what the client wanted and why they wanted it, instead of asking questions to get the answers I wanted to hear. I detached from my needs and prepared myself to move on if I felt my solution didn't meet theirs. I didn't want to "persuade" anymore.

A remarkable thing happened. As I listened to my clients, specific and relevant questions based on the information they shared with me just flowed out of my mouth. I found the conversation started to unfold in a way I had never previously experienced — the client was working with me. Between us, we explored their problem and resolved it together as one, in a way that would never have occurred to me before.

When I reviewed the meeting, I also realized that as well as listening more intently than I had ever done before, I had also asked my client many times to clarify what they had said (simply because I hadn't fully understood what they meant!).

Without knowing it, I had come across the idea of *"feedback"* and clarifying what I thought I had heard.

Unknowingly, I had re-discovered and used a powerful and ancient approach — *Socratic Dialogue.*

A Greek philosopher and teacher who lived in Athens around 400 B.C. — *Socrates'* approach involved asking questions, intense listening and feedback that allowed people to come to their own logical conclusions.

It's a powerful and effortless process that produces incredibly quick results because it allows people to challenge their own beliefs, come to their own conclusions and persuade themselves.

With this accidental discovery, I GOT IT! Magic happened!

Powerful Results, No Fear, No Anxiety, all based on these four Principles...
1. Helping other people solve their problems.
2. Asking the right types of questions at the right time.
3. Listening to what is being **meant**, not just what is being **said**.
4. Feeding back what you think you heard.

These four Principles became the foundation of my approach to sales I now call *"Natural Selling."*

Conclusion

After this discovery, my sales career really took off. I made substantially more money, and achieved a greater sense of personal fulfillment and inner calm than ever before.

As an added benefit, I found that these same ideas worked equally well

177

in my personal life. I found it easier to make new friends, and my one-on-one relationships improved at every level.

These four principles and the relationship-building skills they bring have made an amazing difference in my life both as an entrepreneur and business owner.

As an entrepreneur or business owner, you can succeed without fear, without anxiety and without the uncomfortable feeling that comes from using conventional selling techniques.

You can also "naturally" achieve outstanding sales results and personal fulfillment with effortless ease and inner calm. It's just a matter of thinking and acting differently.

Here's to your own success!

If you like what you've read ... check this out!

FOOTNOTES

Want to know how to be a "Natural" salesperson without using manipulation or techniques? Go to www.NaturalSellingSalesTraining.com or call +17-775-886-0777 and get your free e-course "7 Steps to Natural Selling." Michael Oliver is a best selling author, internationally known speaker, trainer, certified Chopra Center Trainer and founder of Natural Selling Sales Training.

Nowhere to Millionaire

by Wendy Robbins

"**A**re we there yet? Are we there yet? Are we there yet? How much further?" Sounds familiar, huh?

How about letting THERE find YOU? What if you trust that the NEW wants you? Can you accept that you are the one you've been waiting for? You have permission now to be free.

Are you ready to give up your addictions that make you feel small and limited? Are you willing to have the life of your dreams? Would you like more fulfillment in your life? Are you ready to live a life that matters?

I thought so. My business partner, Jorli McLain and I went from $10,000 credit card debt to millions from a hanger that massages your head known as "The Tingler™"(www.everythingforlove.com), and soon again with a plunger costumed as a real plant known as "Toilet Trees™" (www.toilettrees.com) — if I can do it — so can you. Just take the plunge…. I now teach people how to make a lot of money, how to develop a millionaire mind and I teach a step-by-step system to bring products to market (www.nowheretomillionaire.com). This is my reality.

What is reality? Who is thinking your thoughts? Is your "NOWHERE MIND" still trying to run the show? I believe "Reality" is what you think is true based on beliefs filtered through your thoughts, feelings, emotions and perceptions. You think 60,000 thoughts a day. What do you focus on? You can train your mind and your thoughts to think divinely so that your beliefs and perceptions create Heaven on Earth. This will be your reality aka free-ality.

More thoughts: You are the person you've been waiting for. This is the place and time that we agreed to. Welcome home. However and whoever you are is genius. You're breathing, aren't you? You are born in genius.

So, for fun now, let's play! Please allow me to be your inner tour guide. This journey promises you your soul, your passion and your power — Are you in?

Breathe in and exhale deeply — relax — it feels so good to relax — let

179

go of anything that is blocking you right now, any fears, any doubts — the day's challenges — none of it matters right now — no circumstance (aka circus-stance) rules you now or runs your show. Not now. Now, you choose to relax and let go. Whatever happened today — whatever stories you believed, dramas you participated in, now drop. They're too heavy right now. Your dramas don't matter right now. They are not important — what is important is to relax right now.

Take a few minutes right now and **Please** write down your dream life. Contemplate who is with you, who you are, what you do, consider health, wealth, fun, spirit, home, friends, family, contribution, etc.....

Ok, now where did those ideas come from? Who was the thinker behind your thoughts? Did you think in your head or your heart? Did you have a vision? Hear something? Experience it fully. Have you ever thought about it before? Is this new?

FEAR IS YOUR FRIEND — THE TRICK IS TO LOVE IT LIKE ONE

Do you think it's possible to attract those things? Any doubts or fears? Let's talk about fear for a moment, "Who is holding onto the fear?" Who is identified with the fear? If you continue to do what you are doing right now in your life can you attract the vision you just saw? How much has your fear cost you? I ask that we give up the ownership of the fear — just be aware of it. Recognize what's here. Let go of the attachment to the fear.

Fear is the friend you take with you on all your adventures. Fear just wants to be loved.

Which is easier, "To struggle or to be willing?" Which contracts you, to be willing or to be unwilling? What do you do to avoid fear? We can acknowledge the fear and not tell its story. We just meet the fear, ask to bring it on, breathe it in, and transform it with our breath — so each exhale becomes love.

I'm asking you not to fight for your limitations. You've spent a lifetime doing that, and it is now clear that it doesn't serve you. You're not judging yourself or blaming — just realizing that something has been missing, and you are open to be limitless.

So, what are you trying to shield or hide? What does hiding cost you? Are you tired of it? Is it exhausting? It's time to open to that, which we hate, don't understand or what we're not friends with. Then the fear opens and there's an opportunity to clearly understand that fear just wants to be loved. So we love the fear, stress, the anger, the loneliness, the messes — we don't need to fix anything — we are just open and willing.

Fear masquerades as truth – the underlying truth is love – so many of us are simply mirroring and modeling what we grew up with. So we're not as kind or gentle with ourselves, and this is what needs to shift. We can speak to ourselves as we would a small child – because this is who we are. A child. A child

who thinks we are made of dust, exposing an inner knowledge of who we truly are — that we are made of heaven. We are the stuff that stars are made of. We are here to create Heaven on Earth — moment by moment — to be the midwife delivering Heaven. To experience each other as a perfect portion of God or divine self. For fun, today experience everyone you meet as your beloved. Simply love everyone you encounter with no expectations. Notice what happens.

When I asked you to design your perfect life, "Did you experience your utopian life? Did you feel it? How did your heart feel? Were you expanded or shut down? Was it exciting? Were you passionate? Were you scared or wondering how you were going to pull off such a big vision? How you do anything is how you do everything.

Do you think that the world is a safe place? How you answer this has a lot to do with how you interact in the world. It becomes a filter through which you view your life. Your life is a reflection of your thoughts. If you string a bunch of thoughts together you create beliefs. Some are healthier than others — we are not here to judge any of them. We are here to simply notice. We're safe, and I invite you to step into all possibilities — today we are going to wear some new beliefs over our nakedness — and allow these new beliefs that are filled with love, joy, passion, purpose, surrender, intention, gratitude and appreciation to percolate into juicy java that excites us to our core.

Nowhere to millionaire mind, hmmmm. ... DO YOU SERVE GRACE OR DO YOU SERVE THE LITTLE MIND? What are the thoughts that hold onto the resistance? What keeps the stories that are limited — in play? Are you made of dirt and clay or are you made of light? Rest in the clarity and peace of your core. The "nowhere" mind is frazzled — it's been running the show and it's not equipped to do that. I am here to remind us of our truth, which is to simply shift our attention from our limitations to our wholeness. WE ARE TRULY LIMITLESS.

I also believe that we are all part of "one source." I think that separation is an illusion, to me, it doesn't matter if you are a man and I am a woman or someone who is old, fat, thin, black, white, Muslim or Jewish, Iraqi or American — we are all one. Genetically we are. We are the stuff stars are made of. All of us. We just forget this truth and substitute it with a misguided effort to be right. We insist on defending different stories. My God is better than yours. I own this. You are wrong. I am right. So, how is this set of beliefs, perceptions and thoughts working for you? For the world? What if you believed that you are a mirror for everyone you meet and that every person is your beloved? How could anyone be your enemy?

Would you love to be reminded daily of what we're talking about? Would you be open to be coached so that you overcome your fears and doubts easily? That would be helpful, wouldn't it? Can you (on your own) have the life of your dreams? Of course, I've gotta say it's sweet to have a team of support around you, isn't it? I'm open to be that for you — with you.

181

You are the author of your life. Understand that your natural state is of well-being, abundance and health. There is no end to your growth. You are in a state of eternal growth. You have nothing to prove to anyone. You are in a state of absolute freedom.

The possibility right now is for us to take some glue to the little "Nowhere Thoughts" and stop them in their place. Don't feed them! If they're not nourished, they'll simply die.

"Change is hard...this is who I am ... I can't change ... if he or she would have given me_____ I'd be different. He or she's bad for wanting that... It's his or her fault." The victimy, blaming, judging, stuck stories bore me personally. To change is what is natural. Your resistance causes the stress and chaos. Let go of the limiting stories. You manufacture your reality. You create your world, for fun, just really take that in — let it land.

NOW PRACTICE BELIEVING THIS — I AM MAKING THIS ALL UP. So, what are the stories that make "you," you? What are you telling yourself? What are you telling the world? Is it stimulating, passionate, vividly expansive and limitless? If not, just re-tell the story — you are the author. You are making it all up.

Change is the only constant. We hold on so hard to fleeting thoughts, fighting for ground where there is none. We are now becoming the verbs that we are meant to be and not choosing to masquerade as nouns anymore. All in favor, raise your hand and say — Amen, "Awomen."

We are here together to experience liberation — it's a process. So, don't get stuck in the glue that you spew on the way to the NEW. The "New" wants you. Go for the full potential of your soul's blueprint — anything less will have emptiness. Enjoy the process. Appreciate the ride.

Your mission is to make sure the unformed — forms. So, you train your mind, heart and emotions to obey, focus, intend and commit to your visions. This is the game of life you signed up for.

How much further? How much further? This restlessness is the cause of frustration and angst or it can be you simply opening up to the big game... I invite you to relax in the process.

Along the way, make the 3-D reflect what matters — instead of making it — what's the matter. It'll only make you the mad hatter. Let your limiting stories shatter.

Think of taking out a container of Super Glue and pour it over the stories that don't hold you as whole and limitless. Again, if you are not fully nourished in your stories — don't feed them.

Stop your addiction to the stuff that hurts and limits you or has you

speaking meanly to yourself. Notice your thoughts and be in constant awareness and willingness, love yourself. Sounds glib and easy, which it is when you practice and train your mind and heart to fall in love with yourself as a parent loves a child. How can you love anyone or anything if you don't truly adore yourself as your own beloved? It's your kindness and huge heart that reflects a world you are co-creating.

This love from your heart creates light, creates electricity, flow, energy and lovability. Now here's the thing, many of us think we're here to be rich, famous and work for the things — we worship — we strive and anticipate and fear and get gray over the material earth dense 3-D things. We buy into the news and feel the fear when the media tells us we're not pretty, handsome, thin, young enough ... so, from that dry place we attempt to create, and in the crunch and sadness of the crusty life, we manufacture on autopilot without awareness or care; we keep going on wanting, wanting, wanting, not feeling truly deserving or worthy. I am here right now to remind you that Donald Trump or Warren Buffet on their last dying gasp are going to care more about love than making another dollar. One last hug will be worth everything.

If you had six months to live, would you do anything differently? What? What's missing from your life now? You will live a long life — I ask you to stir urgency in you. You choose to live with passion, courage, unity, limitless and purposeful as though every day really mattered. As though today may be the day your physical body would shut down ... remember you are living a long life. You will live a very long life. So, what are you doing with yours?

Remember you are already rich. You are breathing.

If you like what you've read ... check this out!

FOOTNOTES

Wendy Robbins is a speaker/entrepreneur who made millions in two years. She is the Self-Made Millionaire Expert who teaches people how to make money while they sleep. Is it really possible to go to sleep, re-program your brain and become a millionaire? Yes it is. Curious? Go to www.nowheretomillionaire. com. Get a FREE MP3, call and newsletter now! She is available to speak to your group. Check site for testimonials, video, audio, bio, subjects, products, etc.. 800 - 293 - 1984. wendy@nowheretomillionaire.com

183

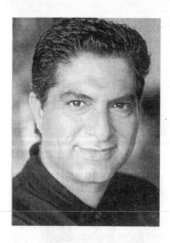

What You Seek, You Already Are

by Dr. Deepak Chopra

When I turned twenty-one as a medical student in New Delhi I had my choice of two kinds of friends. The materialistic kind got out of bed at noon and went to all-night parties where everyone drank Coca-Cola and danced to Beatles records. They had discovered cigarettes and women, perhaps even bootleg liquor, which was much cheaper than imported Scotch. The spiritual kind got up at dawn to go to temple — about the time the materialists were staggering home with hangovers — and they ate rice out of a bowl and drank water or tea, usually out of the same bowl.

It didn't seem strange at the time that all the materialists were Indians and all the spiritual types — were Westerners. The Indians couldn't wait to leave home and go someplace where Coca-Cola, good tobacco, and legal whiskey were cheap and plentiful. The Westerners kept asking where the real holy men were in India, the kind who could levitate and heal lepers by touching them. As it happened, I ran with the materialists, who were all around me in class. Nobody who was actually born in India ever saw himself the other way, as a seeker.

Today I wouldn't have two types to choose from — everyone around me seems to be a seeker. In my mind, *seeking* is another word for chasing after something. My Indian classmates had the easier chase because it doesn't take much to get money and material things, whereas the spiritual types from the West almost never found their holy men. I used to think that the problem was due to how rare holy men actually are; now I realize that what defeated their thirst for a higher life was tied up in the act of seeking itself. Tactics that will successfully get you whiskey and Beatles records fail miserably when you chase holiness.

The spiritual secret that applies here is this: ***What you seek, you already are.*** Your awareness has its source in unity. Instead of seeking outside yourself, go to the source and realize who you are.

Seeking is a word often applied to the spiritual path, and many people are proud to call themselves seekers. Often, they are the same people who once chased too hard after money, sex, alcohol, or work. With the same addictive intensity they now hope to find God, the soul, the higher self. The problem is that seeking begins

184

with a false assumption. I don't mean the assumption that materialism is corrupt and spirituality is pure. Yes, materialism can become all-consuming, but that's not the really important point. Seeking is doomed because it is a chase that takes you outside yourself. Whether the object is God or money makes no real difference. Productive seeking requires that you throw out all assumptions that there is a prize to be won. This means acting without hope of rising to some ideal self, hope being a wish that you'll get somewhere better than the place you started from. You are starting from yourself, and it's the self that contains all the answers. So you have to give up on the idea that you must go from A to B. There is no linear path when the goal isn't somewhere else. You must also discard fixed judgments about high and low, good and evil, holy and profane. The one reality includes everything in its tangle of experiences, and what we are trying to find is the experiencer who is present no matter what experience you are having.

Looking at the people who race around trying to be models of goodness, someone coined the apt phrase "spiritual materialism," the transfer of values that work in the material world over to the spiritual world.

SPIRITUAL MATERIALISM

Pitfalls of the Seeker:
Knowing where you're going.
Struggling to get there.
Using someone else's map.
Working to improve yourself.
Setting a timetable.
Waiting for a miracle.

There's no better way to be a genuine seeker than to avoid these pitfalls.

• *Don't know where you're going.* Spiritual growth is spontaneous. The big events come along unexpectedly, and so do the small ones. A single word can open your heart; a single glance can tell you who you really are. Awakening doesn't happen according to the plan. It's much more like putting together a jigsaw puzzle without knowing the finished picture in advance. The Buddhists have a saying, "If you meet the Buddha on the path, kill him," which means if you're following a spiritual script written in advance, bury it. All you can imagine in advance are images, and images are never the same as the goal.

• *Don't struggle to get there.* If there were a spiritual payoff at the end of the trail, like a pot of gold or the key to heaven, everyone would work as hard as possible for the reward. Any struggle would be worth it. But does it help a two-year-old to struggle to become three? No, because the process of child development unfolds from within. You don't get a paycheck; you turn into a new person. The same is true for spiritual unfolding. It happens just as naturally as childhood development, but on the plane of awareness rather than in the realm of physiology.

185

• ***Don't follow someone else's map.*** There was a time when I was certain that deep meditation using one specific mantra for the rest of my life was the key to reaching enlightenment. I was following a map laid down thousands of years ago by venerable sages who belonged to India's greatest spiritual tradition. But caution is always required: If you follow someone else's map, you could be training yourself in a fixed way of thinking. Fixed ways, even those devoted to spirit, are not the same as being free. You should glean teachings from all directions, keeping true to those that bring progress yet remaining open to changes in yourself.

• ***Don't make this a self-improvement project.*** Self-improvement is real. People get stuck in bad places that they can learn to get out of. Depression, loneliness, and insecurity are tangible experiences that can be improved. But if you seek to reach God or enlightenment because you want to stop being depressed or anxious, if you want greater self-esteem or less loneliness, your search may never end. This area of understanding isn't cut-and-dried. Some people feel tremendously self-improved as their awareness expands; but it takes a strong sense of self to confront the many obstacles and challenges that lie on the path. If you feel weak or fragile, you may feel weaker and more fragile when you confront the shadow energies within. Expanded awareness comes at a price — you have to give up your limitations — and for anyone who feels victimized, that limitation is often so stubborn that spiritual progress becomes very slow. To the extent that you feel any deep conflict inside yourself, a large hurdle stands before you on the path. The wise thing is to seek help at the level where the problem exists.

• ***Don't set yourself a timetable.*** I've met countless people who gave up on spirituality because they didn't reach their goals fast enough. "I gave it ten years. What can I do? Life is only so long. I'm moving on." More likely they devoted just one year or a month to being on the path, and then the weekend warriors fell away, discouraged by lack of results. The best way to avoid disappointment is not to set a deadline in the first place, although many people find this difficult to do without losing motivation. But motivation was never going to get them there in the first place. Discipline is involved, no doubt, in remembering to meditate regularly, to keep up Yoga class, to read inspiring texts, and to keep your vision before you. Getting into the spiritual habit requires a sense of dedication. But unless the vision is unfolding every day, you will inevitably get distracted. Rather than a timetable, give yourself support for spiritual growth. This can be in the form of a personal teacher, a discussion group, a partner who shares the path with you, regular retreats, and keeping a daily journal. You will be much less likely to fall prey to disappointment.

• ***Don't wait for a miracle.*** It really doesn't matter how you define miracle — whether it is the sudden appearance of perfect love, a cure for a life-threatening disease, anointment from a great spiritual leader, or permanent and everlasting bliss. A miracle is letting God do all the work; it separates the supernatural world from this world, with the expectation that one day the supernatural world will notice you. Since there is only one reality, your task is to break through boundaries of division and separation. Watching and waiting for a miracle keeps the boundaries up. You are ever at a remove from God, connected to him by wishful thinking.

If you can avoid these pitfalls of spiritual materialism, you will be much less tempted to chase after an impossible goal. The chase began because people came to believe that God, disapproving of what he sees in us, expects us to adopt a certain ideal. It seems impossible to imagine a God, however loving, who doesn't get disappointed, angry, vengeful, or disgusted with us when we fall short. The most spiritual figures in history were not totally good, however, but totally human. They accepted and forgave; they lacked judgment. I think the highest forgiveness is to accept that creation is thoroughly tangled, with every possible quality given some outlet for expression. People need to accept once and for all that there is only one life and each of us is free to shape it through the choices we make. Seeking can't get anyone our of the tangle because *everything* is tangled up. The only thing that will ever be pure and pristine is your own awareness, once you sort it out.

It's much easier to keep up the fight between good and evil, holy and profane, us and them. But as awareness grows, these opposites begin to calm down in their clashes, and something else emerges — a world you feel at home in. The ego did you a terrible disservice by throwing you into a world of opposites. Opposites always conflict — that's the only way they know — and who can feel at home in the middle of a fight? Awareness offers an alternative beyond the fray.

Last night in bed, I was dreaming. The usual kinds of dream images were passing back and forth; I don't remember much what they were. All at once I became aware of the sound of breathing in my dream. After a second I realized that it was my wife, who was moving in her sleep beside me. I knew that I was hearing her, and yet I also knew that I was dreaming at the same time. For a few seconds I was in both worlds, and then I woke up.

Sitting up in bed, I had the strange sensation that it was no longer important that a dream isn't real. Being awake is more real than a dream only because we have agreed that it is. Actually, the sound of my wife breathing is in my head, whether I am dreaming or not. How, then, could I tell one from the other? *Someone else must be watching.* An observer was aware without getting caught up in being awake, asleep, or dreaming. Most of the time I am so caught up in waking, sleeping, and dreaming that I have no other perspective. The silent observer is the simplest version of me, the one that just is.

If you strip away all the distractions of life, something yet remains that is you. This version of yourself doesn't have to think or dream; it doesn't need sleep to feel rested. There is real joy in finding this version of yourself because it is already at home. It lives above the fray, totally untouched by the war of opposites. When people say that they are seeking, it's this level of themselves that is calling to them in its silent, untroubled way. Seeking is really just a way of winning yourself back.

But to win yourself back you have to get as close to zero as possible. At its very core, reality is pure existence. Meet yourself there and you will be able to create anything in existence. The "I am" contains all that is needed for making a world, even though by itself it consists of nothing but a silent witness.

If you like what you've read ... check this out!

FOOTNOTES 🙠

*Dr. Deepak Chopra has many books that have become international bestsellers and classic texts of health and spirituality. Dr. Chopra is founder of **the Chopra Center for Well Being** in Carlsbad, California. For more information on programs offered by Deepak Chopra, contact The Chopra Foundation:*

The Chopra Center at La Costa Resort & Spa
2013 Costa Del Mar Road
Carlsbad, CA 92009

OR e-mail us at: foundation@chopra.com

*Article excerpts reprinted from the book, **"THE BOOK OF SECRETS, UNLOCKING THE HIDDEN DIMENSIONS OF YOUR LIFE"** published by Harmony Books, Member of the Crown Publishing Group and a division of Random House, Inc. Copyright © 2004 by Deepak Chopra. All rights reserved. Used here by permission.*

SECTION IV

Tips For Making Your Business A Success

© 2005 Kim Muslusky

Top Ten Ways of Thinking Like a Billionaire

by Donald Trump

Here Are My Top Ten ways of Thinking Like a Billionaire:

Don't take vacations. What's the point? If you're not enjoying your work, you're in the wrong job. Even when I'm playing golf, I'm doing business. I never stop, and I'm usually having fun. Now that my kids are joining the family business, I'm closer to them than I've ever been, and I'm finding out that I love relating to them just the way my father related to me — through passion for work well done.

By the way, I'm not the only one who doesn't take vacations. My NBC compatriot Jay Leno works just as much as I do, and maybe that's one of the reasons he's stayed on top in the late-night ratings wars.

2. **Have a short-term attention span.** Most successful people have very short attention spans. It has a lot to do with imagination. Quite often, I'll be talking to someone and I'll know what he's going to say before he says it, before the first three words are out of his mouth. I can tell what the next forty are going to be, so I try to pick up the pace and move it along. You can get more done that way.

3. **Don't sleep any more than you have to.** I usually sleep about four hours per night. I'm in bed by 1 A.M. and up to read the newspaper by 5 A.M. That's all I need, and it gives me a competitive edge. I have friends who are successful and sleep ten hours a night, and I ask them, "How can you compete against people like me if I sleep only four hours?" It rarely can be done. No matter how brilliant you are, there's not enough time in the day.

You may be wondering: Why do I need a competitive edge? You don't, if you're to be an also-ran in life. In "The Natural History of the Rich," Richard Conniff notes that it's common behavior for moguls to seek dominance. Even such traits as who makes the most eye contact in a conversation can be an indication of who seeks to dominate. Conniff singles me out as an example of someone who achieves dominance through my appearance, by leaving my eyebrows untrimmed in order to intimidate negotiating partners. I'm pleased to note that he doesn't comment on my hair.

4. Don't depend on technology. A lot of it is unnecessary and expensive. I don't have a computer on my desk. I don't use an intercom. When I want someone in my office, I yell. It works a lot better than an intercom, and it's much faster.

I don't even have an ATM card- I've never used one in my life. That's the funny thing about being rich: When I go to restaurants, I rarely have to pay. It's usually on the house. The sad part is that if I needed the money, they would make me pay!

I can understand why some people would appreciate the convenience of ATM cards, but a lot of other tech devices are completely unnecessary and get in the way of human contact. If you have something important to say, look the person in the eye and say it. And if you can't get there, pick up the phone and make sure they hear the sincerity in your voice. E-mail is for wimps.

5. Think of yourself as a one-man army. You're not only the commander-in-chief, you're the soldier as well. You must plan and execute your plan alone. People always compare business to war and to sports. We do it because we immediately understand these analogies, not because business savvy equals toughness. It doesn't. It's much more important to be smart than tough. I know some very bad businessmen who are brutally tough, but they're not smart people. They want to act like Vince Lombardi, but they don't know how to win. Lombardi would slap his players, even spit in their faces. He'd have three-hundred-pound men virtually crying. He could do that because he won, and you can do that only if you win.

Billionaires like to win. "The Natural History of the Rich" is full of examples of hypercompetitive plutocrats: Larry Ellison racing his yacht from Australia to Tasmania, Steve Fossett flying a balloon around the world, and Dennis Tito paying $20 million for a trip to space on a Russian rocket. "All of them, one way or another, were showing off," Conniff writes. "To put it in the biological context, they were engaging in display behavior. Animals do it all the time, and their displays, like ours, fall loosely into two categories: They show off with fine feathers, and they show off with risky behavior."

I have my own theory, but it's not as scientific: We do it because it's fun. Work hard, play hard, and live to the hilt.

6. It's often to your advantage to be underestimated. You never want people to think you're a loser or a schlepper, but it's not a good idea if they think you're the smartest guy in the room, either. Because I wrote "The Art of the Deal," everyone is always on guard whenever I negotiate with them. One of the reasons President Reagan was such a successful candidate for office was because rival politicians consistently misjudged him. They assumed an actor wouldn't be able to compete. Through years of insults about his lack of intelligence and political experience, Reagan would smile and remain genial, and in the end, he always exceeded expectations.

Because I'm too famous to be underestimated — I know that sounds

191

egotistical, but it's true- I'm always impressed by ultrasuccessful people who live great lives in a low-key manner. For example, one of my neighbors in Trump Tower is a man named Joel Anderson. For years, I'd see him in the elevator and say hello, but I didn't know anything about him. One day he called my office and said, "Do you think it would be possible for Mr. Trump to attend my party?" He seemed like a nice guy, with a terrific wife, so I figured I'd pop in for a few minutes. When I got to the party, I was amazed to find myself surrounded by the most influential people in New York, including S. I Newhouse and Anna Wintour. I soon discovered that mild-mannered Joel Anderson is the chairman and CEO of Anderson News, one of the countries largest distributors of newspapers and magazines. He's one of the most powerful and generous people I know. I'd been riding in the elevator with him for years and I never knew who he was.

In "How to Get Rich," I discussed how important it is to let people know about your accomplishments. I'll always believe that, but there are times when it's even more impressive if people discover your accomplishments without you telling them directly. A few weeks after Joel Anderson's party, I noticed a long and highly positive profile of him in the business section of "The New York Times." So I want to amend my advice from the previous book: It's often necessary to boast, but it's even better if others do it for you.

7. Success breeds success. The best way to impress people is through results. It's easier for me to do deals now because I've had so many triumphs. You have to create success to impress people in the world of business. It you're young and you haven't had any successes yet, then you have to create the impression of success. IT doesn't matter whether the success is a small one or a big one-you have to start with something and build on it.

8. Friends are good, but family is better. It's better to trust your family than your friends. When I was young, I said to someone who had a fairly big business, "Do you see your brothers and sister?" The person looked at me and said, "Yes, I do, Donald. I see them in court." That had a big impact on me, and I've always tried to stay close to my brothers and sisters, my children, and my former wives.

9. Treat each decision like a lover. Vast fortunes are accumulated through dozens of decisions a day, thousands a month, and hundreds of thousands in a career. Yet each decision is different and special in its own way. Sometimes you decide immediately- love at first site. Sometimes you go slowly- the long engagement. Sometimes you gather people in a room and consider various options- the equivalent of asking your friends what they think of the person that you've been dating. If you treat each decision like a lover-faithfully, respectfully, appropriately- you won't be locked into a rigid system. You'll adapt to the needs of that particular decision. Sometimes you'll think with your head. Other times you'll think with other parts of your body, and that's good. Some of the best business decisions are made out of passion.

Sometimes people are surprised by how quickly I make big decisions, but I've learned to trust my instincts and not to overanalyze things. I like to compare a decision to a lover because it reminds me to keep in touch with my basic impulses- the drives that excite us, attract us, give us inspiration and energy. We are all drawn to beauty, whether it's the allure of a person or the elegance of a home. Whenever I'm making a creative choice, I try to step back and remember my first shallow reaction. The day I realized it can be smart to be shallow was, for me, a deep experience.

10. Be curious. A successful person is always going to be curious. I don't know why this is true, but it's definitely the case. You have to be alive to your surroundings and hungry to understand your immediate world. Otherwise, you'll lack the perspective to see beyond yourself. One of the great aspects of working on "The Apprentice" has been learning about how network TV works. I recently found out that Thursday nights are crucial to the networks because that's when lucrative movie advertisements for the weekend releases air. The higher the ratings are on Thursday night, the more the networks can charge their advertisers. And the more they can charge their advertisers, the more they can pay me to save their network! You see? Curiosity pays!

If you like what you've read ... check this out!

FOOTNOTES

Donald Trump is a billionaire real estate developer that has amassed a fortune through owning key New York properties and Atlantic City casinos. He has gained fame for his flamboyant deals and lavish lifestyle. He is the author of four books and most recently an immensely popular TV show, "The Apprentice."

Article excerpts reprinted from the book, "THINK LIKE A BILLIONAIRE" published by Random House, Inc. Copyright © 2004 by Donald Trump. All rights reserved. Used here by permission.

Unleash the Powerful Promoter Within

by Matt Bacak

Dear Friend,
You are ripping me off.

What?! How? You may be thinking, "We just met. How could I possibly have 'ripped you off' or taken anything away from you?"

But you have! In fact, you are still ripping me off as you sit there. You have valuable information inside of you. You have golden nuggets that could make my life better — easier, more fulfilling or more comfortable. Perhaps your nuggets could make everyone's life better. You may have already developed products, seminars or newsletters, but if you do not market your gold, "how will anyone know?"

Beyond marketing, you must persuade your prospects to buy and actually use your products. People are overwhelmed with all the options they have, so you must help them see your value. However, if you never make your wisdom available, then you are hurting others and you are hurting me.

It doesn't matter if your passion is a security alarm, a beauty product, a business opportunity or anything else, your knowledge, product or service could help people solve their problems. And if you do not think that what you have to offer can help people, why do you offer it in the first place?

I often meet people with the best product in the market. Unfortunately, that product sits on their shelf (or it is still in their heads) and they don't tell anyone about it. And at the very same time, their competitors — with less knowledge and inferior products — are selling those inferior products to people and hurting them by not offering customers the best product available.

Imagine all the people that you could help, imagine all the lives you could change because you have something that could save them time, money or energy. Think of the last time that you searched for something, but could not find what you needed. Maybe the right thing was out there, but because it wasn't marketed well, so you never found it. Give your audience the opportunity to find you.

And that is how you have been ripping me off because you have never shared your unique knowledge and products with me. Not only did you rip me off, but you also ripped off all those you could have been sharing your message with. Quite possibly, you have ripped off the world! You also ripped off someone that should top your list — yourself.

Right now, you could be putting a lot of cold hard cash in your own pocket. It is your job, your duty and your right to market, sell and persuade people to use your services and products. You owe it to yourself and those you care about. But how do you market your products and service so that you can get them out to the world?

The bottom line is very simple; marketing is an exchange between you and someone else. The more important of the two is the other person — your prospect. They have money they worked hard for and they will spend this money somewhere, but it may not be with you. Your job is straightforward; let them know about you and your golden nuggets.

And letting them know about you means that you must promote your product or service. Are you ready to unleash the powerful promoter within you and get rich while promoting your product or service? Great, because I am about to tell you the quickest and fastest way to make that happen.

But first, just a few weeks ago my wife and I lost our baby. The loss devastated us. I had even begun to see my child taking over my empire, growing insanely rich and having more than I ever had in my life; all because I would tell him the real secrets to my success unleashing the powerful promoter within. One day I planned to hand over the reins of my business to him.

I am about to tell you the things that I would have told my son, to prepare him to either take over my business or to start building his own empire. Not just any empire or business, but one that would make him rich beyond his wildest dreams.

Here is what I wanted to say to my child, so now I'm saying it to you:

"You can make a decent income selling products and services, but you can become insanely rich by creating and controlling markets. You see, the Internet offers the cheapest and easiest way to attract and capture people who are interested in what you uniquely have to offer."

How do you capture a market?

With e-zines, newsletters, e-courses or Internet magazines (they are all the same — just named differently).

Think back to the last time that you did a search on the Internet. Were you looking for something to solve your problem? Yeah, tons of people search everyday, doing the same exact thing — and they are looking for you.

www.mentorsmagazine.com

Don't be the average person with an "Internet presence." In other words, just a simple Web site that searchers can view. The majority of searchers check out a site, then they leave forever. (Can you ever find a website a second time? Even if you enjoyed the information on the site, it can be difficult to retrieve later). The people who once found you keep going and you never have any idea who they were, and thus, you have no way to follow-up.

Boy, you are missing out. Big time!

Because the fortune is in the follow-up.

See, if you created an e-zine, newsletter or whatever you might decide to call it, you could capture their email addresses, build relationships and market to them over and over again. Now, you can make millions because you have created and control a huge market that wants your information, products and services.

The second thing that I would say to my own child:

"You must learn to become a great platform sales person. Learn to sell and persuade people."

One great way to generate a lot of cold hard cash from the list, that you create and control, is by putting on teleseminars (FYI: Teleseminars are when a large number of people dial into a "bridge-line," which allows everyone with the secret PIN# to join the group call). I have found that one of the fastest ways to make a lot of money from your market is by giving teleseminars. Many people do teleseminars, but just to deliver information. What I'm talking about is giving teleseminars to sell high-ticket items. You see, I view teleseminars just the same as any other media for selling your valuable information and products, or someone else's. It is just like a live seminar, and if you don't adopt my belief, you will do your listeners a disservice — they want more from you. When you sell, they have the chance to get the full package instead of just a tidbit.

Start by transforming what you already know into persuasive speeches. Then, sell during your public speaking opportunities. If you get asked to speak in front of a live audience, use that time to inspire them to jump out of their seats and rush your table. If you are on a telecall, make sure that they can purchase right away because the likelihood of them buying days later is very slim.

The third thing that I would have told my boy:

"Become a great self-promoter. Become the powerful promoter. Whatever you are passionate about, become great at learning how to sell and market your information, products and services."

A great powerful promoter isn't in love with words, he is in love with people of all kinds, everywhere and anywhere. He is extremely interested in people, watches them closely, listens when they talk, lives their bad moments with them and rejoices in their victories. He is so interested in other people he forgets all about himself, his own needs and wants, and after a time he knows why they think as they do. He recognizes himself in them and knows that whatever they do good or bad — he is also capable of doing. The best way to become a great self-promoter is to love people. Know what every living person fears, hates, loves, and rejoices in. In a sense, it's knowing yourself because others experience what we ourselves experience. Let everything you write say to your reader, "I understand you. I have been in your shoes, I can help you — please let me try."

The fourth thing that I would say:

"There are two common characteristics of highly successful people."

"Highly Successful People" are ACTION-ORIENTED. This means you take action immediately when a good opportunity presents itself.

"Highly Successful People" are EDUCATION-FOCUSED. This means that you take it upon yourself to know everything you possibly can about your field and learn from many different sources.

So, when you see the opportunity to invest in yourself and your business and develop your skills — grab it! Seek out opportunities to learn the art of self-promotion from the leaders. If they were not great marketers, you would not have heard of them — right?

Oh, one last thing — forget about what you learned in school. Follow your dreams, your heart and more importantly, your gut or intuition.

To Be Number 1, You Have To "Get Things Done" With Systematic Automation

by Rob Bell

Did you know your success depends primarily upon your ability to GET THINGS DONE?! Most businesses fail because they can't quickly and easily implement even the most basic tasks. On the surface, businesses appear to have too many opportunities to handle with limited time and resources; however, most businesses waste a lot of effort on insignificant activities that don't yield significant results. Most businesses don't pursue enough opportunities, and the lack of any "Systematic Automation" hampers their ability to exploit those opportunities.

Imagine executing just one tenth of the ideas, sales opportunities and marketing plans you've thought about or been presented with — that's a lot of opportunity! From experience, I know that sales and marketing form the nucleus of any company and lay the foundation of wealth and prosperity. What would it mean to your bottom line (and your personal life) if you could finally turn your business, or department, into that self-functioning "money-machine" you'd always envisioned, instead of a dependent, almost child-like monster that sucks up all your attention, time and energy?

I've used three major philosophies to increase my company's ability to rapidly and easily execute business plans. In fact, these three philosophies helped me to create "Systematic Automation." First and foremost, I decided to outsource all non-essential work and focus on our core strength. Second, I chose to find a mentor — most importantly to avoid costly mistakes, but also to learn winning business systems, policies and procedures to model. Finally, my third philosophy is to always persist. Results don't always happen overnight: sometimes we just need to persist and the reward will eventually come. The implementation of these core philosophies has allowed me *to double my company's growth, year after year for the first three years, and over 35 percent every single year thereafter.*

Do What You Do Best & Forget the Rest

Outsourcing all non-essential activity seems like an immediate and seemingly obvious solution for poor execution. Getting outside experts to help finish tasks and projects faster will allow you to focus on your core strengths.

Many businesses only outsource hands-on, labor-intensive work: like sewing for clothing manufacturers, or coding or programming for software companies. Most companies overlook the opportunity to "outsource internally;" in other words, by using technological systems, many internal functions can be automated. I designed Marketer's Choice software to eliminate much of the manual labor of prospecting, responding to inquiries, customer service, technical support and client communications. I eventually upgraded the program to include upselling, cross-selling, advertising, sales reporting, credit card transactions, and other administrative and sales functions. I sum it up by saying, "Do what you do best and leave the rest."

In fact, companies without "Systematic Automation" will always face challenges in execution because they lack appropriate strategies and systems based on a proven, successful model to copy. My vision for 1ShoppingCart.com has always been to automate as much of the marketing and selling process as possible. Having done this well, we now market the system to give entrepreneurs, small businesses and independent professionals the tools they need to automate much of their activity and to succeed in their sales by using online processes.

The short history and rapid growth of 1ShoppingCart.com Corporation demonstrates this point. The company:

- Opened with two employees and still had less than 25 full-time staff after five years.
- Processed over half a billion dollars in e-commerce transactions for goods and services sold in that same five-year period.
- Sent over 150 million permission-based e-mails per month on behalf of our clients.
- Automatically handled an average of over 1.2 million transactions per day.
- Grew from 250 clients in our first year to over 10,000 this year (2005).
- Expanded globally with a strong presence in the US, Canada, Australia and the UK, with merchants in many other countries.

The power of technology allows practically any size business from an individual sole proprietorship to a huge corporation to apply "Systematic Automation." Today, there's no excuse for a slow response time or poor execution, particularly if you take advantage of the combined power of the Internet and various applications of technical automation. If you do, you can significantly reduce your 'hands-on approach' while increasing your revenues and your free time.

Find a Mentor and Model

Who do you know that is getting the results you want and living the lifestyle you'd love for yourself? Regardless of age, sex or even specific industry, you can always find someone. Prosperous and successful individuals recognize and respect their role in giving back to those following behind them. Many such individuals will surprise you with their willingness to help, provided you approach them respectfully and patiently. Sometimes I've paid for their time — or at least their lunch!

199

Find a mentor, listen to what they have to say and take action. Luckily, my personal mentor was my own father, Robert "Bob" Bell. We spend countless hours talking about business and I could never thank him enough for his words of wisdom (*Thank you, Dad!*).

Model your business on winners. Why try to re-invent the wheel? Use already-proven strategies or systems. Pioneering the West was a risky business; it's no different to arrive first in any market or industry.

Every entrepreneur wants to improve his or her sales opportunities. We all want fresh and plentiful leads that lead to sales. I faced the challenge of finding new customers in my first jobs and these experiences provided the motivation for developing Marketer's Choice software and starting my own company — 1ShoppingCart.com Corporation. I constantly look for multiple ways to leverage my time and get more accomplished. Previously, before the advent of personal computers, I worked as a salesman. Often, I'd be the number one seller just by instituting simple, easily executable systems. One was a fax card request that asked customers what they wanted to buy prior to their exact moment of need. This singular, paper-based system had literally hundreds of leads on my desk before my colleagues made their first phone call of the day. It provided a proven, tested model. Marketer's Choice automated marketing system now provides salespeople with the tools they need in the Internet era.

"Never Give Up"

There are two sides to quitting. One is giving up out of frustration or hard times, the other, stopping a beneficial activity that you've undervalued or perhaps not recognized the importance of.

With respect to quitting when it's hard, I choose to focus on the "reasons why" I'm putting myself under pressure, losing sleep, enduring travel or facing any ordeal. Find out what drives you and keep it in the front of your mind at all times. Actually, I keep my "reasons why" in pictures around my office. My amazing wife, Maria, and our three boys Ryan, Jason and Justin all drive my ambition. Some people have not yet found their true love and a best friend, as I have. We all need to find our "Maria." Maria has always provided me with the freedom to pursue my goals and dreams, and although it's been a rough road many times over, she has always been there to inspire, support, and most of all, empower me to believe in myself. Use caution in the selection of those in a similar position of influence over you – friends, colleagues, suppliers and employers. Make sure your "friends" inspire, support and empower you.

As admirable as it is to think like Winston Churchill and his "Never surrender!" type of determination, you must also look at where you fail by stopping activities that are *actually working for you*! The failure to use more methodical methods involving testing and tracking to reach maximum performance levels causes many businesses to struggle. This means that they don't know what is working, nor do they have any idea what is not working. A marketing campaign may work wonders, but your company (or the ad agency) may scrap it out of boredom. Before you quit for good or bad, test and track all your results in order to make your decision based on facts — not feelings.

Use Internet-based tactics to test your headlines, ads, promotions and offers, even if you intend to use them offline. Sadly, most media attention has focused solely on the ability to "sell online" to the exclusion of many other positive and helpful attributes of online processes.

In Closing

The strategic use of automation truly defines who wins when applying Internet-based solutions. With the right "Systematic Automation," you can put many of the processes needed to sell your products and services and support your customers on "cruise control" by using technology.

Furthermore, you can control your business more easily, and win back more of your time and your LIFE! "Systematic Automation" will allow you to multiply your discretionary time. Whether you choose to focus on your business, travel for fun, do charitable work, take more family time or finally get to your favorite recreation or hobby, you should think about how you can use "Systematic Automation" today!

If you like what you've read ... check this out!

FOOTNOTES

*Go to www.MarketersChoice.com to get your $3.95 no-obligation, 30-day trial for improved automation and immediate execution in your business. **Rob Bell** is the President and CEO of 1ShoppingCart.com Corporation. He has 20-plus years in direct sales, marketing and management.*

From Niche Markets to Fragmentation

by Stephen Pierce

Think about something Bill Cosby said and ask yourself: "How does this apply to my current marketing?" Cosby stated, "I don't know the key to success, but the key to failure is trying to please everyone."

Are you trying to be everything to everybody? Or are you trying to be one specific thing to everybody?

Re-examine your marketing strategy, trim the fat, and focus on specific niche markets. Heck, go even further than niche marketing and fragment that niche into micro-levels.

For example, there are two broad markets that relate to some of our offerings. They are "investors" and "traders." These two very distinct groups of people approach stocks and futures trading in completely different ways.

So, we go to the internal niche markets of "traders" and look at "stock traders" and "futures & commodity traders" and "forex traders."

In fragmenting these markets, we go on a micro-level to create multiple opportunities such as "stock day traders," "emini stock day traders," "futures day traders" and "index futures day traders." How about options trading? You have "stock options traders," "futures options traders" and "forex options traders."

The needs, desires, must-haves, should-haves, and so on, of each fragmented group, are different.

Although, all traders want to make money, how they trade, why they trade and what they trade, require different input and processes to get to that desired outcome.

By understanding this and marketing accordingly, you can more strategically and intelligently build up "monster profits" as you cater to the specific customized needs for each fragment.

Take a look at your market. Are you targeting a niche right now? If not, what are the possible niches within the broader market you are targeting? If you are targeting a niche, What are the possible fragments of that niche?

For example, many would consider gardening to be a niche. Yet, inside this niche, you have "kinds of gardens" like the popular Japanese Garden.

However, when fragmenting the Japanese Garden down on a "micro-level," there are "tea gardens," "rock gardens" and even "water gardens," which all represent different kinds of Japanese Gardens.

A quick look at these different kinds of Japanese Gardens will reveal that although they share similarities, they also have many differences.

What other kinds of gardens are there? How about "organic gardens?" How about a "vegetable garden?" What about plants? How many different kinds of plants do people grow in their gardens? How could these possibly be fragmented? Perhaps "roses" and "tulips" could represent fragments.

How about an "indoor garden," "outdoor garden" or "garden furniture" as some other quick examples for possible fragments?

With stronger micro-positioning, you can shore up greater profits. Discover the power of going beyond the niche market and into fragmenting those niches into even smaller, more specific and specialized sections.

Look to dominate fragments, which can lead to dominance in that niche. Sure, you will end up with fewer clients and customers on a fragmented level, however, these will be better clients and customers; when it comes to fragmented marketing, less is more when the customers are loyal.

Don't Be a Dead Fish

Linda Ellerbee says, "Only dead fish swim with the stream all the time."

When it comes to your marketing, are you a dead fish following conventional marketing, sticking to the status quo and following what has become the "best practices" of chasing fads, copycatting, duplicating and ripping off?

If so, it's time for you to break out of your hypnotic state and start tinkering with your business strategy to unlock a new wealth of opportunities.

Stop being a "me too" copycat in your product offerings and marketing. Stop trying to out-muscle and out-hustle your competition. The winners will be those that *outthink* their competitors.

Don't play by others' rules. Create your own rules that will catch both your market and competitors off guard; to the delight of the customers and to the dismay of your competition.

Strategic marketing is not about copying others and then trying to beat them with speed, muscle and operations. Strategic marketing means out-thinking your competition and making them irrelevant.

203

The best competitive position is to have no competition at all. That's accomplished by changing the rules of play and deploying a distinctive strategy that is in your favor.

Can you finish this phrase: "Those who live by the sword. ..." Chances are you said, "Those who live by the sword die by the sword."

INCORRECT!

The fact is, "Those who live by the sword get shot by those who don't."

It's time you focus your energies and resources on developing and implementing a superior marketing strategy that again neutralizes your competitors.

Being strategic allows you to expand your profits not only by rendering your competition irrelevant, but also by bringing in dollars that reach beyond the small universe you may find yourself stuck in as you continue to recycle dollars between yourself and affiliates/partners in your value network.

Another important reason why you must be dramatically different from and strategically superior to your competition is that you are competing with not only the seen, but the unseen.

Someone in a garage somewhere is creating a product or service that has a bullet with your name on it.

If you do not make your competitors irrelevant, someone is guaranteed to step up and make you irrelevant.

Bill Gates once said, "Microsoft is always two years away from failure."

If Microsoft, which has something like a 90 percent of the market share, fears becoming irrelevant, "What should you be thinking about?

Regardless of the success you may be experiencing today, if you become comfortable and stagnant, you will become part of a "Where Are They Now?" episode.

Whether your approach is "revolutionary" or "evolutionary" in product and service development, your marketing strategy needs to be superior.

Why?

Strategic positions are being overturned quickly, and product lifecycles are shrinking faster than ever.

Every business must prepare for obsolescence. Whatever you sell will become obsolete sooner or later, probably sooner when you consider the quick pace of change.

Polaroid advises: "You should make your own products obsolete instead of letting your competitors do it for you."

So, start looking a client and/or customer ahead.

Allocate resources, not just for today's strategy and clients and/or customers, but for tomorrow's as well.

Like a hockey player, who anticipates and strategically moves to where the puck is going, you need to not only look at where your market is today, but also strategically move to where the market, technology and profits will go tomorrow.

In other words, a strong predictor of your success is your ability to adapt, visualize and change.

Offline Street Marketing Strategy

Here's a barely-legal street-marketing strategy for you. Print up some 3x5 postcards that hype up the benefits of your product and include ordering information and your Web site details.

Then, hit every bookstore you can find and go to a section of books that will draw readers who would have an interest in your product. Pull out one book at a time and slip your postcard into the center of each one.

The alternative is to do something that we do. We recruit local retail outlets to be affiliates and give them referral cards with their referral IDs on them along with a "take-one" display stand that they can put on their counters.

This is a very simple strategy and can usually be approved at the local management level when dealing with chains and franchises.

We have secured locations with National City Bank, Office Depot, FedexKinkos, American Express, Bath & Body Works, Bally's Total Fitness and many other local companies.

"You Got'em, Now Keep'em!"

Marketing strategically requires an understanding of the distinction in strategies between getting new clients and keeping existing clients.

The marketing you use to bring in new clients is different from the marketing you use to keep clients and build loyalty.

Many paralyze their profits because they don't know there is a difference, or simply don't care about the difference.

Although, we would all love to get new clients and customers, the cost of acquisition is much higher than the cost of building momentum with those already doing business with you.

205

Ignoring your current client base or trying to generate continued business from them improperly carries a huge opportunity cost of countless dollars lost and unrealized added value for the client.

Ask yourself, "Do I really need a ton more of new clients?" Perhaps you only need to turn your existing clients into better buyers.

In either case, expand your marketing by using different strategies for *obtaining* and *retaining* clients and customers.

For example, with your current clients try creating a bridge from the old to the new. In other words, acknowledge their previous purchase and create a "benefit link" to a new offering. Show how the new offering can make the prior offering better, more complete and more powerful, etc..

You can also offer different bonus bundles exclusively to current clients and customers that are not available to new clients. Consider "privileged pricing" or "preferred pricing," which allows your best clients to purchase at lower prices.

However you decide to structure your marketing to existing clients and customers, keep in mind that your offers should be skewed to benefit your most profitable client and/or customer group and not to reward your least profitable group.

The point is: "You got'em, now keep'em!"

Serendipitous Innovations

Those with radar-like awareness can take a "chance-discovery" in the environment, recognize its importance, extract the concept and use it to make an innovative contribution.

Serendipity means finding valuable and agreeable things when one is not seeking them.

There are many examples of such finds: penicillin by Alexander Fleming, who accidentally left a dish of bacteria uncovered for several days; saccharine by Constantine Fahlberg, who ate his lunch without washing his hands after his experiment; offset printing by W. Rufel when he failed to place a sheet of paper on a lithograph machine; Charles Goodyear, who spilled a mix of crude rubber and sulphur on a hot stove and discovered vulcanization.

If serendipity suggests "chance-discovery" — the finding of things of value when we are not actually looking for them — the finder must at least be able to see the creative possibilities of his or her own discovery.

Serendipity goes against the grain of narrow-focus thinking, where one concentrates one's mind upon an objective or goal to the exclusion of all else. It invites one to have a wide span of attentions — wide enough to notice something of significance even though it is apparently irrelevant or useless at that time.

We are more likely to be serendipitous if we have a wide span of attention and a broad range of interests. Thus, serendipity needs to be earned first.

Things that happen unpredictably, without discernible human intention, can be incorporated into the process of creative thinking. To see and recognize a clue in unexpected events demands creativity and observation.

To interpret the clue and realize its possible significance requires knowledge without preconceptions, imaginative thinking and the habit of reflecting on the unexplained observations. Some original flair also helps. To quote Louis Pasteur, "Chance favors only the prepared mind."

Get more of Stephen Pierce's "Multi-Dimensional Marketing Strategist" go to www.multi-dimensionalmarketing.com

If you like what you've read ... check this out!

FOOTNOTES

*Stephen's dynamic facilitations take place in an amazing environment that includes collaborative and "experiential" learning to show businesses how to apply innovation and creativity tools to get and keep the competitive edge in product development and marketing. **Innovation Marketers** is a company engaged in strategic thinking, planning and marketing. Visit **www.innovationmarketers.com** for more information. Also visit **www.stephenlive.com** for a free video coaching session from Stephen!*

207

How To Get More Publicity and PR Without Getting Naked, Arrested or Dying

by Martin Wales

Madonna got naked in her SEX book. Janet Jackson flaunted her breast at The Super Bowl. O.J. Simpson and Robert Blake were tried and acquitted of murder charges. Sadly, Terry Schiavo and the Pope both faced serious illnesses and died in the public eye.

All of them were famous or infamous, and the world now knows their names. For altogether, different and more positive reasons, *you need to be famous too!*

Want to reach millions of people, gain massive credibility and attract the best prospects in your target market without expensive advertising? Publicity and public relations (PR) can help you to introduce yourself and your business to new prospects and attract bigger and better opportunities.

What's it worth to you to be recognized as the leading expert in your industry?

You'll never succeed at whatever you do if people DON'T KNOW YOU EXIST.

Unless you're known, you're invisible!

Even if you do have some "visibility," without *the right* experience, appropriate credibility or professional notoriety, you won't see much success either. But, there is a way to change that and there has never been a better time.

Anyone can create their own publicity, PR and media machine ... guaranteed! This is the dawn of the age of Media ME! aka personal media or niche media. Best of all, you can do it quickly, easily and cheaply — even without any experience!

Use the Internet and your voice to reach only your best prospects and your customers — your target market — without paying to reach the general public who don't have a need for your company's products or services.

How do I know and why would you listen to me? I am not a PR agent or publicist. I make my living as a coach and consultant, but now I'm the Director of *Entrepreneur Magazine*™ Radio, Business Development and Affiliate Programs and a successful radio host and TV personality. *I've personally generated over $4 million worth of media exposure in a single year for myself without a PR agency and without sending a single press release.*

Combine Credibility and Celebrity to CASH In Big Time

Have you been struggling to get your name out there? Are you fed up and frustrated about spending your hard-earned cash and precious time you don't have on marketing that isn't getting the results you want fast enough, or that's just plain bombing out?

You're not alone if you have. Many do it the WRONG way. Hundreds of entrepreneurs, business owners, consultants and independent professionals waste millions of dollars and thousands of hours on publicists, PR agencies and press agents every year with little or NO results.

Don't get me wrong. In certain situations, and for many larger companies, the "traditional" PR and publicity tactics can and do work well. But they often take way too long and aren't effective enough if you don't have a HUGE budget (especially if you want national or international attention) and a whole lot of time.

Increase Your Fame and Fortune Today!

You can take advantage of the power of the Internet and some simple pieces of affordable recording hardware and software to create your own media! That's right, why wait at the big (usually closed) doors of all the big name media, like, "The Wall Street Journal," "Forbes," "The New York Times," or to get on all the big city talk radio shows?

With the right strategy, format and presentation, you can create your very own Talk Radio Show. Win yourself that potent and powerful combination of third party referrals, trusted branding, and concrete credibility to create priceless leadership positioning and favored "trusted advisor" status (*Then you can charge what you want and work when you want!*). Stop forever being treated like a commodity! Think about it. How are TV, radio hosts and personalities treated and perceived?

Imagine the benefit of burning your name and company into the minds and onto the tongues of all those in your industry. How does it sound to you to have your name synonymous with the leading and preferred supplier of your specific expertise?

How much value is there in being able to actually hold influence over the market you serve? Just picture customers seeing you as the undisputed source of

209

trusted opinion, helpful recommendations and advice — because you are. That would be powerful — wouldn't it?

Build a waiting list of preselected and pre-qualified prospects who are not just curious about your products and services, but who are predisposed and prepared to buy right now at whatever price levels YOU set — with no objections.

Reach Hundreds, Thousands or Millions With Your Message

Let me ask you: *"If you could easily reach hundreds or thousands of more people on a regular basis with your important message, working from a home office by doing what you love.... 'How would that change your business and your life?'"*

You CAN with the most exciting and rapidly growing publicity and communication tool today — Internet Radio and Audio Marketing.

How many people really know who you are — or your business? If no one has ever heard of you, "How can they even begin to appreciate you or your products and services?" How do they know how to buy from you?

It's tough to say and to face, but "If nobody knows who you are — you're INVISIBLE!" Sounds obvious, but many remain oblivious to this blunt reality.

I know. I used to be invisible myself. For years, I struggled as an independent consultant and speaker. There was lots of stress and little money. Sometimes no money (*Like I said earlier, no one knew who I was*).

Well, as a 41-year-old, ex-high-school science teacher from Toronto, Ontario. ... I've since had the pleasure to hook with up with Tony Robbins, Michael Gerber, Zig Ziglar, Harvey MacKay, Al Ries, Peter Lowe, Jay Abraham, Mark Victor Hansen, Jack Canfield, Robert Allen and Dan Kennedy. There have been a lot of entertainers and celebrities, too, but that was just for fun! I've had the pleasure of interviewing them, meeting them in person, working with them and even sharing the stage.

Most importantly, there have been connections made with executives and influential business figures, such as Steve Balmer from Microsoft and Mark Benioff from SalesForce.com or Jay Nali, an Executive VP of IBM, and so on — too many to name here. Imagine what opportunities could be yours with introductions to these powerful people, industry insiders, trend setters and market movers. All through activities related to publicity.

The Exact Step-By-Step Process and Strategy You Need For More Publicity and PR

You have much of what you need already. You just haven't recognized or leveraged it yet. Reach your goals and dreams by using something *you and only you* have that costs nothing to acquire or operate — something that you use all day, every day anyway! What am I talking about? YOUR VOICE!

Maybe you've already heard about Internet Radio. However, you must realize and recognize that it is so *much more* than just fun and entertainment on your PC.

Internet Radio is the newest medium for audio marketing for professionals like you and it has more than *eight times* the listening audience of satellite radio right now!

Why It Takes More Than A Microphone

You may already know how cheap Internet access and increasingly powerful personal technology have created a world of "broadcasters," but just because someone has a microphone doesn't make him an excellent or average speaker, a presenter or even a talk radio host.

Certainly, anyone with a pulse and a PC can suddenly blog or market his or her way to some notoriety, however, for the serious business professional, entrepreneur, speaker or consultant looking for the best way to use this new world of communications has to ask, "what really makes sense?"

Even if you don't want to be an Internet Radio talk show host, you can still use these exact same concepts, strategies and tactics to improve and profit from audio marketing. It works for your personal phone marketing, your PR interviews, your teleconferences or teleseminars, public speaking and especially any audio on your Web sites.

Internet Radio strategies and tactics are especially useful if you're at all interested or curious about the latest and hottest trends — satellite radio and podcasting. Audio has now gone portable and works wirelessly. Without this knowledge, you'll be left behind as an information marketer. There is an exploding field in personal media and "citizenship journalism."

Why You Can't Fail With This Affordable and Powerful Media

The more people who hear what you have to say, the more they know who you are — and the more in demand you become! For a tiny fraction of a traditional media budget, you can get 10, 100 or 1000 times the benefits through the magic and power of digital media! Consider the following about using Internet Radio and Audio Marketing:

• The first-ever broadcast medium requiring no special equipment or license of any kind!

That's right. If you have a phone and a computer, you basically have the equipment you need to succeed. You can buy special equipment, including high-end microphones and recording gear — but *"you don't need any of it to get started."*

• The first-ever broadcast medium that has flat pricing for 100-person markets or even 100 million!

211

If you have ever purchased, or inquired about air time on traditional broadcast media, including radio, you know that the pricing varies hugely with the size of the actual or likely audience. The larger the media market, the more you have to pay for the air time. On the Internet, and with portable audio, your market can be literally everyone in the world. ***With a computer, your costs do not change.*** With digital recording technology, CDs, MP3s and "podcasting," you can reach your market without needing a live Web connection!

• The first-ever broadcast medium with NO barrier to entry!

You might have a spectacular voice and come up with brilliant insights. You might be able to host "The Tonight Show" with flair. On the other hand you might be a normal person with a pleasant speaking voice trying to sell more of whatever you do for a living. On Internet Radio, these three types are basically equals. If you want to use audio marketing and if you can carry on a normal conversation knowing something about your area of interest, you're all set!

• The first-ever broadcast medium that both copies others and forges new ground daily!

Did you know that Microsoft is currently crafting Internet programs based on the play-lists of dozens of traditional radio stations? The radio stations say that they don't mind, but they're *still* filing lawsuits.

Did you know that a major broadcasting firm with an ethnic demographic skew just spent $56 million to buy what amounts to a couple of Web sites because those Web sites have over half a million subscribers for Internet Radio broadcasting?

Increase Your Visibility, Your Credibility And Your Income Today

Did you know that you can start broadcasting on the Internet for minimal cost with no technical knowledge, no special or expensive equipment and no experience?

From teleconferences and teleseminars, to web seminars, to traditional broadcast radio and television presentations, you must know and decide how to position yourself and your company to create concrete credibility and public recognition.

With the right information and resources, you can get going immediately to create your own media and begin the momentum that leads to mainstream media attention and industry accolades.

Internet Radio and Audio Marketing provides the fastest, most affordable publicity and PR for you. It's *exactly* how to get from where you are to where you want to be in the age of Media ME!

If you like what you've read ... check this out!

FOOTNOTES ♬

*Personal Media Specialist, **Martin Wales**, is the former host of **Entrepreneur Magazine's E-Biz Show**. Martin's traditional radio broadcast experience includes business talk radio in top 10 media markets in North America. Get your FREE Internet Radio Handbook now at **www.RadioTalkShowHost.com** You can reach **Martin** at **martin@CustomerCatcher.com**.*

Bullet-Proof Your Business

What Successful Entrepreneurs Wish They Had Known When They Were Starting Out

by Ellen Stiefler, Esq.

"**If only I knew then what I know now.**" I wish I had a penny for every time I've heard those words from my clients ... especially since they include some of the most successful entrepreneurs in the world.

I am honored to represent many of the brilliant entrepreneurs featured in this book, as well as its publisher and others whose names you would instantly associate with wealth and success. *All of them* have experienced bumps along their paths to success.

Wouldn't it be wonderful if we could learn from others' mistakes and use those lessons to chart a smoother course for our own entrepreneurial journey?

After 20-plus years of experience as an intellectual property attorney working with entrepreneurs, I've seen every obstacle you may confront on the road to success. I've been privileged to be able to help my clients navigate around these treacherous potholes.

Now, I have taken what I've learned in those two decades of experience and condensed them into the **Top Ten Steps to Bullet-Proof Your Business**.

Use my advice as a map on your own road to success. If you follow these steps, you will achieve success faster, have more fun, and save yourself time, money and headaches along the way.

1. Assemble your team. Hire the best accountant and lawyer you can afford and recruit your wisest and most trusted friends and colleagues to serve as your advisors. Hiring professionals is a smart investment. They will more than pay for their cost in tax savings and good advice.

2. Incorporate. There are a number of ways to organize and run your business. You will work very hard to accumulate wealth. Don't lose it. **Bullet-Proof Your Assets.**

To protect your assets, you need a form of business entity that gives you

limited liability protection. This will insulate you from the liabilities and debts of your company. Your personal exposure will be limited to the amount of your investment in the business. Your home, personal investments and other assets will be protected.

There are several limited liability entities to choose among. No doubt you've heard of "S" and "C" Corporations, limited liability companies and limited partnerships. For a thorough discussion of the pros and cons of each choice, as well as more detailed guidance about which form of business entity may be best for you, and step-by-step instructions and forms to set up that entity, go to www. BulletProofYourCompany.com.

3. Don't take action on behalf of your company in your individual name. Having a corporate entity will not protect you from personal liability if you take business actions in your own name rather than as an officer of your company. Never make personal guarantees on contracts or loans and don't act or sign documents in your individual name — only do so in your official capacity.

4. Register your trade name to avoid personal liability. You probably are familiar with the concept of "doing business as" under a trade name. What you may not realize is that if you are a corporation and you drop the "corporate indicator" (that's the "Inc.," "Company," "Corp" or "LLC") you can end up with personal liability for the acts and liabilities of the corporation. For example, Minnesota Mining and Manufacturing Company had to register to do business as "3M" or their officers would have been held personally liable for the acts of that big company.

Your corporate indicator puts the world on notice of your limited liability protection. If you drop that term in your brochure, Web site or other places where you hold yourself out to the public, you can be held personally liable for your company's acts.

To protect yourself, you must file a form registering your corporation as doing business under its trade name. Your attorney can take care of this for you, or you can contact your local county recorder and ask for the form to register a "Fictitious Name" or an "Assumed Name" certificate. After you file the certificate, you will have to publish your registration in local newspapers. You can find more guidance on what to do at www.BulletProofYourBusiness.com.

5. Create a Business Plan. Behind most successful businesses is a good business plan. The old adage is true: *plan the work and work the plan.* The process of writing a business plan will highlight the dangers that you can then avoid once you see them.

Guidance on writing a business plan and templates to work from are available at www.BulletProofYourBusinessPlan.com.

6. Catch a Thief. If imitation is the highest form of flattery, you'll know you are onto a great business idea when others try to copy or steal your ideas.

Here are a few tips that may stop them in their tracks and allow you to catch the thief red-handed.

Waving a big stick deters theft. Prominently displaying notice of your intellectual property rights, whether by using a copyright, trademark notice or a trade secret legend, may make someone think twice before stealing your property.

The best way to catch a thief is to plant hidden "footprints" where they won't be noticed. Then, if the thief denies stealing your software or database or written work, let him explain why your children's birthdates appear in the object code of his computer program, or why small typos that you deliberately included in a sensitive document are reproduced in what he is trying to pass off as his own.

7. Get an Intellectual Property Audit. Your intellectual properties (IP) – copyrights, trademarks, trade secrets and patents — are among your most valuable business assets. To maximize their value to you and your business, you can't afford not to identify, own and protect your IP.

There is no substitute for meeting with a good intellectual property attorney. Ask the attorney to conduct an IP Audit. A good IP Audit will identify your intellectual property, confirm that your IP is protected and give you a plan of action to fix any problems. Then, you can leverage what you own to your best advantage.

You can save time and money by being well-prepared for your meeting with the attorney. You will find an extensive list of questions to prepare for your IP Audit at www.BetterAskMyLawyer.com.

8. Protect Your Intellectual Property. Depending on the type of IP you own, there are different methods to protect it. You will find a detailed explanation of every type of intellectual property and the process for protecting it at www. BulletProofYourIntellectualProperty.com.

Here are some steps you can take on your own to begin protecting your intellectual property:

• **Bullet-Proof Your Trademarks.** A trademark is a word, symbol, sound or color that identifies the source of goods (i.e. Coca-Cola). A service mark performs the same role for services (i.e. American Express). Trademarks come into existence when they are first used and can be renewed forever as long as you continue to use them. You also can reserve a mark before you use it by filing an intent-to-use application with the United States Patent & Trademark Office.

Registration of a trademark is not required although there are benefits to obtaining a Federal trademark registration through the USPTO. Use a "TM" or

"SM" in superscript beside the term you want to develop as your Mark. Do not use the ® symbol until you achieve federal registration.

Even before your IP Attorney conducts a full search to tell you if your trademark is available, you can search to see if it is being used as a domain name, and also run the mark through a search engine and the USPTO records to see what other uses you can find.

Trademark rights are given priority based on first use. There are stories of famous companies like McDonald's and Citigroup having to pay big money to buy out the interests of small users because they failed to check out who had been using their trademarks before they did. If you find that others are using the mark you want to use, consult with an IP attorney before you proceed.

You can find a lot more detailed and helpful information to protect your trademarks at www.BulletProofYourTrademarks.com.

• **Bullet-Proof Your Copyrights.** Copyrights exist in original works of authorship fixed in a tangible medium of expression such as literary, dramatic, musical and artistic works, both published and unpublished. You cannot copyright an idea, but you can copyright the expression of that idea.

Copyrights come into existence the moment they are created. You no longer have to put a "copyright notice" on your work to own a copyright. I still highly recommend that you display a copyright notice on your work in this form: "©"; the year your work was created or first published; and the name of the copyright owner.

You don't need to register a copyright, but there are many advantages in doing so. You will preserve some very significant benefits if you register your copyright within 90 days of first publication of the work. Use that time frame as a guide for action.

You can find registration forms and helpful information on how to protect your copyrights at www.BulletProofYourCopyrights.com.

• **Bullet-Proof Your Patents.** You can patent any new and useful industrial or technical process, machine, manufacture or chemical composition of matter. The system for protecting patents is complex and expensive. Don't sell anything you think may be subject to a patent until you consult with an attorney about filing a patent application.

Prior to meeting with your IP Attorney, preserve your rights in your invention by mailing yourself your invention diary by Express Mail. Then, keep the envelope unopened should the need for it ever arise.

Why do I insist that you use the US Postal Service rather than another carrier? Federal Courts have exclusive jurisdiction over patent cases and the US Postal Service is another Federal Agency, so there is an advantage in using the

217

Postal Service postmark to establish your date of invention.

Another early protection step you can take yourself is to pay $10 and file a Disclosure Document with the USPTO giving you proof of your date of invention. The Patent Office will hold this document for up to two years until you are ready to file your patent application.

You can find more helpful information about protecting your patents at www.BulletProofYourPatents.com.

- **Bullet-Proof Your Trade Secrets.** A trade secret is your competitive advantage. It can be a formula, a database, a recipe — anything you use in your business that is maintained in confidence and gives you an advantage over competitors who do not know or use it.

To establish and protect a trade secret, have anyone with whom you share the secret (i.e. an employee, investor or consultant) sign a Confidentiality and Non-Disclosure Agreement. You should also protect your trade secret using physical measures of security such as shredders, locks and restrictive legends. You can download a full list of my recommended security measures and also a fill-in-the-blank confidentiality form at: www.BulletProofYourTradeSecrets.com.

9. Bullet-Proof What You Own. One of the most common problems for entrepreneurs is not owning the intellectual property in "works for hire." Too often I've seen situations where someone paid good money to have something created for him — computer software, graphic designs, written works — only to discover that he doesn't own the IP rights in what he paid for.

Do not pay anyone to create work for you without having them sign a combination Work for Hire/Assignment Agreement. This agreement will cover all intellectual property rights that could arise in the work and ensure that you own them.

At www.BetterAskMyLawyer.com, you can download a fill-in-the-blank Work for Hire/Assignment Agreement form. Use this form every time you commission something to be created by anyone who is not an employee hired just for the purpose of creating that kind of product.

10. Bullet-Proof Your Website. Using domain registrars like GoDaddy.com, it is relatively inexpensive to buy domain names. Yet, I can't count the times I've negotiated an expensive domain name purchase for a successful entrepreneur who ended up paying far too much to buy the rights in a domain he could have bought for under $10 when he was starting out.

Domains with names similar to yours may become problematic when they divert your potential customers or when there is confusion in the marketplace for your products or services. Early on, it's best to secure not only your primary domain, but also all the common misspellings, plurals and singulars of your domain name. If there is a number in your domain name, don't forget to secure the spelled-out version as well as the numeral. Then, have your server forward web traffic to those secondary domains to your primary site.

If you discover there is a domain closely similar to your own that you want to purchase, using an intermediary to negotiate on your behalf may keep the price more reasonable. Although, there is an anti-cybersquatting law designed to prevent it, some opportunistic people will park a domain with the intention of selling it to the person who failed to buy it when they started their business ... and the price goes up the more successful the buyer becomes.

If you can negotiate to buy the competitive domain name, be sure to get a signed domain name transfer agreement. You can download the form at www. BulletProofYourWeb-Site.com.

If you do find yourself in a spat over a domain names, there are legal proceedings for cybersquatting, unfair competition and bad faith use and registration of domain names. But these proceedings to stop domain name abuses are expensive. When it comes to owning domain names, an ounce of prevention is worth a pound of cure.

In conclusion, if you follow these **Top Ten Steps to Bullet-Proof Your Business**, you will avoid many obstacles on the road to your success, making your journey more enjoyable and problem-free. Please feel free to contact me at Ellen@EllenStiefler.com if you want personal answers to any questions you may have.

"BULLET-PROOF YOUR BUSINESS: What Successful Entrepreneurs Wish They Had Known When They Were Starting Out" © *Amicus Partners LLC 2005. Reproduced with permission of the author.*

If you like what you've read ... check this out!

FOOTNOTES ♺

*You've seen **Ellen Stiefler** on **Good Morning America**, the **CBS Morning Show** and in newspapers across the country. A well-known attorney, author and speaker, Ellen is an expert on growing businesses, protecting your intellectual property and keeping you safe from identity theft.*

*Ellen is the creator of the **BULLET PROOF PROTECTION SERIES**. Go to: **www.BulletProofAdvice.com** to sign up for Ellen's **FREE "Things You Need To Know" Special Reports** (a $149 value) and get your **FREE** download of **THE BULLET-PROOF ENTREPRENEUR** (a ($99 value), a recording of Ellen's appearance on the "Ask the Expert" show on Business TV Channel.com.*

*More Information about Ellen is available at **www.EllenStiefler.com**.* ⟿

The World's Greatest Networker

by Harvey Mackay

So, who is the worlds greatest networker? The President of the United States.

Which President?

Any president.

Whoever is president at any give moment has made it there and succeeded or failed once in office on the basis of his networking skills.

Presidents grub around for votes in New Hampshire snowbanks. They call their friends and their friends' friends begging for money. They bargain with members of Congress, swapping appointments and pork-barrel projects for support for their legislative programs.

Presidents hold press conferences and try to reach beyond the hostile questioning to score points with the electorate. They travel to military installations to show their concern for the soldiers risking their lives for their country. They attend funerals, go abroad, project empathy with minorities and the disadvantaged, kiss babies, visit hospitals, attend fund-raisers, listen to lobbyists and big cigars, tell them how to run the country, they send up trial balloons, suffer fools, point with pride and view with alarm.

In other words, they are the ultimate networkers.

The book "Truman," by David McCullough, contains a story about Harry Truman when he was about to leave office. The Republican candidate Dwight Eisenhower had defeated Adlai Stevenson in the presidential election that fall. Ike had made an issue out of the failures of the Truman administration, and there was no love lost between the general and the former haberdasher.

"When Eisenhower gets here," said Truman, pointing to his desk, "he'll sit right here, and he'll say to do this, do that! And nothing will happen. Poor Ike.

It won't be a bit like the army. He'll find it very frustrating."

Truman was half right.

He knew that the Constitution grants a president only a tiny fraction of what he needs to govern and that the rest depends on his ability to persuade others to carry out his wishes.

But Truman was wrong in assuming that Ike didn't have that ability. Ike succeeded as Supreme Allied Commander in World War II not because he could bark orders louder than the other generals, but because he could handle prickly personalities like Montgomery, Patton, Churchill and de Gaulle.

He listened to their complaints. He mediated their disputes. He let them bask in the limelight. He flattered them. He cajoled them. He asked them their opinions. He thanked them for their input.

And then he won the war.

And then he won the election.

This is how presidents get to be presidents.

They write thank-you notes. George Bush was known as "the Rolodex Kid." Wheelock Whitney, a friend of mine who was a classmate of Bush's, told me that Bush wrote down the name of every person he met at every precinct, city, country, state, and national political gathering he attended over a lifetime, together with "whatever" personal information. He made a point of using that information as a creative way to stay in touch.

I know that's true because I have friends who heard Bush speak at a local political rally when he was vice president and met him briefly at a cocktail party. One of them promptly got a hand-written personal note from him that contained some factoid Bush had picked up from their meeting. The second one got a telephone call out of the blue one day when Bush was between planes at the Twin Cities airport.

Both of those people, substantial business types, have been dining out on their "close personal friendship" with "George" for the last decade and a half.

Bill Clinton the first Democratic president to be reelected since FDR, told "The New York Times" that for most of his life, every evening before he turned in, he listed every contact he'd made that day and entered the names on 3 x 5 cards, with vital statistics, time and place of the meetings and all other pertinent information duly noted.

Richard Nixon found a very creative way to capitalize on all the information he had collected. Say a fellow walked into Nixon headquarters and said what he did for a living, "I'm a barber," he might say.

221

"Okay, why don't you organize Barbers for Nixon? You're the president of the organization. Get a couple of your buddies and make them vice presidents. Get them to get some more people and they're presidents and vice presidents for a new chapter on the other side of town, and so on. And each of you throw in fifty bucks or so into a pot. When you get a few thousand dollars together, come back, and we'll put together an ad for you to run in the state barbers' trade paper."

The umbrella organization Citizens for Nixon had a ton of these groups going. One of them, Mayors for Nixon, had hundreds of members and so much money, the Sunday before the election, they ran half-page ads in "The New York Times" and "The Washington Post." The mayors' group included several who went on to national prominence, such as Dick Lugar, the senator from Indiana.

Politicians make the best networkers. One more story ought to hammer home this point.

Lyndon Johnson began his political career as a congressional aide in Washington. Slaving away in anonymity didn't appeal to the ambitious young Texan. He was eager to make political contacts.

Johnson was living at a cheap rooming house favored by other congressional aides. He began to take a half-dozen showers a day so he could "run into" his peers and build his network. Before long, Johnson was working the rooming-house john as adroitly as some pols can work a Fourth of July picnic.

Johnson didn't waste much time after that. He soon ran for and was elected president of the congressional aides' own network, the Little Congress.

Johnson's choice of venue for networking may not have been the best place in the world to make new friends, but he had the drive to make use of even the most limited opportunity and turn it to his advantage.

Presidents push their legislative programs using networking techniques.

You may think that members of Congress can waltz into the Oval office anytime they want, but most of them never see the president from one State of the Union speech to the next. On the rare occasion they are invited to the White House, they are like bush leaguers called up to The Show.

Many years ago, when Lyndon Johnson was president, the Republican congressional leadership consisted of Everett Dirksen of Illinois in the Senate and Charles Hallock of Indiana in the House. These two hard-bitten partisan midwestern Republicans conducted weekly press-conferences, which the press dubbed "The Ev and Charlie Show." They used them to blast Johnson.

One day, they had been particularly nasty about some legislation Johnson wanted. He invited the two of them to the White House for breakfast — and he got their support.

222

As they left to go back to the Hill, the press converged on them.

"Why did you do it, Charlie?"

"He sure knows how much we Indiana boys like our bacon sliced real thick" was all the dazzled Charlie could think to say. Not only was the pork served to Hallock's liking, but the rumor is he and Dirksen left with a couple of pork-barrel projects for their districts.

This became known as the "Johnson Treatment."

If you don't believe a little thing like that can determine the fate of nations, then I bet you didn't believe Newt Gingrich allowed the government to shut down because Bill Clinton made him and Bob Dole exit from the back of Air Force One when they returned from Yitzhak Rabin's funeral.

Yes, that is how petty politics can be and how much decisions affecting billions and billions of dollars of legislation can depend on networking.

Or, as Ev used to say, "A billion dollars here, a billion dollars there. Sooner or later, it adds up to real money."

MACKAY'S MAXIM
You don't have to be in politics to be a politician. Learn from the best.

If you like what you've read ... check this out!

FOOTNOTES ✝

Harvey Mackay is a bestselling author whose books include the mega-selling **"SWIM WITH THE SHARKS WITHOUT BEING EATEN ALIVE;"** *and a nationally syndicated columnist, whose weekly business advice appears in fifty newspapers around the United States. He is an active corporate CEO and a prominent civic leader. He and his family live in Minneapolis.*

Article excerpts reprinted from the book, **"DIG YOUR WELL BEFORE YOU'RE THIRSTY, THE ONLY NETWORKING BOOK YOU'LL EVER NEED"** *published by Doubleday, a division of Random House, Inc. Copyright © 1997 by Harvey Mackay. All rights reserved. Used here by permission.*

www.mentorsmagazine.com

How To Build Mind Capture

by Tony Rubleski

We live in an interesting age. Never before have people had so many choices, options and marketing messages to choose from. As businesses compete to win new business and retain repeat customers, they face intense, nimble competitors and highly selective skeptical prospects that have seen it all and believe little (if any) advertising they see.

What is MIND CAPTURE?

Mind Capture is simply the ability to stand out, get attention and win new business in a world with too many choices and demands placed on peoples' time.

Why should you care about this thing called "Mind Capture?" Simple. everything revolves around the ability to persuade and sell. Be it politics, education, parenting, religion or business, it all comes down to who can present the most compelling, believable and persuasive argument to win peoples' time, fleeting attention and trust. It may not seem fair, but it's the reality of the world we live in.

Everyone, regardless of social status, is impacted and touched by the forces of marketing. There's no escaping or hiding from it. Marketing messages will always be present and continue to increase. With each new gadget or technology comes a whole flood of new and skilled marketers ready to attack and grab your attention in hopes of getting into your head and gaining "Mind Capture."

Here's the amazing thing about the millions of dollars spent each day on marketing: most of it is overly intrusive, annoying, offensive, ineffective and flat-out pathetic. Businesses of all shapes and sizes try to get cute or clever, and then scratch their heads as to why the marketing function of the business isn't working. Marketing is looked at with disdain and often viewed as a necessary evil. This self-sabotaging behavior keeps most businesses stuck in neutral year after year, or it prevents them from trying to grow. Most refuse to see the importance of marketing, or why they should work at improving it.

So, how do we get busy prospects to listen to our marketing messages? This is a difficult question, but let me throw out an important clue.

Realize the external societal forces you're up against when creating marketing and advertising pieces

Here are six key characteristics of the 21st-century customer that you must acknowledge and consider to achieve maximum success:
- They're extremely cynical.
- They have too many choices.
- They're bombarded with 1,500-plus marketing messages a day.
- They're excellent at tuning out marketing messages.
- They're smarter than ever.
- They're time starved.

Cynical. With the continued meltdown of trust in large corporations (Enron, MCI/Worldcom, etc.) and the ever present skepticism directed at our elected officials, marketers need to realize that people are extremely cynical. Everyday it seems a new scandal breaks, and those individuals once held in high esteem, have been taken down due to poor judgment and blatant acts of dishonesty.

This carries over to marketing as well because consumers have been left high and dry in the past or promised the world from a shady competitor, they're very reluctant to believe your marketing messages. You've got to prove that your company will back up its claims and also make them look good for choosing you.

Too many choices. Open a phone book and look up the section marked "attorney." I'm guessing there are multiple pages listing hundreds of attorneys in your city alone. In many industries the competition is fierce, and customers will naturally hold their supplier's feet to the fire due to the fact that there's a long line of competitors outside the door begging for their business.

1,500-plus messages a day. Between 1,000- to 3,000-marketing messages bombard people every day, so we'll split the difference and assume the average person hears 1,500 messages a day. Today's customer lives in the age of information overload. There's radio, TV, Internet, cell phones, newspapers, mail and e-mail to name a few. Customers are saturated with an incredible amount of marketing messages. Everywhere you turn, someone's trying to get your attention or "Mind Capture."

This marketing noise will continue to grow as creative marketers look for any slight edge they can get to attract attention. I highly recommend you check out the film "Minority Report" starring Tom Cruise if you want to see an interesting look at what futuristic marketing could look like if technology can keep up.

Excellent at tuning out marketing messages. With the massive amount of marketing noise, stimuli and messages being thrown at people each day, they've

225

gotten very good at detecting and tuning out marketing messages. The challenge *ALL* marketers face is getting decision makers to take a few seconds to notice their message and present enough compelling reasons or curiosity for them to read your direct mail piece, e-mail, fax or listen to an ad or live sales rep.

The "BS detector" is always on!

Smarter than ever. With the age of information overload and the Internet, it's easy for prospects to research hundreds of competing products, services, prices and references with the click of a mouse. The Internet may not be as glamorous and sexy as it was a few years ago, but realize that it's not going to go away. People will use it to shop, do research and look for ways to improve their lives and businesses.

Time starved. People are busier than ever. They want convenience and things that will save time. Why do you think FedEx is so successful? They promise speed and peace of mind. If you can tailor your product or service to this way of thinking, your business will prosper.

In every marketing message or piece I create for a client, teach others how to do in a workshop or use for my own business, I continually mention that these six characteristics must not be overlooked. We're trying to get in the mind of the prospect and overcome certain barriers of resistance that we know our marketing message must address if we're going to achieve any degree of success.

So how do you build "Mind Capture" into your business?

It comes down to one key thing. *Using strong marketing EVIDENCE!*

In an age where customers are deluged with more choices than ever, you need to have strong marketing materials or "evidence" to build credibility with skeptical prospects and win more business. The old clichés such as "great service," "lowest prices" and "highest quality" are overused and simply not believable.

You have to prove your case with strong marketing evidence to win more business.

Here are Eight Ways To Strengthen and Build Evidence Into Your Marketing Efforts:
1. Use testimonials.
2. Use before and after examples.
3. Use pictures.
4. Use articles about your company.
5. Create and use a company newsletter.
6. Create client lists.
7. Use a powerful guarantee.
8. Use a "reasons why" sheet.

Use testimonials. This one drives me insane because so many businesses don't use them. In my opinion, they are the single most powerful tool you can employ to build credibility, back up your claims and break down barriers with skeptical prospects. They are one thousand times more believable than any other marketing piece you use to promote yourself or your company.

Testimonials help bridge the gap between skeptical prospects and your marketing message. Use them in all of your marketing!

Before and after examples. Give concrete examples or true stories of challenges a client had before doing business with you and how you solved them. This is a powerful way to clearly demonstrate to someone the old adage "if they can do it, so can I."

The entire infomercial (paid programming) industry uses great "before and after" examples to prove its case and drive people to pick up the phone and place an order — often times on pure impulse. Now that's powerful.

Pictures. Show-off happy customers who use your product or service. Pictures help build interest and curiosity and give visual proof to the sales and marketing message you're presenting.

A picture is worth a thousand words.

Articles about your company. Use favorable newspaper or trade articles about your business or industry to build third-party credibility and interest. People love a good or interesting story. In addition, people have a built-in tendency to believe that your company is legitimate if a newspaper or business publication features you.

Create and use a company newsletter or e-letter. A newsletter or e-letter has so many excellent benefits that I'm baffled why more businesses don't use them. A good, consistently mailed or e-mailed (at least once a quarter, preferably every month) newsletter adds immense value to your customers, prospects and vendors, which allows you the chance to stay in front of them, entertain, inform, offer new products or services, build goodwill and demonstrate your expertise.

Create client lists. Use a bullet page of major accounts (get permission from each client in advance) you serve to add validity and recognition when trying to earn new business. If you can create segmented lists by a specific industry (e.g. banks) this is even better. The whole point of a detailed client list is to show a prospect that you're reliable and have a history of success in the market place or within their particular industry.

Use a powerful guarantee. Back up your claims and offers with such a powerful guarantee that it makes it a no-brainer to do business with you. For example, in my own business, I offer a 100 percent unconditional one-year guarantee on any marketing tools we offer at workshops or seminars, in our mailings, e-letter or through one-on-one consulting. This lets our clients and prospects know that we're serious and passionate about our services helping their businesses.

227

Reasons why sheet. Create a one-page sheet that lists "Five, seven or 10 … reasons to do business with our company." Take your best benefits and solutions and condense them into simple, concise bullet points that clearly demonstrate the advantages of doing business with you.

If you have problems coming up with more than a few benefits, call or survey your existing customers and ask them point blank, "Why do you use our company?" You'll be amazed at the excellent feedback you'll get to add to your marketing arsenal.

Remember to use "Evidence" in **ALL** of your marketing efforts to win new business and positively increase your bottom line.

If you like what you've read … check this out!

FOOTNOTES

Tony Rubleski is currently president of Mind Capture Group. He helps businesses, sales professionals and entrepreneurs move beyond ordinary marketing to a much higher level of bonding with clients. His company specializes in sales and marketing training, advanced direct marketing and public relations campaigns for select clients. He has over 10 years experience in the direct selling and advertising fields.

He's presented to hundreds of audiences on marketing, sales and public relations-related topics the last several years and is a 10-year member of Toastmaster's International. His book titled "MIND CAPTURE: How To Generate New & Repeat Business In The Age of Advertising Overload" has received excellent reviews and interest from some of the top marketing and thought leaders on the planet. His work has been featured in "Bottom Line Personal magazine," "The Detroit Free Press" and the FOX Television news network. In addition, several world class marketing newsletters and experts have featured his marketing creations, book and revolutionary ideas including Dan Kennedy, Bob Burg and Mal Emery from Australia.

Tony publishes a weekly e-newsletter filled with proven and effective marketing and sales strategies to help businesses, sales professionals and entrepreneurs get ahead. You can contact Tony via email, tony@mindcapturegroup.com or by visiting his website: www.mindcapturegroup.com.

Word-of-Mouth Marketing Innovation

Unleash the Hidden Gateway to Exponential Growth

by Tim Sullivan

Are you ready to learn about the World's Most Powerful Marketing Secret? Few, if any, would question that Word-of-Mouth is the most effective, least expensive and easiest way to promote a product, service or idea. Yet surprisingly, most organizations know very little about how to innovatively and systematically best grow their Word-of-Mouth. So, let's begin the journey to help solve this mystery using the following facilitated-thinking pathway.

The Critical Need for Word-of-Mouth Marketing

According to recent market research, the average American adult now receives nearly 3,000 advertising impressions each day. Leading researchers have now determined that people are developing subconscious filters to screen out all irrelevant communication in order to cope with this information overload. Marketers, looking to conquer this symptom rather than the cause, increasingly "pump up the volume" of their marketing to increasingly disrupt people. This desperate approach, however, is proving to have the opposite intended effect, as witnessed by declining marketing recall and response rates.

According to recent US studies, nearly 66 percent of people interviewed distrust and question the motives of marketers, think advertisers disrespect them, believe most marketing and advertising is irrelevant and said they want products that block ads. It's clear that most people simply don't see, hear or act upon most traditional marketing messages, resulting in many sleepless nights for marketers.

Yet, few organizations fully, formally and actively understand, research, capture, nurture and leverage Word-of-Mouth. They simply don't know, hear and act on **what people tell other people about their products**, services, brand, organization and experiences in any organized way — even though this probably is the main reason for their success!

The Word-of-Mouth Marketing Paradox

"... the channel with the greatest influence in America is neither the traditional media of TV, radio or print advertising nor the new medium of the

World Wide Web, but the "human" channel of individual, person-to-person, word-of-mouth." -Ed Keller and Jon Berry, *The Influentials*

1. Paradoxically, Word-of-Mouth is the least-understood, most-overlooked and least-used marketing method — resulting in billions of dollars in lost sales annually. **Yet, Word-of-Mouth is widely regarded to be the most powerful and influential way to communicate your message and value to consumers to create action, and is directly responsible for creating 20- to 100-percent of an organization's customers and revenue.**

2. Ironically, most marketers focus more on trying to improve past marketing campaigns, countering or out-doing their competitors, or following an agency's creative suggestions rather than understanding and leveraging the organic, candid, and influential Voice of the Customer Word-of-Mouth of their "hidden" persuaders.

3. Incredibly, most marketers take Word-of-Mouth for granted and don't qualitatively and quantitatively know all that is being said by people to other people about their organization, products, services and experiences — or that more Word-of-Mouth is negative than positive.

4. Mistakenly, organizations believe that their marketing vehicles are primarily responsible for selling their products. The reality is that people are buying, most often not in a response to your marketing, but in response to what they hear from independent trusted sources.

5. Shockingly, most marketers believe that they can't do much about Word-of-Mouth and almost totally neglect Word-of-Mouth Marketing, thinking that it's too mysterious, invisible and uncontrollable, when in actuality it can be a highly manageable discipline, strategy and process.

6. Surprisingly, instructional books and manuals used for business courses taught at the university level seldom cover Word-of-Mouth Marketing. There is very little detailed public Word-of-Mouth Marketing information, education or training, and thus there are very few Word-of-Mouth Marketing experts. Yet leading organizations are beginning to exploit a comprehensive best practice Word-of-Mouth Marketing Innovation secret weapon that exists today, making Word-of-Mouth the world's best-known marketing secret.

Word-of-Mouth Marketing Definitions

Word-of-Mouth contains the ultimate, honest and influential seed of customer truth and in its natural state is the organic, verbatim Voice of the Customer, which is different and much more powerful than typical customer feedback. It's not what people selectively tell marketers, it's what people influentially tell other people. Thus, Word-of-Mouth Marketing's goal is developing raving fans who tell others about your products. What are people saying about your brand to other people?

When you think about it, you will notice that your friends, colleagues, family and trusted advisors have very strong positive influences on you, and probably vice versa. Word-of-Mouth recommendations and referrals from peers are by far the most powerful influence on buying decisions. What are some of the dozens of things that you bought based on a recommendation that you trust?

As Word-of-Mouth Marketing is a new discipline, there is a significant amount of confusion on precise definitions — you can't manage and improve that which you can't define. To help companies better define, investigate create, evaluate and activate Word-of-Mouth Marketing, we have developed the following standard definitions:

Key Term	Key Term Definition
Word-of-Mouth	Any independent person-to-person communication about a product, service, experience or entity.
Word-of-Mouth Marketing	Any face-to-face or oral marketing activity that stimulates person-to-person communication about a product, service, experience or entity.
Word-of-Mouth Marketing Innovation™	The Word-of-Mouth Marketing strategy, methodology and process for continually investigating, creating, evaluating and activating new and valuable Word-of-Mouth ideas.
Viral Marketing	Any online, pass-along or non-oral marketing activity that stimulates person-to-person communication about a product, service, experience or entity.
Buzz	The sum of all person-to-person communication, the total positive Word-of-Mouth minus the total negative Word-of-Mouth, about a product, service, experience or entity at any given point in time.
Buzz Marketing	Any offline or online person cluster or network-focused marketing activity that stimulates person-to-person communication about a product, service, experience or entity.
Guerrilla Marketing	Any unconventional or unexpected target audience-focused marketing activity to stimulate person-to-person communication about a product, service, experience or entity designed for maximum results from minimal resources.
Person-to-Person Marketing	The person-to-person communication marketing discipline that includes Word-of-Mouth Marketing, Viral Marketing, Buzz Marketing and Guerrilla Marketing.
Person-to-Person Marketing Innovation™	The marketing strategy, methodology and process for continually investigating, creating, evaluating and activating new and valuable person-to-person communication marketing ideas.

Viral Marketing, Buzz Marketing, Guerrilla Marketing, Influencer Marketing, Consumer Generated Media and Customer Activism etc. are built upon the Word-of-Mouth foundation and will be addressed in my upcoming publications.

Word-of-Mouth Marketing Principles

Let's further enlighten your path and marketing mind with this key thought: Getting people to *talk favorably* and *often* to the right people in the *right way about your product* is far and away *the most important* thing that you can do as a marketer. Word-of-Mouth Marketing is not revolutionary; it's evolutionary. It is beginning to cause the extinction of disruptive marketing practices, which may be challenging for traditional marketers. Word-of-Mouth's power differs from advertising in the following Key Principles:

Word-of-Mouth	Word-of-Mouth Principle Detail
Trust	Word-of-Mouth is based on the independence, credibility and honesty of the giver.
Dialogue	Word-of-Mouth is based on people conversing directly with other people.
Natural	Word-of-Mouth is organic and based on people's real experiences.
Remarkability	Word-of-Mouth is created by pleasantly surprising people.
Truth	Word-of-Mouth is based upon the truth inside you.
Benevolence	Word-of-Mouth is advice to help people avoid risks and make them happy.
Relationships	Word-of-Mouth is based on sharing, learning and connecting.
Empowering	Word-of-Mouth is people helping people make the right decisions.
Passion	Word-of-Mouth is people becoming activists for your brand.
Love	Word-of-Mouth is measured by people's love for your brand.
Power	Word-of-Mouth is attractive Power and will always overcome advertising distractive Force.

231

Who benefits by positive Word-of-Mouth & Word-of-Mouth Marketing? Everyone does — both giver and receiver. Studies have shown that the endorphin levels (the body's stress fighters) of people engaged in Word-of-Mouth conversations actually rise. In our research, we witness and measure peoples' muscles physically weaken in the presence of negative Word-of-Mouth and most advertisements, and strengthen when thinking of or receiving positive Word-of-Mouth within the powerful positive attractor fields that are created and sustained around its givers and receivers.

Word-of-Mouth Marketing Elements

To better understand the incredible power of Word-of-Mouth Marketing, it may be helpful to first visualize the following Word-of-Mouth Social Network example of how just *one* person can directly and indirectly influence hundreds of people exponentially.

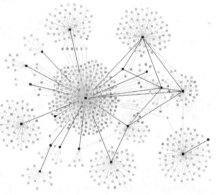

What are your Word-of-Mouth Marketing goals, strategies and vision? The ultimate Word-of-Mouth Marketing strategy is to create Customer Activists who make it their mission to do everything possible to see your brand succeed. To maximize your Word-of-Mouth Marketing success, there are several elements that you must first define and integrate. The organization that first gets this right wins the most customers.

Word-of-Mouth Marketing Element	Word-of-Mouth Marketing Element Detail
1. Roles	What are the connecting roles that people play in recommending your products to others?
2. Connections	What Word-of-Mouth transmitter and receiver connections make the best combinations?
3. Levels	How quantitatively likely are people to recommend your organization and products to others?
4. Classes	What are your Word-of-Mouth transmitter level classes, and how many people are in each class?
5. Polarity	What is the numeric positive or negative Influence Power of your Word-of-Mouth transmitter classes?
6. Motivations	What are the deep, driving motivations for people to transmit Word-of-Mouth about your organization, products, services and experiences?
7. Objectives	What are the overall objectives of people in transmitting Word-of-Mouth to recipients?
8. Formats	What are the formats of people's Word-of-Mouth messages and how can you better leverage them?
9. Characteristics	What are all of the unique personality traits that your Word-of-Mouth messages exhibit?
10. Adopter Types	What are the recognizable archetypes that people fall into when faced with buying your products?
11. Decision Stages	What are the key decision process stages that people go through in experiencing your products?
12. Adopter Concerns	What are people's key issues at each stage of their decision process for your products?
13. Messages	What is the key verbatim Word-of-Mouth that a transmitter uses to influence a receiver at each stage of their decision process?
14. Situations	What are the key places and times that people transmit Word-of-Mouth about your products?
15. Vehicles	From the Top 200 Word-of-Mouth Marketing Vehicles (Testimonials, Blogs, Trusted Advisor Endorsements, e-Mail Forwards etc.) which are best-suited to carry your Word-of-Mouth?
16. Campaigns	What are the best creative ways to integrate and leverage top Word-of-Mouth Marketing vehicles for maximum effect?
17. Success Pillars	What are the best ways to institutionalize Word-of-Mouth leadership into your organization?

The few organizations that are successful at Word-of-Mouth Marketing divulge very few details for obvious competitive reasons; however, a best practice

Word-of-Mouth Marketing Approach will define all of the previous Word-of-Mouth Elements within an innovation framework. Finally, as we are doing with our clients, your Word-of-Mouth Marketing should involve related external and internal disciplines such as Strategic Planning, Product Development, Public Relations, Customer Service, Technical Support and Sales to maximize its power.

Word-of-Mouth Marketing Benefits

If your work is based on sharing information and educating others, you will begin to see how Word-of-Mouth recipients benefit from receiving truthful, valuable information and objective recommendations to improve their lives and careers. Word-of-Mouth as an experience-revelation mechanism has shown to be the most powerful proximal purchase cause, or purchase trigger – essentially the experience that directly precedes purchase.

As an example of the direct benefits of Word-of-Mouth Marketing, a pharmaceutical firm increased sales of a medication by 600 percent through a physician-directed Word-of-Mouth Marketing program. If you could completely harness and nurture your Word-of-Mouth, what do you think your results would be?

Our research supports the common perception to be generally true that on average a happy customer will verbally tell two- to three-people, whereas an unhappy customer will tell four- to 10-people, and when people express their Word-of-Mouth on the Internet, the effect can be amplified a thousand-fold. Word-of-Mouth is the number one cause of Buzz and mastering Word-of-Mouth Marketing will help your organization improve your:

Word-of-Mouth Marketing Improvement	Word-of-Mouth Marketing Benefit Detail
Sales Revenue	Organizations can routinely increase their sales by 200%-1,000% through a disciplined Word-of-Mouth Marketing based program.
Buyer Decision Speed	Word-of-Mouth Marketing is the #1 way to increase the speed in which buyers make decisions.
Growth Rate	Due to its compounding, exponential effect, Word-of-Mouth Marketing increases growth faster than any other marketing or sales method.
Marketing Effectiveness	Word-of-Mouth-enabling all of your marketing vehicles will significantly improve response rates.
Customer Acquisition Cost Efficiency	It takes less time and costs much less to gain customers through Word-of-Mouth Marketing than any other form.
Customer Acquisition	Customers gained through Word-of-Mouth are more likely to spread Word-of-Mouth.
Customer Loyalty	Customers gained through Word-of-Mouth are more loyal to your organization and products.
Profitability	Customers gained through Word-of-Mouth less price sensitive and cost less to serve as they don't suffer from marketing hype expectations.
Customer Insight	Word-of-Mouth research will help you better understand your customers, their needs, what they truly value and their behaviors.
Product Development	Customers gained through Word-of-Mouth provide valuable product insights.
Financial Consistency	Done right, Word-of-Mouth Marketing will bring a constant flow of new customers and revenue.
Competitive Advantage	Whoever wins Word-of-Mouth Marketing wins customers, market share and the market.
Strategy	Word-of-Mouth may be the most solid foundation and focus of your marketing strategy and perhaps overall business strategy.

Word-of-Mouth Marketing can cut your buyers' decision process in half and will turn these new customers into customer activists who further recruit new customers via Word-of-Mouth - creating an exponential sales chain reaction.

Word-of-Mouth Marketing Innovation

Marketing leaders will innovatively capture and amplify their Voice of the Customer Word-of-Mouth advocacy through Word-of-Mouth

233

Marketing to exponentially drive their marketing, customer and revenue growth. The path to Word-of-Mouth Marketing success relies directly on Word-of-Mouth Marketing Innovation — the strategy, methodology and process for continually investigating, creating, evaluating and activating new and valuable Word-of-Mouth Marketing ideas.

Word-of-Mouth Marketing Innovation is simply the top customer-focused method to drive your business — as it is "The shortest path to the biggest pot of gold," according to The Word-of-Mouth Leprechaun. **Word-of-Mouth Marketing amplifies the tremendous power of Word-of-Mouth, and Word-of-Mouth Innovation is THE way to fully unleash the power of Word-of-Mouth Marketing.** However, virtually all organizations lack the following industry-leading 10 Stage Word-of-Mouth Marketing Innovation Process™ Framework and Model for securing successful Word-of-Mouth results.

Word-of-Mouth Marketing Innovation Process™

Word-of-Mouth Marketing Innovation is THE framework for discovering and implementing the most valuable ideas that get people talking to others about your products. The 10 Stages of the Word-of-Mouth Marketing Innovation Process™ support the Accelerated Innovation™ 4 Phases of: Investigate, Create, Evaluate and Activate. Skipping or inadequately covering any of the Word-of-Mouth Marketing Innovation Phases and Stages greatly diminishes your likelihood of exponential Word-of-Mouth success. How might you improve your Word-of-Mouth Marketing Innovation results? The following questions should help guide your thinking.

Word-of-Mouth Marketing Innovation™ Stage	Word-of-Mouth Marketing Innovation™ Stage Key Question
1. Resource *Preparation*™	What Resources do you need to develop a leading Word-of-Mouth Marketing discipline, expertise and programs?
2. Issue *Investigation*™	What are your top business Issues that can be improved through Word-of-Mouth Marketing?
3. Research *Exploration*™	What are the best ways to Research the key Word-of-Mouth about your organization, products, services and experiences?
4. Insight *Interpretation*™	What are the best ways to understand Word-of-Mouth Marketing best practices, research findings and new Insights?
5. Idea *Creation*™	What are the best ways to use experiential facilitated Ideation sessions to create the most and best Word-of-Mouth Marketing Ideas?
6. Concept *Evaluation*™	What are the best ways to refine, evaluate and select the most powerful Word-of-Mouth Marketing Concepts?
7. Solution *Planning*™	What are the best ways to develop your top Word-of-Mouth Marketing Concepts into the most powerful marketing Solutions?
8. Plan *Activation*™	What are the best ways to implement and manage your top Word-of-Mouth Marketing Plans?
9. Results *Appraisal*™	What are the best ways to measure and assess your Word-of-Mouth Marketing program Results?
10. Learnings *Leveraging*™	What are the best ways to maximize and share your Word-of-Mouth Marketing Learnings?

234

Leveraging the Word-of-Mouth Marketing Innovation Process™, we helped a project team set the World Record for Word-of-Mouth Marketing Idea Creation by generating 2,170 Word-of-Mouth ideas in just 8 hours and also helped an organization discover the "hidden" Word-of-Mouth Source, Situations and Messages responsible for their #1 sales outlet. Further, by leveraging Behavioral Science and Quality approaches, we are the first to numerically measure the power of Word-of-Mouth, Ideas, Concepts, Programs and Campaigns. Imagine the advantage of knowing beforehand what Word-of-Mouth elements have the strongest attractor power!

Word-of-Mouth Marketing Innovation Key Recommendations

The power to increase your marketing ROI and sales by a factor of 200- to 1,000-percent through Word-of-Mouth Marketing Innovation is now within your reach if you make Word-of-Mouth Marketing the cornerstone of your overall marketing strategy and:

#	Recommendation
1.	Make listening for, capturing and measuring organic Word-of-Mouth a top marketing priority.
2.	Undertake Word-of-Mouth Research and Analysis to discover and reach new insights.
3.	Leverage a best practice Word-of-Mouth Innovation Framework and Process.
4.	Conduct best practice facilitated experiential Word-of-Mouth Idea Creation Workshops to think outside-the-box.
5.	Design all of your marketing to be a Word-of-Mouth Generation System.
6.	Evaluate all of your marketing by its ability to maximize positive Word-of-Mouth.
7.	Make Word-of-Mouth your #1 marketing focus, and your organization will attract powerful Word-of-Mouth.

As you consider your next major marketing initiative, you should begin to see the many ways that Word-of-Mouth Marketing Innovation can improve upon what you are doing and provide you with the dynamic growth that you need. The question is, are you or your competition going to be the first to unleash this powerful secret competitive advantage?

www.mentorsmagazine.com

If you like what you've read ... check this out!

FOOTNOTES

Tim Sullivan is the creator of *Word-of-Mouth Marketing Innovation™* and the *Word-of-Mouth Power Rating™*. He is the leading advisor to companies looking to improve their Word-of-Mouth results. As a Customer Value Creator for his company, *UNLEASH Buzz*. Tim and his team will deliver best practice Word-of-Mouth Research, Consulting, Facilitation, Training, Agency and Coaching services and products for your organization to dynamically increase your Word-of-Mouth, Buzz, Customer Activism and Growth.

Timothy Patrick Sullivan has been called *"The Word-of-Mouth Marketing Innovation Leprechaun"* for magically helping his clients discover the shortest paths to the biggest pots of gold. You may reach Tim at *tim.p.sullivan@unleashbuzz.com*. To schedule a Word-of-Mouth Project, Workshop or to view more products and services please visit: *www.unleashbuzz. com*. Do a colleague or friend a favor and share this Word-of-Mouth Marketing Innovation knowledge with them today!

Readers receive a special **FREE** *Subscription to the world's leading* **Word-of-Mouth Innovation Blog™**, *a* **FREE** **Word-of-Mouth Innovation Check-Up™** *and a* **FREE** **Word-of-Mouth Innovation Podcast** *for a limited time only by visiting* www.unleashbuzz.com/wwtwe.htm

236

Uncover Unlimited Referrals, Unimagined Business Opportunities & Never Believed Sales Results With NO New Customers!

by Shelby Collinge

If you have all the clients, customers, referrals, affiliates and financial independence you can handle, then you can stop reading. If not, then you have come to the right place. The way we attract and market to our customers in the fast-paced, ever-changing world in which we live is critical.

Too many of us spend a small fortune to market and advertise our businesses, only to end up with little or no results. There has to be a more effective way, and I would argue I have found the secret. ...Think back to the last customer interaction you had that resulted in a sale of your products and/or services. Did you extend every possible option to your customer? Did you "Thank" your customer for their business and ask how you could better serve them in the future or on their next purchase? Did you ask them if they knew anyone who could potentially need or use your product or service? Have you followed up with them to see how things have worked out since their purchase?

When I work with my clients and I ask them these same questions time after time, I get the same answer — "No." Why is it not part of our everyday manners? Why do we think we have to continually fill our opportunity pipeline with brand new customers? Why do we want to make things harder than they have to be? Finding new customers is a difficult and expensive process. You are sitting on an unimaginable fortune right now in your current customer base. Why not spend some time, money, energy and attention on existing customers? Wouldn't you rather sell and interact with someone who already knows the kind of quality products and services only you can provide?

Your current customers have low sales resistance AND they already know you and have done business with you. Why not follow up with these precious gems? Why not leverage these already-existing, established relationships to everyone's delight? Ideally, the most desirable and highly coveted relationship is the "win-win" relationship. When you can provide your customers with service that can't be beat, and products that he or she can rely and depend on, then you are doing them a favor by continually offering them newer and better products and services. You can afford them the luxury to not have to look elsewhere for a solution. They will come to you first instinctively, the first time every time. You

237

should strive to be your customer's number-one call when they need something related to your product or service.

Time and again, I ask businesses and entrepreneurs alike how often they follow up with their existing customers on a regular basis. On average, they typically haven't been in contact in over seven months. Now, I understand that some of you have hundreds, even thousands of customers, but what prevents you from at least making quarterly, pre-planned contact with the top 20 percent of your customers?

The "80/20 rule" applies to this concept in that you will be building deeper trust and rapport with only the top 20 percent of your customers. As you can see, only a few minor changes on how and where you spend your time daily can change your business, and the results will amaze you. I can show you how to plan and execute an overhaul of your current marketing strategy by using your current customer base. I can take you from start to finish.

Imagine for a moment your favorite customer or client. Does he or she spend the most money? Is he or she the nicest customer to deal with? Do they pay on time? Really think about this for a moment and compare it to the majority of your existing customer database. How many perfect customers do you have? How many do you want to have? Wouldn't you like to have ONLY perfect customers?

These perfect clients, which are typically your top 20 percent, need to be and should be your first priority, and you should treat them like valuable gems. Each of these magnificently cut diamonds knows at least 10- to 20 other gems of similar or better quality than themselves. It is a universal law that like attracts like. If you know and understand this time-tested law, then and only then, will you begin to realize its power. Think about one of your perfect customers for a moment. Let's say you take extra special care of him or her as you do with all your customers. You go above and beyond the call of duty, you handle all the details, problems and concerns, no matter how small, and you make the business transaction a relaxing and enjoyable experience. What do you think would happen in a very short period of time? What kind of reputation do you think would start to follow you and your business? What do you think this could do for your annual sales? I promise that these more-than-satisfied customers will refer more customers exactly like themselves and generate more word-of-mouth advertising than you can handle. So, what prevents you (and three-quarters of the rest of the business world) from "mining" your own customer base? Inertia. Your desire to just "keep on keeping on" holds you back. The need to stay within our own pre-defined comfort zones limits us in unbelievable ways.

Sometimes I ask clients what they think they can do to increase business, reduce customer attrition or address other concerns in their business. Usually, their answers are right on the money. This made me realize that most of our business problems don't lie in our problem-solving abilities or our intelligence. Many of us have brilliant business brains. From this exercise, I divined that most our problems lie in our "execution." And there's the rub. We get lazy. We're too busy. Marketing consumes too much time. Think of the biggest challenge facing you today. Do you know how to solve or fix this challenge? Chances are you know how to solve, fix or eliminate this challenge right this very minute. However, getting to that end result is another story. Success lies not only in knowing what to do — it's in taking action and getting started. Overcoming inertia is one of the hardest challenges, but once that movement in the right direction begins, maintaining it becomes much easier and more enjoyable.

What if you could learn ways to leverage existing relationships so that your very own customers bring you additional business, referrals, endorsements or potential new business opportunities? What would that mean for you and your business? What would that mean for your lifestyle? What would that mean for the development of your financial independence? Allow yourself to dream for a moment — right now — about how exciting your job or career would be if everyone around you adored you, your products and services. What if your customers viewed you as their most trusted advisor, told everyone about you and wanted you to be as successful as you could possibly be? Results like this can be easy to achieve when you learn the rules of relationship marketing that I passionately teach.

I want you to think about the many people that you see, interact and talk with from the time you wake up in the morning until the time you go to bed in the evening. I want you to wake up tomorrow morning with a completely different outlook about those same people than when you go to bed tonight. I want you to pretend or imagine that all the people that you see during your day are prospective customers. Now, I don't want you walking around town trying to sell something to everyone you come into contact with, but I do want you to start thinking differently about these valuable resources right before your very eyes.

I want you to positively know, not positively think, but positively know that everyone you come into contact with from now on can and will be a huge benefit to you and your business. Open your mind to the possibility that the waitress waiting on you for your lunch today just might know someone who could benefit from your products or services. One of the local bank tellers may know of a business opportunity or investment opportunity that would be perfect for you. Your hair dresser or stylist could become one of your absolute best sources of word-of-mouth advertising. Can you see the possibilities, new markets and unending opportunities this would open you to?

All you have to do is be friendly, service-oriented, open-minded, and expect that everyone you come into contact with can and will move you closer in some way to your ultimate goals. So, if you don't practice a regular written goal-setting program, then I recommend you immediately start writing your goals down every day. You can't hit a target you can't see.

When I start with new clients, I recommend that they begin writing down their top 10- to 20-goals every day. Get yourself in the habit of writing them down either in the morning or in the evening, and then review them at least once daily. Doing this will only take about five minutes and yet the results are worth their weight in gold. Buy yourself a spiral ringed notebook and do it faithfully every day. Goals are like magnets. The more you write them down, read them, and program them into your subconscious mind, the more attractive you become to your goals and those desired outcomes. Just by writing down a goal on paper you are 10 percent more likely to complete the task.

So, just by writing it down, you move closer to your goals and your goals move closer to you. Momentum also comes into play. Let us use this momentum as a springboard to catapult us to completion of all of our goals and dreams no matter how large and unbelievable they may seem now. Write them all down.

You need to be your own example of what you're searching for. Make one of your priorities to stay connected to your wants, needs and desires, as well as a perfect customer's wants, needs and desires. Make everything you do every day of your life mean something. Make everything you do move you one step closer on your path to your goals and dreams. If you implement the above mentioned recommendations, suggestions and strategies, your success is all but guaranteed. Don't make things any more difficult than they need to be. Do yourself a favor and get out of your own way! Bottom line, if you really want the best for your customers and settle for nothing less, deliver nothing less and earn nothing less!! Allow me to mentor and coach you along the way, and to help educate you in the benefits of leveraging relationships in your journey to the abundant life. I wish you abundant success!

If you like what you've read ... check this out!

FOOTNOTES ✌

Shelby Collinge is president of Relationship Marketing Mastery. If you'd like to leverage your relationships to create unlimited opportunities, unending referrals and unimaginable sales, please visit her site at www.r-m-m.com or call Toll Free (800) 680-4438. Shelby offers group and personal coaching, workshops, audio courses, FREE weekly teleseminars and much, much more.

Are You Steering Your Own Ship?

by Lee Huffman, Executive Partner,
Action International Cornerstone

As a serial entrepreneur I have launched over a dozen successful businesses and heard my share of business metaphors. As the executive partner in one of the largest business coaching firms in North America, my team and I have given a significant amount of counsel.

In my firm, our coaches and partners work directly with successful business leaders around the world. We have found that we can learn something new and interesting from every leader we meet, and we strive to turn what we learn into advice that will help other business leaders accelerate their business development, take their organizations to the next level and turn their visions into reality.

Your Business and Your Life: *Like a Tall Sailing Ship*

One metaphor that has inspired many of the business leaders we counsel is the idea that a business is like a tall sailing ship. For a tall ship to reach its destination, it must have these five things:

1) A star to guide the way.
2) The sea to keep it afloat.
3) A system to steer it towards its ultimate destination.
4) A force to drive it forward.
5) A wise and confident captain at the helm.

Our businesses, and our lives, need all five of these factors in order for us to achieve our goals and have a positive impact on the world around us.

A Star to Guide the Way: *Your Business Vision*

We believe that the star that guides the way for a successful business is "the vision." Evolving this vision is the primary responsibility of the business owner.

241

Every business owner launches his company with a distinct vision in mind. That vision might include enjoying the freedom that business ownership entails, or it might include giving back to the community, increasing one's net worth, or perhaps it might be about spending more time with family. Every business person's vision is unique.

Unfortunately, not all those visions come to fruition. Nine out of 10 business visions fade significantly in the company's first few years of existence. Responsibility lies with the business owner to keep that initial vision alive until either it is achieved, or until it is time to craft a new vision.

But, how do you craft a vision?

You can start by clearly stating the vision that caused you to launch your business in the first place. Many times recalling this vision is enough to reconnect the business owner and his or her team to a brighter future. On the other hand, we often need to establish a short-term vision of making enough revenue to cover expenses; then we can go back and build a long-term vision with the help of the business owner and the rest of their team.

If you own a business, get back in touch with your original vision. Write it down, or create a poster to constantly keep it in the forefront of your own mind and the minds of your teammates. It will remind you of what you are working toward.

The Sea to Keep It Afloat: *Business Plans and an Aligned Team*

Like the captain of a ship on stormy seas, a business owner who can't meet expenses or has high employee turnover, feels like they are riding a financial or emotional roller coaster that is out of control. Owners in such situations often make quick decisions and adjustments that don't always help. They try one quick fix after another, but the storm seems to win each round as their business "ship" is shaken and takes on water.

In reality, most business owners who feel that they are not in control of their businesses only lack a few of the business practices required to get them back into control. We call the use of these practices "Business Mastery." Mastery of business basics can eliminate the chaos, remove the uncertainty and return control of the business to the owner.

Like a tall ship caught in a raging sea, the business leader who feels out of control needs to batten down the hatches, develop a plan to ride out the storm and come out upright and align the team so that the plan can be executed as efficiently as possible when the storm begins to abate.

Battening down the hatches does not always mean letting people go, but that may be necessary. Instead, it means concentrating on the business plan, trimming where possible and aligning everyone in the organization towards common goals. You may have to restructure the business, drop some activities and potentially lay off employees; however, you need to ride out the storm in a way that you position yourself to take the best possible action when the storm subsides.

Don't miss this. Even if you don't feel like you are riding on a stormy sea, a solid business plan and crew aligned with that plan will ensure that your business achieves the highest possible level of success. More storms may lie ahead, but that business plan and an able crew to execute it will help to avoid being blown off course.

A System to Steer It: *Strategic and Quarterly Plans*

Like the rudder and the sails of a tall ship, a well thought-out strategic plan and quarterly execution plans guide the business crew as they sail towards the vision. These plans, like navigational maps, keep the business on course.

In a recent survey, the US Small Business Administration found that six percent of the business owners within the early stages of business (one year old or less) have plans they look at regularly and use to run their businesses. Of the 15- to 20-percent of the businesses that make it to the five-year mark, 68 percent have annual, quarterly or monthly planning processes. So, out of 100 one-year-old businesses, six have plans and out of 100 five-year-old businesses, 68 have plans.

This is a ten-fold increase in the amount of successful business leaders who manage their teams based on solid, well thought-out plans. But not every business starts out with good planning. Even if 100 percent of the business leaders who planned well at their one year anniversary made it all the way to their 5th anniversary, they would only account for 30 percent of the total. These statistics show that over half of the business leaders who made it to their 5th year, learned the power of planning along the way.

We all know that most business plans end up sitting on the shelf collecting dust. Our team has found that there are two reasons for this: (1) Most business plans are designed to impress bankers or investors and don't necessarily address the day-to-day operations of running a business, and (2) There is usually no strategy or process for executing the plan across the organization or a method for tracking progress.

If your business plan is inadequate, create a new one. Write it yourself in such a way that everyone in the company can comprehend and implement it. Let it guide the growth and management of your business.

Bring in someone to lead the business planning process and then create a plan that you intend to execute. Of course, if you have a good CPA, he or she can help with the financial side of this development process, but your team needs to be involved in the execution of the strategic side of the plan or you will not succeed.

The strategic plan will guide you out of the storm and toward that port, which will take your business to a new level of success or security. This strategic plan will answer the following question:

- **What are the strategies that you and your team will execute that will take your business to the next level over the next 12- to 18-months, and who has ownership of each strategy?**

These strategies should be well defined, prioritized and assigned to leaders within your organization, either by title or name.

243

With your strategic plan in place, develop a sub-set of this plan each quarter and measure your team on the execution of this 90-day plan. Using this system, you can steer your business to long-term success.

A Force to Drive It Forward: *Profitability*

While the wind drives the sailing ship forward, the force that drives a business forward is profitability. You must break even just to keep the ship afloat, as we discussed above. However, massive profits are what drive companies to new, more lucrative ports-of-call.

Massive profits come from taking massive action on a guided path toward your vision. Nearly every business leader we talk to wants more customers, more revenue and more profits. In addition, many of them want more time outside of their businesses to spend with their families and friends. However, it is profits that put the wind into the sails and drive the business forward.

By reinvesting part of the profits back into your company, you fill your sails with wind and drive your business forward. By reinvesting some of the profits into your team members, they will realize that their contributions do not go unnoticed. They will work harder and more sensibly towards achieving your business vision. Reinvesting the rest of your profits into yourself and other owners helps pay back those who believed and were willing to take a risk on you and your vision, even before you made it a reality!

A Wise and Confident Captain: *You, Supported By Your Advisors*

No ship can reach port without knowing how to navigate, without having an excellent crew and without a plan for that crew to execute. Even so, the key ingredient in each successful business we have helped expand over the past 30 years, has been a confident captain at the helm of the ship. Inexperienced business owners, like inexperienced captains, often steer their companies into the rocks if left to their own devices.

One of our companies in Silicon Valley provides a great example of this. While the captain of this particular endeavor had vision, charisma and solid business experience, his lack of planning, extravagant spending habits, and inability to listen to his crew all contributed to the shipwreck of his company. But he didn't go down alone — dozens of his best people left in order to find a more seaworthy ship. Even a confident captain can sink a ship, especially when they do not solicit advice and take action on input from their advisors.

A wise leader of a very successful enterprise once told us, "Wise people know what they don't know and they are not afraid to go to those who do know." Wise leaders surround themselves with the best advisors they can find and then they listen to and act upon the input from these advisors. To become as successful as possible in your enterprise, and to become a wise and confident captain, seek out the advice of others. Would you like to avoid shipwrecking your business? Seek out the advice of others, but not just business leaders like yourself; seek out men and women whose ideas differ from your own.

Sure, it is nice to have one or two advisors who can say they have

successfully sailed ships that are very similar to your own, but you might receive additional new ideas from people in other industries and other business disciplines. So, if you own a retail business, find an advisor from the manufacturing or service sectors. If you own your own service business, find people in the medical or dental fields, and so on.

Of course, we always recommend that you find a successful, well-trained, fully-certified business coach who can give you even more ideas and support you as you grow your business. Remember to select your coach wisely, keeping in mind that not every coach or mentor has the same experience, training or knowledge.

Summary

I hope that you find the analogy between the successful business and that of the sailing of a tall ship warrants further investigation in your own business.

You and your business must have the following traits ...
1. **Vision:** A star to guide your way.
2. **Business Basics:** To keep your business afloat.
3. **Strategic and Quarterly Plans:** To steer your course.
4. **Profitability:** To achieve and maintain the wind in your sales.
5. **Wisdom and Confidence:** Both your own and that of those who advise you.

Without all these things, your ship may be headed for the rocks. We help business owners and business leaders grow their businesses and share in the massive abundance that we see in the world around us. If we can do anything to help you in this way, please feel free to contract our office.

If you like what you've read ... check this out!

FOOTNOTES ♔

*Lee Huffman is a serial entrepreneur, a business catalyst, and a certified Action business coach. His firm, **Cornerstone Business Coaching Services, LLC** has been awarded several **Action International Business Coaching** franchises where they coach successful business owners all around the world.*

*Included with the purchase of this book, qualified business owners will **receive a complementary business coaching session** from an Action International Business Coach **valued at $295.00**. To qualify, you need to have five or more employees and have been in business for six months or longer. To sign up for your introductory business coaching session, go to **www.ActionCoaching.com/ Cornerstone** and click on the picture of the doctor. This will take you to the **Business Health Check** questionnaire that you can complete to see a snapshot of the health of your business. After you complete this questionnaire, an Action Business Coach will be in contact with you set up your complementary business coaching session. If they can be of service to you, please do not hesitate to contact them at **Cornerstone@Action-International.com**, or +001 770 932-2525.*

The Secret To Achieving Your Financial Goals

by John Assaraf

Have you ever asked yourself what your highest income-producing activity is?

If you're like most people, you probably go about your day-to-day business never really thinking about the moment-to-moment activities that consume your day. I'd like to walk you through an exercise that has helped me and my clients stay focused on earning their highest possible revenue per hour.

We each start with 365 days in a year. If we take away weekends (104 days), five major USA holidays, two weeks of vacation, and personal religious holidays (average 3), that leaves each one of us with approximately 238 days in which to earn the income we desire. Of course, we can add or delete days based on our own schedule and desires.

If you multiply these 238 days by an average of 10 working hours per day, you are dealing with 2,380 hours of real work time for the year. So, let's do some math.

If your yearly income goals are:
- $25k = you must be earning an average of $10.50 for every hour of work.
- $50K = $21 per hour
- $100k = $42 per hour
- $250k = $105 per hour
- $1 million = $420 per hour
- $5 million = $2100 per hour
- $10 million = $4200 per hour

In order to earn the income per year that you really want, you absolutely must be doing activities every hour that cause your income to line up with this chart. If you catch yourself doing anything that isn't your absolute highest-producing income activity all the time, you are, in effect, making it much harder to achieve your desired financial goals.

www.mentorsmagazine.com

Ask yourself the following questions:
- What activity or activities generate your highest producing income?
- What are you spending your time doing?
- Are you focused on the real money-makers or the real time-wasters?
- Are you making it easy for yourself to be a high income earner, or are you doing the things that can be done by someone whose income goal or ability is less than yours?

I can tell you that when you start to look at each hour this way, you'll stop doing the small stuff and start doing the real stuff that yields results.

Just look at your most recent three- to five-days and count the number of hours you spent really making the big bucks vs. all the stuff that creeps up on all of us. What you discover will amaze you.

Here's To You Having It All!

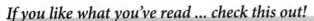

If you like what you've read ... check this out!

FOOTNOTES ♡

John Assaraf, aka "The Street Kid" is a New York Times & Wall Street Journal Best-Selling Author, Trainer & Entrepreneur. Go to: ***http://www.cloningofsuccess. com*** *to get your **FREE** four-Lesson Course on **"The Neuro-Science of Financial Success"** (a $97 value) and get your **FREE** subscription to **"The OneCoach Weekly Report, More Money, More Life"** (a priceless value) if you are in business for yourself.*

247

Who's Got Your Back?

by Reggie Cochran

As an entrepreneur and a life coach, I believe in earning multiple streams of income. I also believe that for most people to run more than one business successfully, they will need to form various types of partnerships. This is a very serious process that one definitely should not rush into.

The right partner can create a synergy more powerful than the both of you ever thought possible. The wrong partner can lead the both of you to bankruptcy in record time. Over the last 20 years as an entrepreneur, I have seen, studied, and been on both ends of the spectrum. So, for the next few minutes, I want to share with you some of the things I have learned from my experiences.

When I was actively fighting in martial arts competitions, I constantly looked for workout partners better than myself that had a variety of fighting styles. In contrast, I observed my peers constantly training with people with very similar fighting styles or people not as good as themselves. I went on to win world titles, while most of my buddies struggled to make improvements in their fighting.

In my coaching practice, I often see clients making similar mistakes when forming business partnerships. They either connect with people similar to themselves in knowledge and skills, or they team up with someone who has different skills and abilities, but also has very different goals and attitudes. In time, both situations can lead to major problems.

To me, the ideal partner should be like-minded in attitude and goals, but possess skills and knowledge that you yourself lack. In addition, the person should possess high moral and ethical standards. If possible, they should also share the same work ethic, and in some cases, you may even have to take into consideration the potential partner's religious beliefs.

I would only consider someone who does not fit this basic guideline as a silent partner; in other words, someone investing in the project with finances and/or resources, but with little to no involvement in the actual day-to-day activities of the business. Even with silent partners, I strongly urge you to take into consideration the candidates financial, moral and ethical standards — and again — sometimes one may need to consider their religious beliefs.

www.mentorsmagazine.com

Now that I have explained the basic qualities one looks for in a business partner, let me walk you through a couple of examples of how I found a couple of great partners for current business projects.

A few years ago I found my career moving quickly from marketing and training into consulting, coaching and information product development. After carefully meditating on this transition, I decided I really liked this new direction and wanted to continue on this path.

Once I made that decision, I took time to research and study people that had already experienced success in these areas. I then determined which of those individuals I would model to become more successful myself. In this process, I kept detailed notes of my role models' strengths and weaknesses.

I then went through a brutally honest self-evaluation to determine my own strengths and weaknesses. I compared my own assets and liabilities to those of my role model's. After having finished this appraisal process, I saw the need for a couple of different partners to accomplish my new goals faster and easier.

Because of the steps I had already taken, I had a list of attributes I needed my future partners to possess. Then it became a matter of determining which partners I needed first based on the priority order of my goals.

In addition, I had to decide what I would offer the right person in exchange for becoming my partner. From that point on, the search began for the people that possessed the skills or resources I wanted.

So let's recap what I had accomplished thus far — I knew what type of person I needed and I felt like I knew where to find them. I also felt like I had an acceptable offer for the right person. I now had to make sure I was in the right frame of mind to start prospecting.

Many times people go through action steps to start searching for partners but don't have the proper mental positioning and attitude in place before they begin. Some take a weak position and lack confidence in their approach; as a result, they come off looking like beggars hoping to secure a partner. Who wants to partner with someone who lacks confidence?

Others don't check their ego at the door and come off acting like egomaniacs. They scorn the intelligence of potential partners' if they decline the offer of partnership. I have seen people insult each other when a prospective partner rebuffed an offer. No one with any salt wants to become a partner with someone who can't control their ego.

Before you actually make your first contact with a potential partner, practice your approach on video camera. If you don't have access to a video camera, practice in front of a mirror and record yourself on cassette for review.

If possible, practice your approach with a person you can trust to take the exercise serious. You want someone who will critique you, but not verbally beat you up. Find someone who will support your goal and not try and talk you out of fulfilling those goals. I also recommend you hire a professional coach who can help you with this process. It will be money well-spent.

Now, even if you do find a partner that possesses what you want and wants to take you up on your offer, you still have a lot of work left to do. In the business world, people like to compare a partnership to a marriage of sorts. So, let's use that example for a minute. Traditionally, we like to think of an engagement period between a couple before the marriage takes place. Then, if things continue to work out, the actual wedding takes place. Before that wedding comes together, a ton of planning goes on between the couple and their families. All the loose ends have to be tied up before the event takes place that legally binds that couple together. A similar process should occur when taking on a new partner.

Once you feel that you have found the right person, find out as much as you can about the person's personal and business background. Your potential partner should be scouring your background as well. Together you should also work with your legal and financial advisors to make sure the partnership protects both of you as much as possible from problems within the partnership as well as liabilities that may occur while doing business. With a successful venture in place, don't forget to plan potential exit strategies in the event of either partner's retirement or premature death.

If you go through all of this and still feel like you are a match, then move forward and finalize the partnership. There's the honeymoon phase and then there's the dreaded "honeymoon-is-over" phase. Once you and your partner are running your new venture, both of you will have to constantly work at keeping your relationship going.

The space of this article does not allow me to go into all the techniques you can use to keep your partnership performing at peak levels. But I will add this: honesty and open communication must remain a priority to both partners. Since we reap what we sow, make sure you keep your ego in check. Have fun at what you are doing, and always be the type of partner that you want your partners to be.

No crystal balls can guarantee that the partners you pick will work out the way you planned; however, if you take into consideration the things I have mentioned, you will have a better chance of success.

In closing, I want to thank you for taking your time to read this book. The authors who contributed these articles care about your success. Success really is a choice and I pray this book will allow you to make more of the right choices. God Bless.

If you like what you've read ... check this out!

FOOTNOTES ✪

Reggie Cochran is an internationally known *Peak Performance* coach, speaker and retired world champion martial artist. He is currently co-authoring a series of books with Chuck Norris and Ted DiBiase that will help raise money for nonprofit foundations. Reggie is available for speaking and peak performance coaching. For further information, regularly visit the following sites:

> *www.blackbeltsuccess.com*
> *www.kickstartbooks.com*
> *www.mentalskillscoach.com*

Why You Want To Be My Best Friend

by Ariane Thorne

As the Art Director for "Mentors™ Magazine" and the "Walking With the Wise™" book series, I work with celebrated speakers and mentors from around the globe. Very few understand the lingo we use about how to send files, photographs and written articles unless they've hired a publicist.

But alas…. Because I've been dealing with a fair amount of frustrated people, Linda Forsythe suggested that I sit down and write this article to educate everyone on what is involved when sending press-ready artwork, advertising or marketing materials to a publisher. I've included some of the most typically asked questions I receive on a daily basis, so here goes….

Q: What the heck is a DPI and why do you keep sending my pictures back saying I don't have enough of them?

A: When we ask you to send a picture over in a certain amount of DPI, I usually wind up listening to dead silence on the other end of the phone. DPI stands for "Dots Per Inch." When you look at pictures in print or on the web, you are really looking at thousands of little dots that come together to form the picture. This is what you would actually see if you were to put it under a "magnifying glass" (aka a loupe). When we ask you to send something in 300 DPI, it means 300 Dots Per Inch. DPI is the resolution of the picture, therefore, the more dots it has, the more clarity it has. You need higher DPI for print than you do for the web. This is why a picture from the web cannot be used for print purposes because all you would see are fuzzy or blurry images. A picture on the web is generally only 72 DPI.

Q: OK … then why do you ask me to send you Pixies?

A: YIKES!!! Unless you have flying Pixies, like Tinkerbell, housed in a box somewhere, I'm not interested in having you send them. What we are asking you to send are called, "pixels." Pixels are just another name for dots.

Q: Then how do I know if I'm sending something to you in the right DPI or pixel definition?

252

A: Do a little investigating for yourself to check the information of the file that you are sending. Right-click on a PC and go to "Properites" or on a Mac, you would hit "Command or Apple" key and the "I" key on your keyboard. You'll see what kind of file it is and you might even see what program it was created in... but what you're REALLY looking for is the file size. It's going to say something like, "164KB" or "164K." Any file that is 300 DPI at 164KB or lower is not a high enough resolution to print on a press, unless it is only 0.7" by 0.7" in size. In other words, if you were going to give me an image the size of 2" x 3" at 300 dpi it would have to be 2.06M (MB) in size to be press ready. Another way of saying this is that you must know the physical size the picture will print at and THEN look to see if the DPI is the right amount for that particular sized picture.

Q: OK, now what's the difference between MB (megabytes) and KB (kilobytes)?

A: The first thing to clarify is that K=KB=kilobyte and that M=MB=megabyte. Secondly, the way easiest way to compare the two is to the metric system. 1000KB=1MB, just like 1000 millimeters equals 1 meter. It's that simple, the prefix "kilo" means 1000. This is a very important piece to the puzzle; just like you don't want to get your teaspoons and your tablespoons mixed up when you're baking or you could end up with a Napalm bomb!!!

Q: What is the difference between RGB and CMYK?

A: RGB stands for Red, Green, and Blue and CMYK stands for Cyan, (C), Magenta, (M), Yellow, (Y), and Black (K). RGB is a color space that is used for the web or more specifically, it is designed to be seen on a monitor. It is an additive color space ... meaning that Red, Green, and Blue are combined together to form other colors. The additive color system was discovered when it was found that these three colors combined made up light when it was emitted from an illuminated source, ie. your computer monitor. There is a very specific reason why RGB is not used for printing purposes and I'll explain that in a minute.

CMYK is a color space or color model that is subtractive in nature, meaning that it is made by mixing colors. Now, don't jump ahead of me, I know that you'd think that if you mixed colors together you'd be ADDING them into the mix, however it's based on the theory of looking at colors under white light and how we as humans perceive that color with our eyes. Under white light, a banana appears to be yellow because it absorbs all of the other colors in the visible color spectrum and it reflects yellow light ... that's the subtractive part. We aren't looking at a printed book or magazine through an illuminated light source, we are looking at it under white light, therefore all of the pictures that you submit for press need to be CMYK, unless they are just printing in black ink. The various shades of Black are actually shades of Grey, therefore if you were submitting an image that would only be printed in Black ink, it would be saved as "Greyscale" (more commonly referred to as Black and White). What's also important to note in the CMYK spectrum is that Cyan is the opposite of Red. Remember that infamous color wheel from first grade? Cyan is opposite from Red on the color wheel and Cyan absorbs Red, therefore adjusting the Cyan of your image will determine how much Red will appear on an image.

253

Q: What do you mean when you say you are printing something in four colors?

A: When you send magazine or a book to press, the printer makes up what is called a plate (similar to a negative) for each particular color that is printed, for every page. One plate would be all the of the Cyan information that was displayed in that particular page, the next plate would be all the Magenta for that particular page, next all the information or data that makes up the Yellow part of the page and finally the last would be all the Black data of that page. When printed on top of each other, the final result would be a "four-color" picture which is the finished color picture you see in a full color print. If you look at a printed magazine under a magnifying glass you can see dots of all of these four colors.

Q: How do I compress a file?

A: What's more important here is why to compress a file. You cannot send me a file that's larger than 10MB over e-mail. That's because it would take way too long for me to download and I don't have that kind of time. I need to access my e-mail efficiently and this is why I don't want you to send me files larger than this capacity. So, to answer your original question, if you are running Windows XP, you can open up a Windows Explorer window and browse to and select the file(s) that you want to compress, rightclick and scroll down the pop-up window to "Send to- Compressed (zipped) folder." Or if you have an older Windows Operating System you would need to get a program called WinZip on your computer. You'll follow the step-by-step WinZip wizard to create your zipped file. When you've created a file that has a .zip after it, you've accomplished this task. A zipped file (.zip) is actually an archive for storing and compressing other files. Attach and send that file to me, not the 26MB JPEG. If you're on a Mac, you'll use a program called Drop Stuff and you'll drop your file on the program window and it will compress, just like magic (only you will have the option of creating it as a Stuffit archive (.sit or .sitx) or as a zipped file. Now, if you don't want to download this kind of software from the web because you're on Windows XP and your Norton Internet Security or the firewall on your server won't let you, you can have your web-master set up an FTP site that's specifically designed for transferring large files.

Q: That's nice to know but what is an FTP site?

A: It's something separate from e-mail. You can send me a file by way of a different program other than Microsoft Outlook, so your computer doesn't slow down to the point where you're freaking out because you think you have the latest virus. An FTP site is designed with more space in mind so that you can store larger data files on a server.

Q: Why is it so important that I get my materials to you in a certain period of time?

A: I'm a very busy person with my own deadlines to meet you know!!! (Besides I'm the one that gets yelled at because YOU are late). Deadlines are extremely important in print because each section of the production process takes a certain amount of time. Then when it goes to press, the printer also has to meet a deadline, and finally it is distributed. If the article contributor is late … it slows up the whole process.

Q: Can you make my picture look better? How about taking 50 lbs. off my hips?

A: This is the part that you should really pay attention to! Here's why you want to be MY new best friend: I can make you skinney, give you teeth, give you hair or take away wrinkles. There is this amazing filter in Photoshop called Pinch. In your case I would use the Pinch filter as a sort of virtual liposuction, but it's not that simple, it takes a lot of cloning as well. Yes, I can easily make a virtual clone of yourself that's a heck of a lot hotter, but you gotta dish out some extra dough for that. Actually there's a tool aptly called "the clone tool." Using this tool I can remove unsightly shadows from other, "trimmer" parts of your body, thus reducing the overall plumpness of you. I can also take pieces of you and replace them with other pieces of you if you get on my bad side (*smile*).

I hope I answered some of your questions. Please know that if you take the time to understand some of the above rhetoric … then you have a higher percentage of becoming published or becoming more aware of when you aren't being represented correctly. You have worked very hard as an entrepreneur and how you are represented to the public has EVERYTHING to do with your ultimate success.

If you like what you've read ... check this out!

FOOTNOTES

Ariane Thorne is the art director for "Mentors™ Magazine" and the "Walking With the Wise™" book series. She has a Bachelor's degree in visual arts with an emphasis in graphic design. Although she is commonly referred to as an art director, she prefers the term "visual logician." Ariane is currently working on her theories about design as logical juxtaposition. She would love to answer any other questions you may have if you send her an e-mail to design@mentorsmagazine.com.

What If The Navy SEALS Taught Real Estate?

Tactical Mentoring

by Todd Dotson

It was just past 5:00 A.M. on a cold winter morning, a handful of individuals and I quietly boarded the aircraft and settled in for a two-hour flight. What should have been a routine flight was soon interrupted by turbulent weather and the pilot's voice over the intercom telling us to lock down for the remainder of the trip. The rough weather did little to interrupt the focus of my team and me, only depriving us of a little extra shuteye.

Not long after, the pilot was back on the intercom reporting that inclement weather had forced us to change the primary drop zone and land the plane at a secondary site. Once on the ground, my team quickly assembled and headed to the predetermined staging area to rally with the indigenous personnel.

We quickly headed over to our AO (Area of Operation) only to be slowed by icy conditions and rough roads. Slowed temporarily, we arrived at the target area and began conducting immediate operations.

It wasn't long before we identified multiple targets and moved to take down the primary target.

Needless to say, it was another successful OP....

What I've just described wasn't a SEAL team conducting military operations, but the Tactical Real Estate Team conducting property operations on behalf of our students. It's what I refer to as a "property sweep," and Rochester, N.Y. was the target.

As the sun began to rise, we debriefed over breakfast. In all, we had identified just over 100 targets, prioritized our takedown and put the first five under contract — one target property was bought for a dollar and sold in "As Is" condition for $2,300.

"If the Navy SEALS taught real estate investing, there's no question they would be teaching Todd Dotson's Tactical System. I know because I was a Navy SEAL...." — Ty Valkanas Real Estate Investor/Mentor/Former Navy SEAL.

The following week we were in San Jose. Favorable weather conditions allowed for a smooth drop into the staging area. East San Jose was the first AO — you remember, Area of Operation. Multiple targets identified with two under contract. The first was bought for $352,000 and sold in "as is" condition for $375,000. The second was a pre-foreclosure taken down "Subject To" and sold utilizing a short sale with the lender.

Two weeks later, we dropped into Orange County, Calif., and quickly proceeded to Santa Ana and then to Long Beach. Next we headed to Phoenix, Ariz., and dropped into the "Presidents Streets" to target ugly houses and then reassembled in Scottsdale to work some luxury homes. ...

The outcome? It's always the same.... When the Navy SEALS hit, they leave a body count. When Tactical Real Estate hits, we leave a property count.

I trust you've enjoyed the operational breakdown. It's funny — when we go out to mentor students they're always expecting us to bring the "Magic Bullet"! When our time together concludes, they realize they're the magic bullet. We just helped them strategically grid their market, successfully acquire the target, quickly line up the weapon of choice (wholesale, subject to, lease option, short sale, etc.) and tactically pull the trigger!!! You see it's not how much information you have that counts; it's the quality of the "Intel" that really matters. It's being able to evaluate, understand and implement where you live — that's my expertise.

If what I've just described gets your juices flowing, then welcome to Tactical Real Estate™. If not, I'd prefer to know now. Not everybody makes the cut, and just because you have a Gold Card doesn't mean you qualify. Contrary to what many of the Gurus on the mass market tell you, not everybody is cut out to be a full-time investor. When we come to train you, the only easy day was yesterday. "When we drop in, it's on."

Regardless of who provided your foundational training, Tactical Real Estate™ can help you implement where you live.

Listen, if you haven't replaced the income on your job and you want to, you can't afford not to have us drop in and conduct operations on your behalf. I've found over the years that those that have a strong burning desire to succeed and haven't turned the corner are precisely the ones that need Tactical Mentoring the most. People are smart if you'll just show them how. People don't mind paying for training as long as the training pays for itself. Is it any wonder I developed the slogan, "The Checks Don't Lie™." It's my call to the industry to produce results or make way for someone who can.

By now, I'm sure I've piqued the curiosity of some and ruffled the feathers of others ... GOOD! I'm not here to win friends, just influence people. You can do it. More importantly, you deserve to be able to do it!

"Your no nonsense approach to training helped us build our business the right way. Today we are creating cash and building wealth as evidenced by the attached check of $149,492.91. The checks certainly don't lie!™"
— Katy McKinney Real Estate Investor/Mentor

While I'm thinking about it, be sure to check out my June 2004 cover story in "MENTORS™ Magazine." Better yet, call my office at 1-800 RE DEALS and request the bound copy of my reality-based interview with Linda Forsythe. I don't think she would mind me saying that my command of the nation's real estate markets even surprised her!

5 Keys to Your Success
Sustained success in this business comes down to five key ingredients:
• Creating Inventory
• Successfully Tracking/Contacting Owners
• Quickly Determining Your Prospects
• Writing Simple, Reality-Based Offers
• Having High-Speed Exit Strategies

"Thanks for finally taking us out of the audience!"
— Roger M., Phoenix, Arizona

Since we just covered five keys to sustained success in this business, let me address three common misconceptions or myths about real estate investing.

Three Myths About Real Estate Investing

1. **MYTH** — Investing in real estate is a sure-fire road to financial independence. FACT — Most real estate investors don't survive their first portfolio of properties. ...

2. **MYTH** — Real estate investing is all about Location, Location, Location. FACT — Location is important if you live there or you're holding for appreciation. Otherwise, it's all about the DEAL, the DEAL, the DEAL. ...

3. **MYTH** — If you buy it, they will come. FACT — You're not Kevin Costner, and this isn't the "Field of Dreams." Buy it right and they will come, buy it wrong and you're in trouble. ...

I hope you've enjoyed this article, but it's time to "Fast Rope" into the LZ (Landing Zone) and get after it. If you are just getting started and always had a strong desire to succeed in real estate, now is your chance. If you are starting over and are a casualty of training that was long on promises and short on delivery, it's your chance to do it right. If you're already on the fast track and want to make sure you stay there, let us ensure your success.

What If the Navy SEALS Taught Real Estate? They don't, but fortunately we do, and we are coming to a city near you. Understand, reality-based training

easily pays for itself. Without it, most are doomed for failure. If you are serious about real estate investing, you are going to pay for my "Mentor Program" one way or another. Going it alone may well cost you time, money and quite possibly financial freedom. A former student, close friend and current mentor on my team said it best:

"Todd, your training was life changing. As a West Point graduate and Army Ranger, I understand what it means to be reality-based. As a member of the elite Army Rangers, we had a saying, 'No one gets left behind.' Today I'm privileged to be part of another elite unit. At Tactical Real Estate™, we have another saying, 'No student gets left behind.'"
— Lt. Colonel John Angell, U.S. Army Retired, Real Estate Investor/Mentor

My friend, don't get left behind in the wasteland of books, tapes and generic real estate boot camps. ... Let us drop in and escort you to safety and financial security.

The Checks Don't Lie™

P.S.: Remember, real estate investing is not a Hobby, and Hope is not a course of action. Get In, Get Out and Get paid!

If you like what you've read ... check this out!

FOOTNOTES ⚘

Todd Dotson of Arlington, Texas is the founder of Tactical Real Estate™ and the Nation's foremost authority on getting in, getting out and getting paid. With an emphasis on "buying and selling" to create immediate cash and a system for parlaying that into wealth, he brings a reality-based approach to the business of real estate investing.

As the developer of the country's first nation-wide on-site mentoring program, Todd has the unique advantage of having mentored students in every major market in the country — a claim that only he and his team can make! Hands-on experience allows him to seamlessly combine wholesale buying and purchase option strategies —Anywhere, USA.

Todd instructs his students to go "ugly often" and "pretty when it's profitable!" The results speak for themselves as does Todd's trademark slogan, "The Check's Don't Lie."

To learn more about Todd Dotson and Tactical Real Estate™, visit his Web site at www.TacticalRealEstate.com

The following is from the Highly Acclaimed

"7 Habits of Highly Successful (Wealthy) Real Estate Investors!"

by Sherman L. Ragland, II, Wharton MBA, CCIM

John Jacob Astor; Oliver T. Carr, Jr.; Trammel Crow; Harry B. Helsmley; Gerald D. Hines; Richmond McCoy; Victor MacFarlane; Jim Rouse; Mel & Herb Simon; Fred & Donald Trump; and Sam Zell. These men's lives testify to the fact that in America anyone can become wealthy through savvy real estate investing. Like Sam Zell or Donald Trump, hundreds, if not thousands, of other people have become wealthy and live life on their own terms — in control of their lives and destinies. So, how did they acquire their wealth? A burning desire to become real estate investors started them on their path to prosperity. A few of these elite investors have also made it their business to share their experiences and how they achieved financial freedom. Some do it for publicity, some for money, while others simply see this as a way to "give back" when so much was provided to them.

In 1984, I had the first-hand opportunity to learn about opportunities in commercial real estate from James W. Rouse, a nationally-recognized real estate developer who was the visionary behind Harbor Place in Baltimore, Faneuil Hall in Boston and South Street Seaport in New York. At the age of 22, my interactions with Mr. Rouse left a lasting impression on me. That same year, I entered The Wharton School of Business to earn an MBA and started a lifelong study of what separates highly successful, wealthy real estate investors (at all levels) from those who never move past "dreaming" about success. Based on 20 years of research, one-on-one interviews with very wealthy/successful real estate investors, running the largest Real Estate Investors' Association (REIA) in the greater Washington D.C. region, and applying these same rules to my own investing, it is my pleasure to share with others the seven commonly shared habits of highly successful real estate investors. Anything practiced for 21 days in a row has the ability to become a habit. It is my hope that you will incorporate these seven concepts into your own investing and one day interview you on Real investor's Talk Radio™ as you share with us your successes in real estate investing.

"You Learn By Doing It!"

Without a doubt, the number one success secret of wealthy real estate investors we studied is the overwhelming need to "do." Although, all of the successful investors profiled mention the need to "gain knowledge" and to "study your craft," these highly successful investors differ from others who would seem to (at times) suffer from "paralysis of analysis." Successful investors practice the habit of learning as they do; if they feel the need to go into a new line of business, such as moving from developing successful warehouses to operating their own hotel chain, they do not spend an eternity studying all there is to know before "doing." No, these savvy investors study **while they take action**. In fact, the very elite not only learn by doing, but they also possess a sense of urgency — the attitude of "DO IT NOW."

Guidance- The Power of a Mentor

While learning by "doing it" was the number one habit of successful real estate investors, seeking the guidance of competent mentors came in a very close "second." In numerous interviews, Donald Trump discusses the critical importance of the guiding hand of his father in his own decision to pursue real estate development as a career. And while he and his father's opinions differed greatly with regards to young Donald's desires to "make it big" in Manhattan, the lessons learned sitting across the desk from his father doing deals in Queens helped Donald get a "fast start," which propelled him into the ranks of elite investors at a relatively young age. Bill Rancic, Trump's apprentice shares this same philosophy.

Not everyone has the opportunity to be the son or daughter of a developer or be born into a family of real estate investors. However, many leading investors today cite the importance of not only having a good mentor, but in having the humility to actively seek one.

Visualization & Goal Setting — Start with the End in Mind

The ability to see the big picture, even when you are just a very "small fish" is a key trait of all successful real estate entrepreneurs. Very few highly successful real estate investors started with either an expense account or a trust fund. In fact, many started penniless. However, their ability to "see beyond their circumstances" often helped them get started and stay on track. Many also attribute the very act of setting goals as a key to their success. Committing your dreams to a piece of paper helps you to take action. In the words of one highly successful investor: "The best way to set goals is to start with the end in mind. Figure out where you want to be when you declare yourself 'successful' and work your way backwards. Each day have a plan of attack for taking one step closer to achieving your goal, and as soon as you have your goal in sight, raise the bar and set a new one."

"When All Else Fails, Persistence Prevails" — Commitment

So reads a saying on the bottom of a motivational poster: "These pearls of wisdom contain much truth. Highly successful investors understand the power of selecting a goal and then **remaining committed to it, no matter what**."

Commitment has best been described by one millionaire investor as: "What you decide to do on the Saturday morning, which happens to also be the

91st day of your 90 day Plan and everything you absolutely positively knew was going to happen during the 90 days has failed to materialize — despite your best efforts ... and every one of your 'so called' friends and family members has made it a point (or so it seems) to call you over the past five days and ask you, 'are you still doing that real estate thing?' " At that point you have to make a decision — get out of bed and start all over again or pull the covers over your head. What is really going on is that you are being faced with a test, the "commitment test," which is a test of your commitment of what you told everyone what's important to you such as achieving financial freedom, providing for your family and having choices in life. The reality is that many, if not all, of the things you want to see happen will fail to show up when you want them to show up and it might take you longer than it has taken others. However, you have to decide, "Are you going to keep at it, no matter what?" or was it all "lip-service? I too, faced the "commitment test" many times. Fortunately, every time I faced it, I passed, which is why today I can choose to stay in bed any day of the week while my "so called" friends and family **have to** go to work. As I look back now, what difference does it make if it took 90, 180 or 365 days, the thought of punching the clock for someone else was all I needed to realize that if everything failed to work, I would just start over again for another 90 days, but this time do it exactly like how my mentor said to do it. Making the decision to keep at it, no matter what, is called "commitment," and I learned first hand that often times it is the single difference between success and failure.

Applied Knowledge — Knowing the Rules

Ownership of real estate is one of the few opportunities actually protected by the U.S. Constitution. When you own real estate, you own a lot more than simply concrete, glass and dirt. With the ownership (or even simply the control) of real estate, you also possess the right to say who can and who cannot use your property and how it can be used. As the owner, you determine who can build on your property, who can extract the minerals under your property and who controls what happens above your property. While many of these rights have been redefined through fair housing laws, zoning ordinances and air-traffic control regulations, when you "control" property through outright ownership, or by mutual agreement with the ultimate owner, you often have "absolute" control. Sometimes this control extends past the time when you yourself pass on into the 'great unknown." In Manhattan, absolute ownership (oftentimes called "fee ownership") created great fortunes, but control of real estate through ground leases, "master" leases and air-rights agreements also made many wealthy too.

When Donald Trump decided to build Trump Tower in 1983, he obtained the rights to the airspace above next door neighbor Tiffany's & Co. By securing the "air rights" above the Tiffany's flagship building on 5th Avenue, Trump prevented anyone from ever constructing any building above the 7th floor of the Tiffany building; moreover, he was able to construct a larger building on his site next door, which provided condominium purchasers in Trump Tower unobstructed views of Central Park over the Tiffany's building. Trump has successfully repeated this strategy of using "air rights" to create some of the most exclusive and expensive real estate projects in Manhattan. Everyday, investors can use this same "control without ownership" strategy to control single-family houses through lease-options.

Every real estate investor needs to understand the appropriate rules for his or her particular property niche. I'm not referring here to the broad "rules of thumb" the average person with zero real estate experience may have picked up from talking with another uninformed person, but savvy investors know that for their product type, for their market, for their part of town successful investing requires applied knowledge. Each area of investing will have its own rules — savvy investors make the time to master them.

Focus: "The Strangest Secret"

In his landmark recording "The Strangest Secret," Earl Nightingale, the dean of modern day motivational speakers said, "The strangest secret is that we become what we think about." Upon closer examination, Nightingale said that **we become what we focus on**. Many "would be" investors never seem to break out of the mold of mediocrity simply because they lack the discipline of focus. If you invested one- to two-hours per day focused on a goal and took steps to achieve that goal, you could easily achieve that goal within a year or two. One-to two-hours per day over the span of two years is 1,095 hours, or 45 days. Think of it this way, "If you could completely focus on one thing, temporarily sacrificing television and other distractions, and then use that time to become completely and totally focused, could you achieve the simple goal of putting together a deal within 45- to 90-days?" For most people the answer is "Absolutely — YES!" A lack of focus often prevents people from achieving their most cherished goals.

Core Beliefs - The Power of Knowing What You are Supposed to Do, Then Doing It

Core beliefs is not about "right vs. wrong." Core beliefs is about "integrity." The investor/developer who tells people he is "only doing a project to make money" has much more integrity with a community than the developer who publicly claims to be doing a project "for the benefit of the community," who in reality is **only** doing it for money. Ultimately, as they say, "the truth comes out," and more importantly what you say to others is the "line" you use on yourself. As one highly successful investor put it, "If you tell yourself one thing on Monday about why you are doing a deal, and come Friday you have a totally different criteria for having made that same decision, then the person you have really lied to is yourself. As time goes on, the more you lie to yourself, the harder it is to make good decisions. Far better to figure out what motivates you and stick to your guns. People will respect you more for what you believe–even if they do not agree with it — than if you are constantly saying one thing and doing something totally the opposite." The first step is, of course, to understand what your core beliefs are. For some people it comes relatively easy while they're still at a young age. For others, this may very well take a lifetime. The most effective real estate investors honestly believe that their real estate activities are in fact simply a public demonstration of their "mission" in life, the natural outcome of their core beliefs. As a result, they achieve well above what the average investor normally accomplishes. These highly successful investors also make the time for self-discovery — to understand what their "purpose" is.

263

Knowing your core beliefs helps lead to action. One highly successful investor summed it up this way: "It was if something finally clicked inside and I knew I was doing what I was suppose to do; from that moment forward every decision became so much simpler, and every action had so much more power behind it. Making good, powerful decisions made it easier to take my game to a whole new level, which is what propelled me ahead of my peers."

To order your FREE Copy of: "Seven Habits of Highly Successful Real Estate Investors," please go to: **www.GoingInMotion.com**

If you like what you've read ... check this out!

FOOTNOTES ♊

*Sherman L. Ragland II, "The Wharton MBA," is the host of **Real investors' Talk Radio™**, a nationally syndicated radio program. He is an active investor and is dedicated to assisting all people to learn the correct way to invest in real estate. Through his appearances in leading magazines and national business publications like **"Fortune"** and **"Investor's Business Daily,"** and as a frequently invited guest lecturer at leading graduate institutions like The Wharton School of the University of Pennsylvania, **Ragland is widely regarded as one of the Top 10 National Teachers** on the subject of Real Estate Investing Strategies for Professionals. Ragland emphasizes that: "With focus, team building and applied knowledge, you do not need an MBA to "Go in Motion" and succeed in the real estate game!"*

"Who Else Wants to Discover the Timeless, Proven Success Principles Used by Renegade Millionaires to Create Wealth by Trading the Markets?"

by J. Daryl Thompson

Did you know that the book "Think And Grow Rich" by Napoleon Hill has probably produced more millionaires and billionaires than any other self-help or success-related book in history?

Ask virtually anyone in that high-caliber category where they received their original inspiration, motivation or simple ideas about what it takes to honestly become wealthy and they will name this book as the source. Even if they do not recognize the book, they probably used the principles detailed in the book anyway.

Personally, I have used the principles outlined in the book to propel myself to the top 10 percent of American Society in terms of net assets, and the vehicle I chose to accomplish that feat has been stock market investing.

I recently went back and re-read my dog-eared version of "Think And Grow Rich — the Action Pack Edition." In the "Notes" section, I had scrawled "I have the Burning Desire to become a world-class stock market investor." I scribbled those notes on May 29, 1992.

Since that date, using "Think And Grow Rich" principles, plus some "Accurate Thinking" investing systems I developed along the way, I have averaged around 80 percent a year by investing in common stocks. I feel my "Burning Desire" has become real.

My research over the past seventeen years proved to me that 99 percent of the world's investors make investing and trading way too complicated. I discovered that successful investing only requires two things:

• The right mindset for trading and investing in the real world.

• Investing and trading systems that work in the real world.

As you can see, I am not at all interested in anyone's pet theories about how things "should work" in investing or in any other endeavor. To me, and to any other "Accurate Thinker," the only thing that counts is what works in the real world — helping each other to succeed.

In his book "Think And Grow Rich," Hill described in detail 13 success

265

principles compiled over many years of interviewing the most affluent people of his day. I simply applied the same principles in my quest of becoming a world-class investor in the stock market. Let's talk about the first three of those principles now.

Trade And Grow Rich With ... The Astonishing Power of The Burning Desire

"There are no limitations to the mind except those we acknowledge,"

-Napoleon Hill, "Think And Grow Rich*"*

I like to keep things as simple as possible.

And most of the time, the simplest ideas and concepts are the most profound.

As I wrote in the Notes section of my copy of "Think And Grow Rich" in 1992, and as I rediscovered many years later, here in one sentence is the foundation of all success and wealth:

"Great accomplishments start out as a single thought."

In my case, that thought was that I would become a world-class successful investor.

But just a thought is not going to get you anywhere. Obviously, anyone can think about being rich or whatever the goal might be — but this is not enough. And this is also a popular misconception about the whole aspect of "Think And Grow Rich."

Many people who did not fully understand the "Think And Grow Rich" philosophy got the impression that all you had to do to attain riches was just to sit in a dark room and think about it and then money would just fall from the heavens into your lap!

No, although all great accomplishments do start with a single thought, much more needs to be done after that.

For one thing, the thought must be turned into a "Burning Desire." You must develop a "white hot frenzy" of desire to attain your goal at all costs.

And these "costs" cause most people to lose hope and abandon their goals, desires and ambitions long before they attain them. Some of these people just do not understand certain unchangeable universal laws, like the law of "Cause and Effect." Like the law of "What you reap; therefore you will sow," and like the simple law of "there ain't no such thing as a free lunch."

And, the second thing needed is "Definiteness of Purpose." This simply means knowing exactly what you want down to the finest detail possible.

For example, Hill outlined six practical steps to turn the desire for riches into its financial, real world equivalent.

1. Fix in your mind the **exact** amount of money you desire.

2. Determine exactly what you intend to **give** in return for the money you desire.

3. Establish the definite date you intend to **possess** the money you desire.

4. Create a definite plan for carrying out your desire and begin **at once** whether you are ready or not, put this plan into **action**.

5. Write out a clear, concise statement of everything you have done in the first four steps.

6. Read this written statement aloud twice daily, once just before going to bed at night, and once just after arising in the morning. As you read, see, feel and believe yourself you are already in possession of the money.

Here I have to be honest with you again. I did not carry out these steps to the letter in the attainment of my goal. I was a tad vague in some of the steps and this led to taking much longer to achieve my goal — including a near-disaster I will tell you about later.

Also, there is a huge difference in merely **wishing** or **hoping** for a thing and just being ready to receive it. There is a saying that describes this concept: "Be careful what you wish for, you just might get it".

So, when you have a definite purpose, with a burning desire to achieve it, the other side of that is you must be **ready** to receive it and **believe** you will receive it.

And this leads to my near-disaster.

I started to receive what I desired, like **gangbusters**! After learning "Accurate Thinking" investment systems, I began actively investing in the stock market.

For five years straight, I averaged 80 percent a year in the market. Everything was going along according to plan, but then I started thinking about what was happening.

I had read in all the investment books that if you could average around 20 percent a year in the stock market you would soon have the world "beating down your door" to give you their money to invest. Indeed, I was working for a world-class money manager at the time who had become a billionaire from making our investors 12- to 16-percent a year.

So there I was, an investing novice, averaging 80 percent a year! So, I proceeded to play "mind tricks" on myself. I began thinking "this can't be real, I don't **believe** this is happening, and I am **not ready** for this."

Then, I proceeded to *undo* my success. I sold all my stock holdings and started buying real estate. My rationale at the time was that I needed a *new challenge*.

267

I soon found out that my talents were related to stock investing and not real estate! I promptly lost all my gains from the stock market. To this day, my wife Barbara still asks me, "What were you thinking?"

Anyway, I implore you to use my real-world example of what can happen when you fervently desire something, but in the end are not **ready** for it — do not **believe** it when you start to **receive** it!

Oh, by the way, one of the stocks I owned was a start-up company called Cisco Systems. I bought it at the optimum buy point of the decade in October of 1990. It went on to become one of the best performing stocks of the decade; up about 75,000 percent from October 1990 to the top in March 2000. I read somewhere my modest initial investment would have been worth about $28 million: oh well, live and learn!

Trade And Grow Rich With ... The Amazing Power Of Directed Faith

"Both poverty and riches are the offspring of faith," Napoleon Hill, "Think And Grow Rich"

You may feel the above quote from Hill is a little harsh.

After all, how in the world can **poverty** be caused by faith?

This is partly because most people in the world probably associate the word "faith" to something positive, and in the Biblical sense, this is certainly true.

But in "Think And Grow Rich," Hill uses the word "faith" in a different context. Here is his definition: "Faith is a state of mind which may be induced, or created, by affirmation or repeated instructions to the subconscious mind through the principle of autosuggestion."

In this context, poverty can certainly be produced by faith. Hill goes on to say that "There are millions of people who believe themselves 'doomed' to poverty and failure because of some strange force over which they believe they have no control. They are the creators of their own 'misfortunes' because of this negative belief, which is picked up by the subconscious mind and translated into its physical equivalent."

So, it is obvious that you must **absolutely control** what you think about! And here we get into the area of "Directed Faith."

"Directed Faith" simply means exercising that conscious control over what you choose to continuously believe in life. "Directed Faith" mixed with strong emotion can produce some very interesting outcomes in your life!

In his book, Hill seems to equate **belief** with **faith**. Based on my own results in the context of becoming a successful investor, I see them as two slightly different things.

www.mentorsmagazine.com

I feel that belief must come **before** faith. To become a successful investor, I think you must first **believe** you can do so. Without that fundamental belief, having faith is a much harder thing to do. However, at least in my case, once I was able to actually **believe,** I could become a world-class investor; my **faith** that I could do so practically took care of itself.

And, I must admit, there was an enormous additional factor involved that may make my case a little different from the usual.

That factor came in the form of **immediate success**. As I said before, once I discovered an "accurate thinking" investment system that made sense to me, I was able to use it and immediately started averaging 80 percent a year investing in the stock market.

Nothing builds self-confidence faster than immediate success! However, you also have to be careful not to let that success "mess up your mind" like it did mine about five years after I started investing (see my "near-disaster" story in "Trade And Grow Rich" success principle number one).

So, the quickest route to solidifying your belief and faith, at least in the context of being a successful investor or achieving your other goals, is experiencing positive, reinforcing outcomes as soon as possible!

What do you do if that does not occur as soon as you want it to? In the case of an investing system, it usually means that one of the following is happening:

1. Your investment system is faulty to begin with.

2. You are not executing your system properly.

3. Your system is not the right one to use for the current market conditions.

I am going to tell you right off the bat that I am not a proponent of "black box" canned systems. I mean, think about it! If someone developed a "Holy Grail," automatic system that worked in all market environments; Why in the world would they be trying to sell the system to you? They would be keeping it to themselves and making enormous fortunes with it.

But we are getting off track. My point is that you must develop belief and faith in *yourself* rather than in some "black box" system.

Trade And Grow Rich With ... Mastering Your Destiny With Autosuggestion

"Every adversity carries with it the seeds of a greater benefit."
– Napoleon Hill, "Think And Grow Rich"

Maxwell Maltz calls it "Entering the theater of your mind."

Shakti Gawain calls it "Creative Visualization."

269

Vernon Howard calls it "Psycho-Pictography."

And, Napoleon Hill calls it "Autosuggestion."

What is "it" I am talking about?

Let's start with Hill's definition: "'Autosuggestion' is the agency of communication between that part of the mind where conscious thought takes place and that which serves as the seat of action for the subconscious mind."

Basically, "autosuggestion" is any kind of self-administered stimuli received through any of the five senses by the conscious mind and transmitted to the subconscious.

These stimuli can take several different forms, such as talking to yourself aloud, affirmations, "day-dreaming" and seeing clear, vivid pictures in your mind — you achieving your goal and the desired results already taking place.

But Hill states emphatically that there is one aspect that must be added to that stimuli and where most people go wrong. In his words, "Your subconscious mind recognizes and acts only upon thoughts which have been well mixed with emotion or feeling."

This is why simply having a passion, that "**burning desire**" for what you want is so important. It's what keeps you motivated to achieve your goal at all costs, eliminating or avoiding any obstacles in your way.

In my case, I immediately developed a passion for stock market investing, and I used autosuggestion in several different ways to keep that passion alive.

The first form of autosuggestion I used was seeing myself discovering the "perfect investment system." I imagined a "secret formula" (similar to "Think And Grow Rich") for producing a return much greater than the "accepted" stock market rate of return of seven- to nine-percent annually I had informally read about.

So, I started out by devouring every book I could find related to the stock market. I read about fundamental analysis, technical analysis, the Elliott Wave theory, the Gann theory, Bollinger Bands and everything from the old "classics" to the latest computer-driven techniques.

But for a long time, nothing seemed to "click" for me. Strict fundamental analysis just put me to sleep. Since I was a mathematics major in college, technical analysis was more exciting, but I thought that something was still missing. My passion for the stock market kept me searching for the right system for me. Somehow I knew it was out there waiting. I kept telling myself, "keep on searching, keep on searching, it's out there," my second form of autosuggestion.

Then I read the book "How To Make Money In Stocks" by William J. O'Neil, founder of the Investors' Business Daily newspaper. The CAN-SLIM system outlined in the book put all the "pieces of the puzzle" together for me.

270

CAN-SLIM was immediately appealing to my love of mathematical formulas. As I said before, I like to keep things as simple as possible. If I can reduce a complex idea to a simple, easy-to-remember formula, I am a "happy camper."

In my opinion, CAN-SLIM is the perfect hybrid of "just the right amount" of fundamentals and "just the right amount" of technical analysis. It is based on the "Real World," not on someone's theory of how things "should work."

I firmly believe you can use autosuggestion to "master your own destiny." After my immediate success as a stock market investor, I began to "dream even bigger dreams." I envisioned myself as a full-time investor helping thousands of other people to that same dream, or even just to discover how easy it is to make money in the markets with the correct system.

I also started envisioning my new lifestyle ,which would unfold as a result of becoming a full-time investor and educator. I began to design this lifestyle in my mind. Here were some of my qualifications and other desires:

1. Become financially independent and "retire" by the age of 50.

2. Be able to do what I love to do, when I want to do it, with anyone I choose anywhere in the world.

3. Own beachfront property in a gorgeous part of the world.

Well, in February of 2003, I was able to "retire" from the corporate world at the age of 50. I am now a full-time investor and educator, doing just what I want to do and because of the Internet, I can do what I do virtually anywhere in the world. I have met many new friends I would not have met if I were still at my old job.

And my wife and I now own a beautiful piece of paradise — because of our stock market investments, we were able to purchase a villa on the gorgeous island of Contadora.

Contadora belongs to the country of Panama, and is about 43 miles off the Pacific coast from Panama City. It is part of the Pearl Islands, where the "Survivor" series shot several episodes. As a matter of fact, the "Survivor" production crew set up operations on Contadora — it is truly a beautiful, magical place.

So, now you see why I now absolutely believe in autosuggestion, in setting goals and designing the lifestyle you desire in your mind mixing those thoughts and "thought-pictures" with strong, positive feelings. You can truly become "The Master Of Your Own Destiny."

I'm here to tell you, **IT WORKS!**

Next, here is the secret to making all this work, practically speaking….

Oops, my publisher says I'm out of space for this book. For the rest of the secrets, you will have to visit my website at www.tradeandgrowrich.com.

271

In Conclusion. ...

There is a reason why certain laws of nature are called "universal laws." Just like gravity, they will always work, no matter where you are in the great space/time continuum.

There is not a shadow of doubt in my mind that anyone who studies and seriously applies the 13 success principles outlined in "Think And Grow Rich" can become wealthy and successful — if that is the intention. And, after 17 years of success, I feel I have the right to say that Napoleon Hill's "Universal Laws of Success" have worked for me. I urge you to let them work for you!

If you like what you've read ... check this out!

FOOTNOTES

J. Daryl Thompson is the owner and CEO of Trade And Grow Rich LLC. Mr. Thompson is a highly successful investor in the stock market, and is now devoting his life in educating other investors on how to use uncomplicated, real world strategies to achieve unusually high performance returns in the stock market.

Mr. Thompson's grand vision is to create an international Master Mind Group of highly successful investors, who will use some of their investment returns to aid and support humanitarian efforts around the world.

For more information, and the rest of Mr. Thompson's 13 investment success principles, please visit www.tradeandgrowrich.com.

Rare Exclusive Interview with Chuck & Gena Norris

by Linda Forsythe

"MENTORS™ Magazine"
(Transcript from LIVE Interview)

Welcome to our cover story interview here on this beautiful Monday evening, brought to you LIVE from "MENTORS™ Magazine." This is Linda Forsythe, your host each Monday for these free interview calls from some of the most renowned millionaire mentors, celebrity speakers, and best-selling authors in the world! Be sure to check back frequently to find out who will be featured each week on our show. Since all of these LIVE calls are taped, we use the transcripts from our best interviews and place them as cover stories in our hard copy of "MENTORS™ Magazine." All of this information is listed on our web site at www.mentorsmagazine.com. On our site, you may also sign up for a FREE weekly newsletter that will be delivered directly to your In-Box each week. Included in your newsletter will be articles of inspiration and guidance from one of our many wonderful mentors.

This evening, I'm extremely honored to have not one, but two honored guests! These individuals know how to overcome adversity and shine. We have action film star, Chuck Norris, and his beautiful wife, Gena. Many of you are already familiar with Chuck Norris as the World Champion Martial Arts Fighter and movie star, or even as Cordell Walker, from the hit television series "Walker, Texas Ranger." Over the course of this interview, you will get to know more about Chuck and, as an added bonus, his wife, Gena. Both of them have a fascinating rags-to-riches story and work together as a well-oiled machine. This dedicated husband and wife team has successfully mastered the art of acting as great parents while still running several major business projects.

Both are highly involved in Chuck's nonprofit organization for kids, called the Kick Start Foundation. And if that isn't enough, they are also involved in Christian ministry projects, as well as Chuck's martial arts organization, the United Fighting Arts Federation. I have a long laundry list of accomplishments in front of me for both of these dynamic individuals, but I know our audience is anxious for me to start this interview. Chuck and Gena are the ultimate entrepreneurs, and we have much to learn from them!

LINDA FORSYTHE: Welcome, Gena and Chuck. I want to thank you both for taking time out of your extremely busy schedules to share with us today!

CHUCK NORRIS: That's quite all right, Linda. We consider it an honor that you chose to interview us. My real name is Carlos, by the way, but for the purpose of this interview, you may call me Chuck.

GENA NORRIS: Thank you, Linda. It's our pleasure to be here.

LINDA FORSYTHE: Probably the best place to start is by talking a little bit about each of your lives and careers before you married each other. So, I'll ask this first question to Chuck: From what I understand, your childhood was filled with family and financial hardships. If you don't mind, could you tell us a little bit about your childhood?

CHUCK NORRIS: I'd be happy to. Amazingly, I faced incredible challenges from birth, because my mom was in labor for a week, waiting to deliver me ...

LINDA FORSYTHE: A week?!

CHUCK NORRIS: Yes, and when I was finally born, I was what they call a "blue baby." I wasn't breathing, so the doctor had to work frantically to get me breathing. Finally, after a few moments, of course I made it, but then I had to go into intensive care for about four days before Mom could even see me. When they brought me in to see Mom for the first time, she held me in her arms and looked into my face and said, "God has plans for you." (My mom told me that all of my life).

But anyway, I grew up mainly with my mom and granny. My dad was an alcoholic and a philanderer, so he was very seldom in my life. Because of this and not having a male image around, I grew up extremely shy and introverted. I also didn't participate in sports. Many people have a hard time believing that, but it's true! It was a very difficult time in my life, and I grew up extremely poor in Oklahoma. Mom was on welfare for about 10 years. Amazingly, Linda, as poor as we were, I was very rich in love. My mom and granny showered me with love every day, and I never *felt* poor growing up because of this.

LINDA FORSYTHE: You are correct in that a house filled with love is extremely important. I'm sure your mom's planting seeds in your mind about how God had plans for you was also uplifting. I'm curious though — how does joining the Air Force eventually lead you to become a six-time world fighting champion and internationally known movie and television star?

CHUCK NORRIS: Good question. Well, you know, as I said earlier, I was extremely shy. In fact, I never even had the nerve to stand in front of a classroom and give a book report all through school. Never once could I bring myself to get up and speak. When a teacher would ask me to come up and do a book report or whatever, I would just shake my head and say "no." I'd rather have taken an "F" than get up there and embarrass myself. Of course, by not getting up, I became embarrassed anyway. I went all the way past high school graduation with this shyness.

LINDA FORSYTHE: Looking at you now, it's hard to believe you had this terrible shyness!!! Is that why you ultimately joined the military? Was it to toughen you up?

CHUCK NORRIS: No. Actually, my ultimate goal after graduating was to be a police officer. I thought, "Okay, I'm only 18 years old, so I can't join the police department. Maybe if I join the military for four years, I'll get some police experience there." So I joined the Air Force and went into the Military Police. Then I was sent to Korea. When I was over there, I decided to learn Judo." This was in 1960, so the only thing I'd ever heard of was Judo. I never heard of Karate or Tae Kwon Do. After enrolling in a Judo class, two weeks into my training I broke my shoulder and had to have my arm in a sling!

LINDA FORSYTHE: A situation like that would probably discourage most people about continuing to learn Judo, but obviously that didn't happen to you. What happened next?

CHUCK NORRIS: Actually, breaking my shoulder is what led to other events. After my accident, I was walking through Osan Village one day. As I'm walking, I looked up on a knoll and could see these heads jumping up and down. I remember thinking, "What's going on up there?" My curiosity got the best of me, so I climbed to the top of the knoll. What I saw there absolutely amazed me!!! I saw these Koreans jumping up in the air and doing these incredible kicks. I couldn't believe the human body could do something like that, so I stood there mesmerized. At the time, I had wanted to ask them what they were doing, but they looked WAY too mean to me. When I eventually went back to the Base, I asked my Judo instructor what he thought those men on the knoll were doing. After he explained everything to me, I said, "I'd sure like to learn that!" After my shoulder healed, my Judo instructor introduced me to an instructor of Tae Kwon Do. After training, I left Korea as a black belt in Tae Kwon Do and a brown belt in Judo.

LINDA FORSYTHE: That's incredible!!! Did achieving this eliminate your shyness?

CHUCK NORRIS: It helped, but I still had more work to do on myself. After Korea, I arrived at March Air Force Base in Riverside, California. I remained very shy through this whole period. When stationed at the Air Force Base, I decided to start a martial arts club there. This meant I would have to give a demonstration if I was going to encourage people to join. I wanted to overcome my shyness and remember thinking, "If I give a demonstration, this means I will have to give an opening address to the audience." That terrified me, but I moved past the fear!!! The only thing that encouraged me was the thought of memorizing a half-page speech. Then I could make the presentation without having to think. So, I worked on this half-page speech for two weeks. Now this was in 1961, and I can *still* remember this vividly. It's in the evening, in the gymnasium, and there are about 500 people attending. (Sigh) The microphone was lying on the floor. As I went to pick up the microphone, my hands were sweating. I started with, "Good evening, ladies and gentlemen, my name is Chuck Norris, and I'd like to welcome you here tonight." The next thing I remember, I was walking out into the middle of the gym to do my martial arts demonstration. To this day I wonder if I ever finished my speech or just laid the microphone down. I'm still not really sure.

But the bottom line is this: It was my martial arts experience that gave me the strength to begin to crack that egg of insecurity I had carried around for 21 years. After the military, I applied for the LAPD.

LINDA FORSYTHE: So, you finally obtained your dream of becoming a police officer?

276

CHUCK NORRIS: Not quite. It's amazing how everything happens for a reason. At the time, I was married with a child, so I went to work at Northrop Aircraft in order to support my family while waiting for a decision from the LAPD. When working at the aircraft factory, I certainly wasn't making enough money to support my family, so I had to find a way to supplement my income. It was because of this I started teaching martial arts in my mom's backyard. As I was teaching, I decided, two weeks before I went to the academy (they finally accepted me), to become a full-time martial-arts instructor instead.

LINDA FORSYTHE: It sounds like your dream focus changed.

CHUCK NORRIS: Not totally. My dream focus materialized with more clarity in the direction I wanted to go. The only difference was I now had to figure out a way to draw students to my school in order to obtain a good income because working for yourself means you make only what you can draw in. It was because of this that I decided to become a competitor, mainly to draw students to my school. I remember thinking, "If I could just win one local tournament, then I could receive 'write-ups' in local magazines, papers, or maybe even in a martial arts magazine."

LINDA FORSYTHE: *This* **was the reason you started competing? Wow! When you actually think about it, your idea was an excellent marketing strategy!!!**

CHUCK NORRIS: The only thing was, I had MUCH to learn about business. My first tournament was in Salt Lake City, Utah. I took three of my students, and we drove all the way there in my old car. I smile when I remember back at how we just barely made it with my rusty heap. All three of my students won, but I lost. I decided to keep trying, so when I got back, I entered another tournament and won the Los Angeles All-Star Championship (This was a local tournament).

LINDA FORSYTHE: I think that right there is an excellent testimonial about never giving up.

CHUCK NORRIS: This is the amazing thing about goals. Once you accomplish a goal, then you want to set new goals. It just seems to happen that way because it builds confidence. It was because of that small *win* that I began to think, "If I can win a local tournament, maybe I can win the state title." I went on to fight for the state title in 1965, and won that, too!!! Now I was REALLY motivated, so then I thought, "Well, if I can win the state title, maybe the national title should be next." Guess what? I won the national title. Of course then my next thought was, "Well, if I can win the national, why not the international?" In 1967, I won the international. Everything started by taking one small step toward one small goal. It took action to move past my fear, and the action propelled me forward in a big way ultimately.

LINDA FORSYTHE: That's an amazing story of accomplishment and goal setting!!! So what happened to your business in teaching the martial arts?

CHUCK NORRIS: I was going to quit at the time and just concentrate on my teaching, but the promoter of the International Championship said to me,

"Chuck, if you win two years in a row, you could get your name inscribed in this huge silver bowl." This sounded intriguing to me, so in 1968 I fought another time and won the Grand Championship again. I again made the decision to retire but then was given an offer to fight for the World Title in New York City. It was at that time I decided to become a professional fighter — which I did. I then won the World Title and held it for six years!

LINDA FORSYTHE: I bet at this point your school would have had a substantial enrollment if you decided to go back to teaching, right?

CHUCK NORRIS: You are correct. I did wind up having three successful schools because of my reputation, but it was at this time I made a fatal error. A company came to me and said, "Chuck, we want to buy your schools and open Chuck Norris Schools nationwide. Are you willing to do that?" It sounded exciting, so I sold my schools. Two years later, we were bankrupt.

LINDA FORSYTHE: Oh, no!!!

CHUCK NORRIS: But again, some things happen for a reason. I wasn't going to quit, so I started teaching private students and giving seminars to support my family. Steve McQueen was one of my students.

LINDA FORSYTHE: Really?

CHUCK NORRIS: Yes. I remember Steve saying to me, "Well, what are you going to do now that you no longer have the schools?" And I said, "I'm really not sure." He said, "Well, have you ever thought about acting?" I started laughing because I'd never even done a high school play, much less anything else. I said, "What in the world makes you think I could be an actor?" He said, "Well, acting is more than just taking acting lessons. It's a certain presence that the camera picks up, and I think you may have it. I would encourage you to try."

LINDA FORSYTHE: Was THIS the point where you became an actor? Did you jump on it?

CHUCK NORRIS: Actually, I thought about it for four months. There is a strong philosophy I developed through the martial arts, and that philosophy was, "Once I make my mind up to do something, by hook or crook I'm going to finish it!" It was important for me to make up my mind whether this was a goal that I wanted to pursue until the end. Finally I decided that I would.

LINDA FORSYTHE: I think all our readers know that it usually isn't easy to become a well-known or successful actor. Was it easy for you? How did you start?

CHUCK NORRIS: No, it wasn't easy by any means, but I had stubborn determination on my side. I started checking around for the acting schools in Hollywood, and they were very expensive. Finally, I found an acting school where I could go on my GI Bill. About four months into my acting, I thought, "I've got to go out and find a job!" I went to something the industry names "a cattle call" for a part in a movie. When I arrived, there were over a hundred guys trying for the same position, and some of these guys were people I recognized from television. In fact, there was this one particular actor I'd seen before that was trying for the same part, and I wanted to go up and ask him for his autograph.

LINDA FORSYTHE: Well, did you get the role?

CHUCK NORRIS: I didn't get that particular role, but I did wind up writing my own screenplay called "Good Guys Wear Black."

LINDA FORSYTHE: You're kidding? You mean you decided to write your own screenplay to star in, instead of begging permission to act in someone else's film? (Laughs) I love it!!!

CHUCK NORRIS: It wasn't until four years later that I finally found a producer who would do my film. From that point on, it's history. After "Good Guys Wear Black," I wound up doing 23 films and then finally doing "Walker, Texas Ranger."

LINDA FORSYTHE: Whew!!! Well, you certainly stuck with your goals until the end. Isn't it amazing when we choose to "get over" our fears, how much we can shine?

CHUCK NORRIS: Absolutely!

LINDA FORSYTHE: Chuck, you *obviously* have! Well, you know what, Gena—it's your turn. You've been very quiet sitting here, and I want to hear your story. I understand it's quite interesting.

GENA NORRIS: Aww!

LINDA FORSYTHE: Please tell us about your life prior to becoming Mrs. Chuck Norris.

GENA NORRIS: Well, it's interesting because my young adult years were fairly parallel with Chuck's. My family was also very poor, and my mother had always been an extremely hard worker to support her family. I'm the eldest of six children, so that came with a huge responsibility. Like Carlos (Chuck), I had a career change in my 30's as well; I decided to go back to school. I started taking classes to go to work in law enforcement in order to support my children. The pay scales were much different then (lower), so it took dogged determination and hard work. I don't know — I guess you just have to be really, really brave in order to do that. As a single mom, you do what you have to do. You're pushed into one of those situations where that inner strength comes shining through if you let it. I just got busy and took action. I did what it took to achieve my goal of supporting my family.

LINDA FORSYTHE: I really appreciate you sharing that with us. I can certainly understand what it is like to be a single mom! So you both have a history in law enforcement behind you?

CHUCK NORRIS: Linda, law enforcement is still very dear to my heart. That is why, out of my 23 films, in 11 of them I played some type of law enforcement officer. In fact, that's what motivated me to do "Walker, Texas Ranger." It's also the main reason I did the series.

LINDA FORSYTHE: Well, it's good that both of you have the same

background together. Now how did the two of you meet — or can I guess here?

CHUCK NORRIS: It is an interesting story. Quite a few years back, my best friend, Larry, was in Dallas and living with me. At the time, I'd been divorced for a number of years. He said, "You know, even though you're successful in all these arenas, you're still a very unhappy man. There is this lady I know who's a real strong Christian and a beautiful woman. You should meet her!" I agreed, and he invited Gena out to visit in Dallas. In the meantime, Gena had also been doing modeling, so she obtained a modeling assignment in Dallas. Anyway, a bunch of us were at a sushi bar, and I was with one of my sons and his wife. There were about 12 of us total. I also had a date with me. I was kind of nose-to-nose talking with my date, and Gena came walking into the sushi bar. Larry introduced Gena around to everyone at the table, but I was still talking with my date and not really noticing. Larry had to push to get my attention, so when I finally turned around and looked at Gena, I said, "Holy mackerel!!!" I couldn't take my eyes off of her. When I eventually turned back around to my date, all I could see were daggers in her eyes. Then my date got up and left.

LINDA FORSYTHE: I'll bet.

CHUCK NORRIS: So, anyway, Larry took Gena back to the hotel and the next day we went to breakfast with her. I also decided to get her an acting position on "Walker, Texas Ranger."

LINDA FORSYTHE: So Gena was on Walker? I didn't know that.

CHUCK NORRIS: We dated for a while and later, I went to one of her modeling assignments, where she was modeling wedding dresses. When I went there and watched her go down the walkway with different wedding dresses, there was one time when she came down the walkway ... Is that what they call it, Gena?

GENA NORRIS: The runway.

CHUCK NORRIS: Okay. So Gena's walking on the runway, and this flower pot lands and falls onto her train, and she started dragging it with her. As I watched the potted plant on her train go by and the way she handled it ... It was at that point I realized how deeply in love with her I was. Later, I asked her to marry me.

LINDA FORSYTHE: What a beautiful story!

GENA NORRIS: We laughed for a long time about that, and this was almost eight years ago, Linda.

LINDA FORSYTHE: (Laughs) Let's move on a few more steps in this story. After you both became happily married, I know both of your kids developed good relationships with each other. When was it you both decided to become new parents? Tell us about your twins.

CHUCK NORRIS: When we got married, the last thing on my mind was having children again. I already had three grown children. She had two teenage children. We really didn't have any aspirations of starting another family.

GENA NORRIS: Don't forget to tell about our nine grandchildren!

CHUCK NORRIS: Yeah, nine grandkids. But something happened that everywhere we went, we would run into friends of ours who had started second families. They would always say, "Chuck, you cannot imagine how great it is! You're more mature now and you will enjoy children so much better. When you had children the first time, you were a child yourself (which was true)." So, anyway, everywhere we went, we'd run into friends who ...

GENA NORRIS: Chuck, start mentioning the names of some of these friends. There was Allen Autry.

CHUCK NORRIS: Yes, there was Allen Autry who was the Mayor of Fresno, California.

GENA NORRIS: Mary and Burt Sugarman ...

CHUCK NORRIS: And Bernie Koppel, who was on the "Loveboat." So, anyway, it was at this point we started talking about it.

GENA NORRIS: (Laughs) Talking about it?

CHUCK NORRIS: Well, yes ... I did have to think about it first because there was a slight problem. You see, I'd had a vasectomy 25 years earlier, so I wasn't sure if I was even *able* to have children. Finally, I came home from shooting "Walker" one night, and Gena had drawn a bath for me. I'm lying in the bathtub and thinking about Burt Sugarman (Mary Hart's husband). He was also in his second marriage. Burt just had a new son. Earlier, I had gone to see his baby, and I saw this glow in his face. As I lay there remembering that, I thought, "Golly, I want to have that glow!" So I got out of the tub and put my arms around Gena. I said, "Gena, if it is at all possible, I would like to start a family with you. But having a vasectomy 25 years ago, I don't think it's humanly possible." She says, "Well, now that you mention it, there's a doctor in Houston that I've talked to ..."

LINDA FORSYTHE: (Laughs) Gena, it was good that you already had done the research!

GENA NORRIS: (Laughs) I wanted to make certain I had all bases covered just in case. Anyway, this particular doctor specialized in a new procedure called ICSI, and we went to go see him.

CHUCK NORRIS: His name is Dr. Lipshultz. I said to him, "Look, doctor, you know these reversals are tough and the chances of this working are very minimal. I don't think I want to go through all that and then become disappointed because it didn't work." He said, "Oh, no, no, no!!! I'm not going to do a reversal. I'm going right into your epididymis and *get* what I need." (Laughs) That statement kind of set me back on my heels. Gena and I both decided to go through the whole procedure, but then we kind of ended up with six embryos.

LINDA FORSYTHE: Oh, oh.

CHUCK NORRIS: They suggested we implant all six embryos into Gena, and I'm thinking, "Golly! We could wind up with quadruplets here!!!" So, Gena and I talked about it, and we finally decided on four embryos. Gena became pregnant. Later, we went for the first sonogram. This doctor was talking while doing the procedure and said, "I see one little tyke!" and in a few minutes said,

281

"Oh, oh ... looks like there's another one!" I kind of felt a little dizzy and I said, "Really? Twins?"

GENA NORRIS: You weren't the only one who felt a little dizzy!

CHUCK NORRIS: As the doctor continued to evaluate, she then said "Oh, look, there's three!!!" I said, Three?!!!" She said, "Well, we won't know for about a week." Ultimately it did wind up being just two. (sigh)

LINDA FORSYTHE: Well, still. Wow! What an abundance of blessings. (YIKES!)

CHUCK NORRIS: But, you know ... the thing is, Linda, it really HAS been a blessing. When Gena became pregnant, I knew I had to slow down on my work schedule because I was working 16 hours a day on a series. I knew I had to finally stop and concentrate on Gena's pregnancy and to be there for her. After eight-and-a-half years on "Walker" and 203 episodes, I decided to end it. Thank God I did, because Gena almost died three times during her pregnancy! Through the grace of God, she and the babies survived.

GENA NORRIS: After all this, I told Chuck he needed to write a book about everything that has happened.

CHUCK NORRIS: I thought about what she said and decided she was right. So, I decided to write the book called "Against All Odds." I wrote about my childhood and the obstacles I had to overcome in order to achieve the successes that I've achieved in my life. The book goes in depth about all the trials and tribulations I went through and what Gena went through with the pregnancy and so forth.

LINDA FORSYTHE: Oh my! This truly was a miracle considering the things you both went through. Now look at all the wonderful blessings you both have because of moving forward in faith.

GENA NORRIS: Right, although at times it certainly was challenging, especially being an older mother and carrying multiple babies in a pregnancy. This alone is challenging in itself without also having medical complications. You *must* have a certain mindset. You *must* stay strong and positive. I just *knew* that, no matter what, I wasn't going to let negative things come into my mind because I had two other lives inside of me. I wanted to make certain they were going to get here. We knew that God had special plans for them. They are now here and are healthy, happy, beautiful babies. We're so blessed!

LINDA FORSYTHE: All of this speaks volumes about your strength, Gena. Let's go ahead and move forward to today. In addition to Chuck's acting, the two of you are juggling several other businesses and personal projects. How do you manage to handle so many projects and still be active with all your children, not to mention taking care of each other's needs?

CHUCK NORRIS: Well, we prioritize. Our family comes first, and our Foundation comes in second. Then my career and our relationships and my UFAF (United Fine Arts Federation) — they come in third.

GENA NORRIS: It's a balance for sure, Linda. Carlos and I have a

great friendship. We're best friends, and we talk about everything. It is challenging sometimes, but we work well as a team.

LINDA FORSYTHE: That's certainly obvious, especially since divorce rates show that having a successful marriage can be tough. Do either of you feel that being a celebrity couple adds additional hardships to a marriage compared to couples not in your situation?

CHUCK NORRIS: Not really. See, I don't take being a celebrity that seriously. I've also never taken my acting career seriously because it can be going strong one day and gone the next. I'll ride the wave as far as it will take me, and once it's over, it's over. I'm not going to have any remorse about anything, and I will continue to set new goals in my life. I worked as hard as I could to make whatever I did successful, but I never allow myself to get wrapped up in the celebrity thing.

LINDA FORSYTHE: I must say that there's a very down-to-earth nature to both of you. Plus, your accomplishments say much for what you're offering the world. If each of you could share just one word of wisdom with other married couples, based on what you have learned from your marriages, what would you tell them?

GENA NORRIS: Communication.

CHUCK NORRIS: Yes, definitely communication. That would be the top of the list. You must learn to communicate with each other. When one of you is down, and you see that, you must do what you can to pull him or her back up.

LINDA FORSYTHE: Chuck, a few months ago, we interviewed one of your black belts, Reggie Cochran. Reggie shared with us your "code of conduct" and how it played a role in his success. He also mentioned you offered a poster at www.chucknorris.com. Can you take a couple of minutes to tell us about your "code of conduct" and how it came about?

CHUCK NORRIS: I really call them my "Principles of Life" because those 12 principles pretty much determine what my life is about. The first one is, "I will develop myself to the maximum of my potential in all ways." That's always been my philosophy. Whatever I decide to get into, I step forward with all the strength that I have. The next one is, "I will forget the mistakes of the past and press on to greater achievements." That's important, too, you know. Don't dwell on the mistakes and the failures you've had; concentrate on the future. It goes on and on. You can read the rest of these principles on www.chucknorris.com.

I've decided, I will always be in a positive frame of mind and convey this feeling to every person that I meet, and that's another important thing for me. I always want to be in a positive frame of mind and portray that positiveness to everyone.

LINDA FORSYTHE: In addition to your "Principles of Life," as you called it, are there any other tools or techniques you would like to share with our audience that will help them become successful in all areas of their lives?

CHUCK NORRIS: Well, I think the key thing is setting goals. You must set realistic goals on what it is that you want to achieve. On any goal worth accomplishing, there are going to be obstacles in the way, and that's when you must have the determination and the perseverance and the faith in God and yourself to achieve those particular goals. You know, when I first started and became a fighter, my goal wasn't to become the World Karate Champion because that was so far beyond my comprehension that I didn't even think about it being possible. Remember, I had set a realistic goal of winning a local tournament, and once that was accomplished, I went to the next goal.

LINDA FORSYTHE: One step at a time.

GENA NORRIS: And that requires a commitment to learn.

LINDA FORSYTHE: Yes. Throughout our lives we need to become lifelong learners.

CHUCK NORRIS: Exactly.

LINDA FORSYTHE: You also have this incredible Kick Start Program. I would love to hear more about that. How did it get started? What was the purpose behind it?

CHUCK NORRIS: Well, you know, being a martial arts teacher for 15 years, I worked with thousands of young kids, many of them coming in with a LOT of insecurities. They may have had physical, mental or social problems; low self-esteem; and low self-worth — that sort of thing. The philosophy of the martial arts helped raise their self-esteem and instilled the discipline, respect, and the self-worth that many of these kids were lacking. So I thought, "Well, this is all well and good, but these kids who came to my school had parents who could pay the tuition. What about the millions of youngsters in America whose families don't have the money? How could I reach them?" This had always been in the back of my mind, but I didn't take the time to do anything about it.

Then when former President Bush was running for President in 1988, I was asked to go on the campaign trail with him. I did this for four months, and we became real good friends. I was having lunch with him after he became President, and he said, "Chuck, do you have any future goals outside of the entertainment world?" I said, "I'd like to teach the martial arts to inner city schools, primarily to the 6th, 7th, and 8th grades, because middle school kids are at a stage of drifting in one direction or the other. I told him that it was the children around the ages of 11, 12, or 13 who are at the crucial stage of life direction. I knew if I could get at them through the martial arts, I could help guide these kids toward a positive direction in life.

Bush agreed. So through the President's influence, of course they agreed to let me teach a middle school in Houston, Texas. But guess what? The school they gave me was the toughest school in Houston, in the Third Ward.

LINDA FORSYTHE: Oh, my!

CHUCK NORRIS: They said, "Okay. Let's see what you can do here."

www.mentorsmagazine.com

They thought I was going to fail. To make matters worse, I was getting ready to leave for Israel to do a movie, so I had to put one of my instructors at the school to teach. We were to teach five classes a day. (They're like PE classes with 30 kids in each class). So, we were going to have 150 kids to teach in one school. The instructor's name was Roy White. Roy White was a blonde-haired, blue-eyed kid with glasses, and now he was asked to teach in a tough, all-black school.

Anyway, Roy calls me the day before I leave for Israel. He says, "Mr. Norris, I don't know. This is the roughest school I've ever seen in my life! They've already called me every name in the book. I don't know if it's going to work." I said, "Well, Roy, I'm leaving tomorrow for Israel. Can you hang in there until I get back?" He then asked, "How long are you going to be gone?" I said, "Well, about four months."

LINDA FORSYTHE: I'm sure poor Roy loved you for that one!

CHUCK NORRIS: He said, "Well, hopefully I'm still alive when you get back." When I came back four months later, I flew to Houston to this school. I see it, and it's all "barbwired" in. It looked like a prison! I pulled into the school, and the principal was waiting for me. He walked with me to the gymnasium, where all 150 kids were waiting. As we were walking across the school ground, some of the kids in the classroom spotted me. They started running to the window, yelling my name and waving. As I'm waving back, one of the kids yelled out to the principal, "My dad's going to kill you!"

When I finally arrived at the gym, I saw the 150 kids standing at attention. As I walked in, they said in unison, "Mr. Norris, it's a pleasure to have you here, sir." I then shook all their hands. We did a Q & A for about an hour. They ended by doing an excellent demonstration. After it was over, I said to Roy, "What happened? Four months ago, you were ready to throw in the towel." He said, "Boy, it wasn't easy!!! But every day I just kept chipping away and instilling positive affirmations of how they can succeed in life." He said he would do this everyday before starting the class, and slowly but surely the kids started to get it. It started soaking in.

Roy went on to say, "But the turning point came with this boy, who was 6'2" and 180 pounds. He was also an 8th grader and a real muscular kid. I was teaching a class with him in it, and the kid interrupted by saying, 'Mr. White, can you and I spar?' I berated him and said, 'Look, you don't challenge the instructor in a class!' After I finished the class and the other students left, I had him stay back. I said, 'Do you still want to spar?' He said, 'Yes, sir.' I said, 'Okay.' So we sparred, and I tapped him around the head to show him I was in complete control. After losing, he then said, 'Well, I'm a better wrestler.' So we then proceeded to wrestle, and I got him into a choke hold. The kid finally said, 'Thank you, Mr. White. Thank you very much, sir.' After he left, he went out and told everyone, 'Don't mess with Mr. White!' That kid became my strongest advocate, and from then on, things started changing."

LINDA FORSYTHE: Do you have any success stories you like to share because of your Kick Start Program?

CHUCK NORRIS: Yes, absolutely, because there are so many!!! Since that one school, we've now expanded to 38 schools in the last 12 years. We currently have 5,500 kids in the program, and we graduated 35,000 kids over the last 12 years.

285

A particular kid I'd like to tell you about, Linda, is one that we really like to brag about. His name is Gerardo Esparza. Gerardo was a kid who would get into a LOT of trouble. He got in so much trouble that they were getting ready to send him to reform school, or juvenile hall.

Our instructor petitioned the principal and the authorities to let him have the boy on a probationary period, just to see if he could help him before they incarcerated him and made him worse than he already was. They agreed, and Gerardo started in our Kick Start Program. One of the stipulations in order to be in our Kick Start Program is you *must* break all gang ties. This was very difficult for Gerardo because he was with the gangs. The alternative of going to jail persuaded him to break off gang ties. Our instructor was watching him very closely and sometimes would catch him with his gang buddies. He would tell Gerardo, "You are NOT going to associate with gang members because *your* gang is your karate friends."

So, anyway, he does wind up finishing the 6th grade, with a "D" average. During the summer (we teach year around) he didn't associate with his gang friends and ended up developing loyalty to his karate friends. He broke off all gang ties. He then went from 6th grade with a "D" average to 7th grade with a "C" average and on to 8th grade with a "B" average. Finally he went on to the 9th through 12th grades with straight A's. In the end, he earned a scholarship to MIT.

GENA NORRIS: What is even more wonderful is he just graduated.

LINDA FORSYTHE: Oh my goodness! What an inspirational story!

CHUCK NORRIS: I really feel, Linda, if we would have had these types of boys in our Kick Start Program in the past, terrible things may not have happened at some places such as Columbine High School. Many of these children are just wounded spirits who are trying to make a statement, but in a very destructive way. I truly believe if we had these boys before, we could have prevented something like that from happening. Our goal with our Kick Start Program is to work with kids that have this destructive potential, but ultimately redirect them toward a very positive and good way of life.

GENA NORRIS: Know this, too, Linda: Every child is at risk. We're living in very challenging times right now. A program like this would be extremely beneficial to every child in the country.

LINDA FORSYTHE: I'm glad you brought that up because I was going to ask you, How can we get more of these programs into the schools? I personally have a son in high school who just turned 16. I worry all the time about him. What you're telling me could really be a "Godsend"! Not only for my son, but for all boys in high school.

CHUCK NORRIS: It is. Well, look what it did for me. It's turned around the lives of many, many kids who were suffering from whatever insecurities they were carrying with them. The main obstacle facing the Kick Start Program is financial. Our Foundation is funded wholly through our own fund-raising efforts. The cost runs about $60,000 a year per school, which equals about $500 per child. When I talk to my sponsors, I say, "Look, we can spend $500 now saving these kids or spend $60,000 later when they're incarcerated in prison."

GENA NORRIS: $60,000 per prisoner on a yearly basis.

LINDA FORSYTHE: That is a sobering thought! When you put it that way, it sure puts things in clear perspective. We don't have a choice, do we? We MUST get busy and do something that will help our youth. Especially since they are the future!!! You and I are going to have to talk about how our magazine can work with you. I want to help get the Kick Start Program funded so that a number of the boys who require the type of help that you have to offer will get what they need.

GENA NORRIS: Actually, Linda, 40 percent of our students are girls, by the way.

LINDA FORSYTHE: Really?!

CHUCK NORRIS: Many of them are growing up in dysfunctional homes. I'll give you an example. Our instructor noticed one of the girls in our Kick Start Program was very distant all of a sudden. Earlier in the year, she had been extremely outgoing. The instructor sat her down and said, "Is there something bothering you?" It turns out that the girl's uncle was molesting her. The instructor then asked, "Have you talked to a counselor about this?" She said, "No, I don't want to talk to anyone about it." She didn't trust anyone, but yet she would confide in our instructor. He said, "Look, we MUST go to a counselor because you need help right now." He sat her down with the counselor, and she told the counselor what was going on. They took care of the problem. It's important that the reader understands that this is what my instructors do. They're not only teachers; they're mentors and they're spiritual guidance counselors for these kids.

GENA NORRIS: A more appropriate name might be surrogate parents.

CHUCK NORRIS: Yes, they're like surrogate parents. It's an incredible program. To me, it's probably the best program, dollar-for-dollar, going in the country today to help these kids.

GENA NORRIS: You know what, Linda? It's important to let people know that if they want to get involved with this program, 90 cents of every dollar we raise goes directly to our children. The other 10 cents is for administrative costs. So it's really flipped in relation to how most programs are run.

CHUCK NORRIS: Most of them are 90 cents for administration and 10 percent to the program; ours is just the opposite.

LINDA FORSYTHE: I hope our audience is hearing and understanding what you are saying because your program is vital!!! Please go to www.chucknorris.com and look into the Kick Start Program. See what you can do to help.

Since we are close to being out of time, I need to bring up one last question. I understand, Chuck, that you just filmed a new movie. Are there any other projects in the works that you would like to share with us?

CHUCK NORRIS: We are getting ready to do a two-hour "Walker, Texas Ranger, Movie of the Week" for CBS. We start shooting in April (2006). And we're also moving back to Texas. Linda, the Kick Start Foundation requires our time there, and we just can't do it from Los Angeles. So we've got to move back to Dallas and put the time and effort into the Foundation. We are doing everything we can to make it grow — plus I'm going to be doing most of my filming in Texas, too.

287

LINDA FORSYTHE: Before we end this interview, I wanted to hear a little bit more from Gena. Gena, is there anything that you would like to add or say to our listeners about what you have going on?

GENA NORRIS: Well, you know what? We're always looking for help with our Kick Start organization. If you go to www.chucknorris.com, you can link right into Kick Start, or you can go directly to the kickstart.org website.

LINDA FORSYTHE: Chuck and Gena, this is going to be the beginning of a very beautiful relationship because I am going to do everything in my power to help you further all of these endeavors. You are making a huge difference in the world!!! How far do you want the Kick Start Program to expand? What is your end goal? Do you eventually want to go into all 50 states?

CHUCK NORRIS: We would love to. I think it is of vital importance to our youth, but we need help in order to make this happen: financial help, good instructors, and moving past the bureaucracy so we can implement the program into more schools.

LINDA FORSYTHE: All of our readers heard you, and I know they will go to your website in order to find ways to help make this dream a reality. I want to thank you both so much for taking time from your very busy schedules to do this interview!!!

CHUCK NORRIS: I appreciate your helping us get the word out. We are all capable of doing incredible things in this life. Sometimes we need a little extra help to move beyond our fears or choose the right path. It may take a little guidance, but after all, that's what mentoring is about! With the right type of guidance, we can accomplish miraculous things. We can shine!!!

LINDA FORSYTHE: Beautifully stated! With that being said, I think this is the perfect time to end this interview by quoting the "MENTORS™ Magazine" motto: *"Move forward with BOLDNESS on your quest, and mighty forces WILL come to your aid."* ... Goodnight, everybody.

If you like what you've read...check this out!

FOOTNOTES ✿

Chuck Norris is the star of more than 20 films and the long running TV series "Walker Texas Ranger." He is also the author of several books, including his latest best seller, "Against All Odds." His lovely wife Gena is a very accomplished entrepreneur and philanthropist. Both are highly involved in Christian Ministry and the growth of Chuck's Kick Start Foundation. For more information on Chuck and Gena, please visit the following sites: www.chucknorris.com, www. kick-start.org and the soon to be launched www.kickstartbooks.com.